AF560679

Environmental Geography

ENVIRONMENTAL GEOGRAPHY

Girish Chopra

Environmental Geography

© Reserved

First Published : 2011

ISBN 81-7169-993-6

Published by :

Ajay Verma
For COMMONWEALTH PUBLISHERS
4831/24, Prahlad Street,
Ansari Road, Darya Ganj,
New Delhi - 110002
Ph. : 23272541, 23257835
Fax : 91- 011- 23257835
e-mail : campusbooks@hotmail.com

Typesetting by :

Arjun Computers
Delhi - 110051

Printed at :
Roshan Offset Printers
Delhi

Preface

Environmental geography is the branch of geography dealing with the dynamics of Earth's surface features and their evolution through the actions of weathering and erosion. This type of study is linked to hydrology, environmental geology, and other facets of both geography and geology. A major part of environmental geography is the examination of landforms and waterway patterns resulting from the actions of water and streams. This is also referred to in geologic circles as geomorphology.

The link between cultural/environmental geography and geology was at one time very real. As technology has increasingly insulated our cities and commerce from the difficulties presented to communication and transportation by mountains, hills, rivers, and just sheer distance, geomorphology has become less relevant to geography.

Environmental geography represents a critically important set of analytical tools for assessing the impact of human presence on the environment, measuring the result of human activity on natural landforms and cycles. It involves several aspects of the relationship between humans and the environment. This begins with a recognition that what we call 'natural resources' are socially constructed. That is, something only becomes a resource if humans make it so through a variety of cultural, technological, and economic filters. It is not possible to understand environmental problems without understanding the demographic, cultural, and economic processes that lead to increased resource consumption and waste generation. Many of these processes are complex and transnational. Potential solutions arise only from understanding the 'normal' functioning of biogeochemical cycles as well as the technologies that humans employ to interfere with those cycles.

This book provides a comprehensive introduction to the major aspects of environmental geography, the ecological systems; ecological process engineering; the energy-atmosphere system; soil, water, biomes and the eco-restructuring. It also deals with local, regional and global environmental problems at micro and macro-levels. It is hoped that it will be highly useful to geographers, environmentalists, researchers and policy makers.

Girish Chopra

Contents

1

Environmental Systems

The total earth system consists of the geosphere and the biosphere. The geosphere is conventionally defined as the lithosphere (rocks), the hydrosphere (oceans, rivers, and lakes), and the atmosphere, together with the pedosphere (soils) and the cryosphere (ice). It constitutes the substrate for the biosphere, which is the earth's integrated life support system. On the other hand, the biosphere can also be subdivided into terrestrial and marine subsystems, with living organisms further subdivided into animal and vegetable species (plus bacteria).

The animal world consists of humans, other mammals, birds, fish, insects, and a number of other orders, phyla, and families. The human section (which dominates the rest) is sometimes called the anthroposystem. This can be further broken down into the sociosphere and the "technosphere." The latter, in particular, influences the other different natural systems of the geosphere, and is in turn influenced by them. The human impact on the other components of the earth system has now reached a level comparable to - and in some respects greater than - that of natural processes.

Anthropogenic activities include the extraction of raw materials, their physical and chemical separation and refining, as well as their conversion and distribution.

Manufacturing represents only a small fraction of these activities. Indeed, from some environmental standpoints it is not necessarily the most important. Extractive industries, including agriculture and forestry, and also "final" consumption (including personal transportation) often generate more harmful waste materials and residues than cutting, or shaping, or forming, or assembly.

In spite of the adoption of waste-minimization policies, the continued use of new "virgin" materials and fossil fuels still imposes a heavy burden on the biophysical environment. This can be overcome only in time by more appropriate research and development strategies, including information systems that facilitate the optimization of the exchanges between industry and nature. An interesting and different approach is offered by the concept of "landscape ecology." This has developed out of a kind of merger between traditional geography and ecology.

A "landscape" is, by definition, a kind of shorthand for the complex spatial interaction patterns of natural and human systems. Widespread landscape transformations have now become a pressing global problem. There are no landscapes, except perhaps in Antarctica, free from human influence. The industrial type of landscape in particular reflects a very high level of technological and environmental interference by humans.

Climate System

The basic objective of the Framework Convention on Climate Change was to further a political process leading to "stabilization of greenhouse gas concentrations in the atmosphere at a level that would prevent anthropogenic interference with the climate system" and to do so in such a manner as to allow ecosystems to adapt naturally, and so as not to interfere with food production and economic development. Needless to say, it is also important to understand better the processes that are influenced by the earth's atmosphere on a global, regional, and local level. These include biophysical, geochemical, hydrological-oceanic, and socio-economic processes. This calls for an improved understanding of the socioeconomic consequences of climatic change and for further investigations of the response mechanisms to mitigate such changes.

The climate system is mainly driven by solar radiation. The major engine of global atmospheric circulation is the so-called hydrological cycle. Solar heating of the ocean surface causes evaporation of water. The moist air rises until it cools to condensation point. The water vapour condenses and returns to the earth, partly over land. The condensation process releases heat in the atmosphere. Water from precipitation then flows from the land back to the sea, carrying nutrient elements (and causing salinity gradients).

Thermal imbalances between high and low latitudes drive both winds and ocean currents, redistributing energy and matter within the atmosphere and the hydrosphere. As a result of the interactions between solar radiation and the geo/ biosphere, the climate system changes continually. This has occurred throughout the history of our planet. However, in the recent past a new factor has appeared: increased emission of "greenhouse gases" or GHGs (e.g. carbon dioxide, methane, nitrous oxide, chlorofluorocarbons). These emissions are strongly linked to human activities, especially the combustion of fossil fuels and high-intensity agriculture.

The build-up of these gases in the atmosphere has made it act somewhat like a mirror for heat radiation. This has led to a marked global warming process, whose magnitude and rate are still under discussion. The task of determining likely "winners" and "losers" resulting from this ongoing climatic change is extremely difficult. It will affect mainly agriculture. Among the industrialized countries, agriculture accounts for only a very small part of the economy. This has led some economists (mainly in the United States) to conclude that climate warming is not a great concern and that major efforts to counteract it would not be economically justified. Yet it is undeniable that agriculture is essential for human survival and that it counts for a much larger part of the economies of poorer developing countries.

The Intergovernmental Panel on Climate Change (IPCC 1990) projects that the results of global warming, such as increased precipitation and longer frost-free periods, could bring about rather limited immediate benefits to some regions, located mainly in the northern hemisphere. In the South, however, where food supplies are regionally more limited, difficulties related to food security problems may increase. Since climate warming would also be accompanied by sealevel rise, it is of even more immediate concern to small low-lying island nations and countries such as Bangladesh with large populations heavily concentrated in estuarine zones.

One of the most significant results of climate change is likely to be the shifting of agro-climatic zones, although the spatial distribution of such shifts is still difficult to predict. Also sealevel rise affecting low-lying coastal areas by flooding will influence industrial planning and development. The establishment of international funds to counter the adverse consequences of climatic change and the creation of an International Insurance Pool (IIP) to provide insurance against the consequences of sealevel rise are under discussion. An important implication of the IPCC's work is that uncertainty is itself costly.

In other words, it is important to find out (and quantify) the real costs of action (or inaction) in the area of climatic change and to establish economic incentives or disincentives for achieving the stabilization and eventual reduction of greenhouse gas emissions. In this respect, a narrow application of the "polluter-pays" principle would adversely affect economic development in some countries (notably China and India) that are heavily committed to the use of coal. Hence, there is increasing interest in "joint implementation" and such devices as tradable permits. Other important aspects of human activities on the global level include stratospheric ozone depletion and its potential biospheric effects, as well as the processes involved with acid deposition. Both can be directly linked to industrial emissions of gaseous pollutants.

Stratospheric ozone is important for the biosphere because of its absorption of ultraviolet (UV) radiation, which is harmful to humans, animals, and plants. But long-lived chlorinated fluorocarbons (CFCs), which gradually diffuse from the lower atmosphere into the stratosphere, are broken up by UV radiation, releasing atomic chlorine (Cl) atoms. These, in turn, react with ozone (O_3) molecules, which are converted back into ordinary molecular oxygen and atomic oxygen, leaving the chlorine atoms free to attack more ozone. Each chlorine atom can destroy hundreds of thousands of ozone molecules.

Hence, CFCs are literally capable of destroying the ozone layer. Acid deposition is caused by the emission of chemicals such as nitrogen oxides (NO_8) and sulphur dioxide (SO_2) to the atmosphere, mainly from combustion processes. Nitrogen oxides are produced in high-temperature flames when there is excess air. This happens mainly in coal-burning electric power generating plants and internal combustion engines.

The nitrogen in the air itself is oxidized. Sulphur dioxides are produced when coal, containing a small percentage of sulphur, is burned or from the smelting of sulphide ores of copper, nickel, lead, or zinc. These gaseous oxides are further oxidized in the air or on the surfaces of small particles, which act as catalysts. These oxides, reacting with and dissolved in water, become nitric and sulphuric acids, respectively. They may travel hundreds of miles through the atmosphere and descend in the form of rain, fog, and snow or even in dry form. These acids are eventually deposited by rain on the surface of the earth or on the surfaces of trees and other vegetation,

This acid deposition has had great effects on aquatic ecosystems by increasing the acidity of rivers and lakes. This has negatively affected both the flora and fauna. It also has a marked direct impact on terrestrial vegetation, mainly because of its effects on soils. The acidification of forest soils releases and mobilizes metal ions (especially aluminium) that were formerly bound to clay particles. Some of these metals are toxic to trees. The ongoing discussion of the complex causes of "Waldsterben" (forest die-back) is largely related to acidification.

An interesting integrated approach to climatic impact assessment that takes into account the primary, secondary, and tertiary sectors of the economy has been proposed by Parry et al.. This interaction concept not only focuses on climatic parameters but also includes social factors such as poverty, war, or hunger as necessary for a useful evaluation of the effects of climatic change. In addition to policy implications, this allows for feedback regulating and enhancing possible change effects. For instance, a change in climate may lead to a change in natural vegetation belts, which itself will influence the climate through changes in fluxes of gases or through changes in surface reflectivity. This integrated approach will allow a more comprehensive treatment of interactions between climate and society.

The concept of vulnerability is central to any research into climatic change. The World Meteorological Organization (WMO) has defined the objective of its climate programme as "determining the characteristics of human societies at different levels of development which make them either specially vulnerable or specially resilient to climatic variability and change." Vulnerability can be seen as "the degree to which a system may react adversely to the occurrence of a hazardous event". This concept has often been used in relation to climatic and global change research, being linked to terms such as resilience, marginality, susceptibility, adaptability, fragility, and criticality.

In the tropics especially, a wide-ranging integrative approach encompassing all aspects of vulnerability is needed. This includes biophysical monitoring, modeling, and studies on the transformation of the physical environment. In this respect, only an improved understanding of the socio-economic, cultural, and demographic factors will provide the necessary insight into the situation of social groups at risk.

BIOLOGICAL DIVERSITY

Biodiversity describes the abundant variety and variability of living organisms, which, in the context of different ecosystems, have evolved over the past 3 billion years. The biological evolution responded to unstable situations (open cycles) by "inventing" new processes to stabilize the system by closing the cycles. This self organizing capability has been called "Gala". In the latest stage of evolution, humans, as the dominant species, have been responsible for major habitat changes. For instance, land use changes resulting in deforestation and desertification have often brought about a loss of biodiversity, both at the level of ecosystems and also within ecosystems, leading to a loss of genetic and species diversity. This loss has many wide-ranging potential and real effects on both man-made and natural ecosystems and the human populations depending on them.

In return, humans have also, over thousands of years, exploited and manipulated the genetic wealth of biodiversity by selecting and breeding crops and animals. It could perhaps be argued that the effects of climatic change upon agricultural crops would be negligible, because of their great variability. However, one of the main problems is the trend towards great genetic and ecological uniformity. This has occurred through the introduction of commercial seeds that have good yields under optimal conditions but that produce very little in less favourable environments. Therefore the conservation of indigenous varieties, bred and specialized to local conditions for centuries, is potentially advantageous.

The recent global warming trend has the consequence that these localized specialized varieties with limited distribution will disappear sooner than the more uniform commercial crops. This underlines the vulnerability of agro-ecosystems and the general importance of an increased emphasis on preserving biological and genetic diversity. The consequences of intentional or unintentional "invasions" of living organisms, through export or exchange between different ecosystems, should also be increasingly considered. This has long been a problem associated with human commerce and colonization.

Many desirable crops - including maize, potatoes, and tobacco - were brought to Europe from the Americas, for instance. Pineapples were taken to Hawaii from South America. Rubber trees were taken to Malaya and Indo-China from the Amazon valley. But pest species also migrate. The rabbit plague in Australia, Dutch Elm disease, the starling, the grey squirrel, the Norway rat, the water hyacinth, and dozens of other examples could be cited. Meanwhile, in many cases other competing species were eliminated by the interlopers.

As another response to this biological "erosion," various forms of biotechnology have emerged, ranging from traditional fermentation techniques to modern breakthroughs in genetic engineering and recombinant DNA technology. Biotechnology can offer new possibilities for food production, medicine, and energy supply, including special chemicals for improved environmental management. In addition to the protection and conservation of the biosphere, the international Convention on Biological Diversity (UNEP 1992) advocated better handling of biotechnology and improved distribution of its benefits as key elements for successful economic development.

WATER

Fresh water supply is a key factor for the maintenance of terrestrial ecosystems. A good example is the hydrology and water balance of the tropical forests, which has also become important for its impact on human land use. Estimates for the Amazon Basin suggest that a complete replacement of the rain forest by grassland (if it were possible) would increase soil and surface temperatures by 1-3°C, with rainfall and evapo-transpiration declining by 26 per cent and 30 per cent, respectively.

The main global water uses are for irrigation, electric power generation, and industry. Municipal uses, for washing, cooking, drinking, and sewage disposal, are comparatively minor at the global level, though locally important - especially in dry regions. Concerning water consumption, there are important differences between the industrialized countries ("North") and the developing countries ("South"). In Europe, for instance, industrial use (including electric power) is dominant, with only 37 per cent for all other human uses, including agriculture. In Africa and Asia in the 1980s, by contrast, withdrawals for human use and agriculture were over 90 per cent of the total.

In industry, much water is recycled several times before it is finally discarded as waste water. (In the United States, the petroleum refineries use water - mostly for cooling - nine times before it is discarded.) On the other hand, industrial waste water is often toxic. If it is discharged into surface water or groundwater without treatment it creates serious environmental problems. During the past 20 years some progress has been made in water resources management.

However, recent experiences in Eastern Europe have shown that problems of water quality in the former communist countries are much more serious than it was previously thought. It is estimated that agricultural use of water for irrigation in the South will decline further, at least in many areas such as northern China, owing to falling water tables. The share of industrial water use will rise and it is expected that an adequate supply of fresh water will constitute the most critical resource "bottleneck" at the turn of the twenty-first century.

SOIL

Topsoil is a fragile and elusive interface between the biosphere and the lithosphere. The soils (i.e. the pedosphere) have been deeply affected, and even (in some cases) created, by human action. No analysis of vegetation, land cover, and land use can be undertaken without a comprehensive knowledge of the soils, their nutrient status, and their stability. Because of the great variety and variability of soil development, in both time and space, a sharp distinction between natural and anthropogenic changes is quite difficult to make.

Human-induced changes are mainly caused by agricultural land use (crops and livestock), and by transportation and settlements. Roads and settlements have decreased the total area of productive soils (especially fertile top soils) in ali urbanized societies. This process is of great concern now in Asia, where most of the population still live on farms but migration to cities is accelerating. In a number of studies of the relation of agricultural production and the population carrying capacity, the importance of soil constraints within the biophysical framework has been stressed.

Several soil zones have been identified where present food demand exceeds the agricultural production potential. These are designated as critical zones of food insecurity. Climatic and soil data have also increasingly been used to assess vulnerability. This has been done on a global scale by emphasizing biophysical driving forces. It has also been done at the local and regional scale by associating vulnerability with changes in crop yields, harvest failures, and agro-ecological potential. In this connection the ecotoxic impacts of industrial wastes and agricultural chemical usage on the biosphere have not been treated adequately.

Lithosphere

Global change processes involving the lithosphere(The solid earth) are often ignored. However, as the main supplier of mineral raw materials, this part of the geosphere plays a leading role in relation to important bio-geochemical and nutrient cycles. With the exceptions of carbon and oxygen, the anthropogenic mobilization of most nutrients and trace metals by industrial activities can already be compared with the natural rate. In many cases, the anthropogenic mobilization is considerably greater than the natural flux. This applies, for instance, to most heavy metals.

Processes of erosion, deposition/sedimentation, tectonic movement, and volcanic eruption can deeply affect human use-patterns, especially of the soils. Earlier assumptions about the humid tropics have increasingly been questioned. These include the assumption that weathering and chemical denudation proceeded there much faster than elsewhere and the idea that tropical rivers were only "passive conveyors" without eroding their own bed. New work on quaternary climatic changes and tectonic diversity has contributed significantly to our knowledge of the stability (and instability) of tropical landscapes.

Of course, geomorphological factors can influence technological development. An interesting example is the construction of multipurpose dams for both irrigation and power-generating purposes in the subtropical zone of excessive "planation" (or retarded valley formation). Most tropical dry savanna regions belong to this zone, which is also sometimes referred to as the savanna planation zone. These land forms are basically related to climatic factors such as sheet flow on sloping surfaces with extreme peaks of river discharge.

Although it is generally perceived that big rivers cut deep gashes into the bedrock, in the semi-humid and semi-arid tropics reality is somewhat different. Here most rivers flow in shallow river beds. On tectonically stable blocks, placation surfaces are dominant even at altitudes over 1,000 m. The geomorphological term for this type of valley is "trough valley" or "Flachmuldental". In these geomorphic circumstances it is quite difficult to find suitable sites for irrigation or power dams. Large technological and financial investments for this purpose can be much less profitable than in other tropical regions.

It must be recognized, therefore, that the seasonally wet and dry outer tropics suffer from persisting constraints caused by land forms and river discharges which also affect the economic development of this very important climatic zone. Aside from Africa, many examples can be cited from the Deccan Plateau in India and the Planaltos on the Brazilian Shield.

Land-cover and land-use changes have become global in scale. For the better understanding of these changes, more work on the linkages between biophysical and human-induced driving forces is essential. Generally speaking, land cover refers to attributes of parts of the earth surface including vegetation, soil, groundwater, and topographical features. Broad categories would include, for instance, the boreal forest, tropical savanna, cropland, wetland, or settlements. On the other hand, land use refers to the purpose for which land cover is exploited. These uses can be as varied as agriculture, industry, recreation, or even wild life conservation.

Looking at it globally, at the scale of the earth system land-cover changes over the past three centuries can be described briefly as follows: considerable net loss of forest, a marked gain of arable cropland, partly former forest and partly from wetlands, and considerable loss of wetlands that have been partially or completely cultivated or otherwise drained and changed. The direct impacts of these changes on the bio-geochemical budget are not yet clear. But the following can be assumed:

— The conversion from natural to human-induced systems over the past 150 years has resulted in a net flux of CO_2 that is almost equal to the net release by fossil fuel burning over the same period.

— The present release of CO_2 from land-cover changes amounts to about one-third of that from fossil fuel consumption.

— Land-use and land-cover changes represent the largest source of N_2O emissions, which contribute to greenhouse warming and (possibly) also to stratospheric ozone depletion.

— The two largest land uses in spatial terms are crop cultivation (14 - 15 million km^2) and livestock production (with pastures and range-lands, about 70 million km^2). Settlements with industries cover only a small percentage of the world's land area.

Among the main driving forces of land-use changes, population growth, socio-economic and cultural organization, and technology play leading roles. Technological development changes the use of and demand for land resources. Other societal factors related to political and economic structures and to change in attitudes and value systems add a new dimension to environmental change.

Impact of Human Economic Activities on Earth Systems

Human economic activities have now reached an order of magnitude where their influence on the natural earth systems is quite significant. If we accept the analogy between biological and industrial metabolism, the latter can be defined as "the whole integrated collection of physical processes that convert raw materials and energy, plus labor, into finished products and wastes... with the economic system as the metabolic regulatory mechanism". The firm (factory/plant) as a basic unit of the economic system can be compared to living organisms in biology. This analogy, taken a step further, leads into the notion of "industrial ecology."

Similarly, the "cycle" concept of the geo-scientists (e.g. the hydrological, carbon/oxygen, nitrogen, or sulphur cycles) can be adopted as "materials cycles" of the industrial system, starting with raw materials from the earth and returning them to nature as wastes. Industry converts primary resources into products useful for humans. In the course of these transformations, large amounts of waste are generated. It is important to measure these fluxes and processes. A number of measures of industrial metabolism have been proposed, which also require a sound knowledge of the biophysical basis. They include measurements of dissipative losses, of recycled materials, and also of the economic output per unit of material input, which can be called material productivity.

Clearly, more exact measurements based on geophysical and geochemical data are desirable. This is because, collected at a sectoral level, they would allow improved analyses of the entire process of industrial metabolism. The establishment of an information system on industrial metabolism has been proposed.

One attempt to introduce a universal measure for ecological disturbances is "materials intensity per unit of service". The underlying idea is that the potential for disturbance is closely related to the mass of materials moved or processed in the whole chain of processes beginning with extraction and ending with disposal or recycling. The difference between the mass of the product itself and the total mass moved indirectly in the chain has been given the evocative term "rucksack." The size of the rucksack of a material product is a rough measure of the potential for disturbance resulting from its production and use.

In the case of West Africa in order to get a clearer picture of the biophysical base and the human impacts on it, including brief comments on associated economic activities, it is helpful to "go down" in scale from a global to a continental or even to a sub-continental or regional scale. For a first overview one could adopt the zonal classification of "landscape belts" (Landschaftsgürtel), which can be used as an expression of the existing combined attributes of climate, vegetation, soil, and land use. In West Africa, this sequence of "landscape zones" extends from the rain forest to the desert in a fairly regular fashion.

An analysis linking this major biophysical pattern with corresponding patterns of land use and economic development poses some interesting questions. Political boundaries have cut right across this ecological zonation, usually encompassing several landscape belts within each state. Development of land use, including industry, has been strongly influenced by history, i.e. mainly by events in the pre-colonial, colonial, and post-colonial periods. Within this biophysical donation, agricultural activities and mining industries play a more dominant role than manufacturing. Similarly, rapid urbanization has influenced the patterns of development.

West Africa belongs, broadly speaking, to the group of less and least developed countries, although some states such as oil-rich Nigeria or the resources-rich Gabon and Côte d'Ivoire have been (erratically) nearing the level of the newly industrialized economies (NIEs). In many African countries, economic development has been assisted by foreign aid programmes. Much of the rest has been driven by natural resource development projects controlled by large foreign based oil and/or mining companies. There is no history or deep-rooted tradition of political democracy.

Ethnic and tribal identities are stronger than national loyalties. "Checks and balances" are weak. Government, when based on parliamentary forms, is likely to be single party in practice. The alternative is military dictatorship. Owing to the political situation (in Liberia, the Sudan, Angola, Mozambique, Rwanda, Somalia, etc.), so far only very limited chances for any eco-restructuring exist. In a few of the better-functioning African economies, industrial activities cover the whole chain of production from the extraction of raw materials to materials processing and manufacturing and final waste disposal. Industrial enterprises are the main consumers of renewable and non-renewable natural resources, including mineral ores, energy, and agricultural products in all forms. Industrial processes often produce toxic wastes, gases, and other effluents. Furthermore, many goods imported from the North cannot be recycled and become difficult or even hazardous wastes.

For many West African nations, access to land resources is important for sustainable development. Land resources provide the basis of most human activities, including the management of soil, water, and energy. In urban areas, in particular, access to land is becoming difficult because of growing conflicts between industry, housing, transportation, and recreational needs. But in rural areas too the increasing use of fragile, marginal land calls for improved planning and management of land resources. As a first step to combat unsustainable practices, a sound land-use policy, with improved land tenure structures, possibly even introducing a more efficient land registry system, will be important. Population growth in Africa is generally correlated strongly with the expansion and intensification of agricultural land use.

Often this results in deforestation, if not desertification. On the other hand, studies have shown that population density and growth may rank well below economic factors causing environmental degradation. However, these relationships are by no means clear. They often depend on rather complex local circumstances and require further situational assessments of considerable subtlety. Whereas there are a number of very well-documented studies on the Amazonian forests, we know very little about the corresponding African situation. One of the marked differences is the much more limited impact (or even absence) of livestock farming or ranching in the cleared forests. This is mainly because of the adverse effects of the tsetse fly, carrier of "sleeping sickness" (trypanosomiasis) in tropical Africa.

So far, only very few comparative aggregate studies have researched the role of environmental driving forces in Africa on a statistical/empirical basis. Most micro-type studies have been of a more descriptive nature, often in relation to population carrying capacity and landscape transformation. Perhaps the UNU project on Population Growth, Land Transformation and Environmental Change (PLEC) and also UNU's Research and Training Centre on Natural Resources in Africa (INRA) will provide some further insights into regional and local dynamics of environmental land-use/ land cover changes leading in many cases to land degradation.

Only a small number of African problems can be mentioned explicitly here.

Air pollution: In many urban areas, air pollution resulting from electric power generation, transportation, local industries, and domestic cooking is already a major problem. In addition to the normal sources, atmospheric pollution is also the result of widespread forest-clearing operations, especially forest burning by small holding farmers and bigger agricultural enterprises. Another source is the large-scale transportation and deposition of dust by desert winds. Estimates of the quantities of dust moved are quite large: 13 million tonnes per season, mainly from the Saharan and Sahelian zones, are deposited on land all the way across the Atlantic. This material not only "fertilizes" the Latin American and Caribbean forest belt; it also provides trace nutrients (including phosphorus) that permit the growth of oceanic plankton.

Water pollution: Through clearing of vegetation and the transformation and intensification of land use, both for ploughing and for the accumulation of "bricks and mortar" (urbanization), surface runoff has increased and a number of river beds have become significantly silted. In the bigger urban centres the industrial impact on the hydrological cycle is quite marked. The dumping of liquid and solid wastes of all kinds has polluted the urban water supply almost everywhere. Waterborne wastes include industrial waste water from timber and paper-pulp mills, mercury pollution from gold mining, pollution from leather tanning, and pollution from cellulose-based industries. There are presumably significant saline water wastes from oil drilling and pumping operations in Angola and Nigeria.

Solid waste: Data on solid waste are very scanty. Pollution by solid waste is generally high in countries with major mining operations (e.g. iron ore in Liberia and Mauritania, tin/columbite mining in Nigeria, gold mining in Ghana, or bauxite mining in Guinea and Cameroon). These operations cause major potential environmental hazards but they also often constitute the only source of hard currency - along with cocoa or coffee - for the national economies. Manufacturing waste is far less voluminous than mining or agricultural waste. Municipal waste is an increasing problem, however. In many urban agglomerations, "waste economies" are an important part of the informal sector. Special situations arise when social groups live on (and from) waste dumps, as for instance in Cairo.

Industrialization and urbanization: In West Africa, industrialization is still in a very early stage. So far, West Africa is suffering many of the disadvantages and enjoying only a few of the benefits of industrialization. Local small-scale industries often concentrate on repairing and renovating industrial products. Urbanization has fuelled industrialization. Energy supply, transportation facilities, public infrastructure, and proximity to political power (because of security and influence considerations) are important location factors for the siting of industries in the big cities. Metallurgical and chemical industries exist on a very limited scale, if at all. The same applies to electronics industries. There is, however, a certain growth of small-scale industries in rural areas and in smaller regional centres.

The main resource-based industries such as mining, quarrying, and agricultural enterprises are generally not closely linked to urban centres. The socio-political influence of the transnational corporations has declined in Africa in recent years. These enterprises often operate in isolated "enclaves," such as mining or plantation areas, with minimum interaction with the larger society. Pollution control and other regulatory measures, including recycling and cleaner forms of production, are in a very initial phase. In most African countries environmental control mechanisms exist only "on paper." For instance, Nigeria has its Environmental Protection Law of 1986, but, as in most developing countries, actual enforcement remains difficult.

Besides demographic growth (generally around 3 per cent per annun or more), African development is strongly influenced by the situation of the political economy and the access of countries to resources. Critics of a one-sided climatic explanation of hazards and disasters often quote the Sahel crisis of the 1970s as an example to prove the dominant role of socio-political parameters in coping with a famine initiated by drought. However, it seems clear that only consideration of both biophysical and socio-economic and cultural factors can explain the vulnerability of the "political ecology" within this zone.

If one looks at it spatially, one finds that the most vulnerable groups do not necessarily live in the most vulnerable locations. It is the combination and overlap of the two that leads to the most problematic cases of marginality and sensitivity. In this respect the impact of technology may vary. Irrigation, for instance, may reduce biophysical vulnerability. On the other hand, irrigation practices may lead to salinization and waterlogging. The heated controversy over the consequences of the "Green Revolution," with its technology packages (improved water supply, seed selection, chemical fertilizers, etc.), for resulting development is typical of this debate.

Structural Adjustment Programmes (SAPs)

SAPs have been adopted by more than 30 countries in sub-Saharan Africa, more especially in the 1980s, although African states were already affected by World Bank and IMP policies in the 1960s. Because world recession problems had to be overcome, African governments cooperated with the Bank and the IMP in various ways. Sometimes "shock treatments" were implemented in less than two years to resolve a crisis. In other cases more gradual reforms were spread over longer periods, also affecting the industrial sector. It was claimed that the beneficiaries of SAPs were the rural poor, because they were protected in relation to the urban poor by the stimulation of exports and an increase in farm incomes, offsetting in part the decline in wages.

However, it seems unsafe to argue on the basis of the rural-urban dichotomy alone. What, for instance, is happening to rural incomes that are often dependent on remittances from urban and industrial workers? On the whole, and in most parts of the world, one of the most generally recognized impacts of SAPs has been increased social differentiation, including the rural poor. Although this process seems to have been stronger in Latin America and Asia than in Africa, even the World Bank initiated special policies directed at the poor to complement the existing SAPs.

It is interesting to note that environmental problems, such as, for instance, the dependence of economic productivity on the conservation of the endowment of natural resources, have so far hardly been considered in the design of SAPs. Although it can be reasonably argued that in some cases SAPs have been a success (e.g. the Economic Recovery Programme in Ghana), on the whole sub-Saharan Africa has had a long history of poverty, war, and famine extending over millennia: "vulnerability, inequality and threats to the social fabric in Africa are not a product of the 1970's and 1980's, much less of Fund and Bank prescriptions for stabilization and adjustment. Nor are they purely imported colonial phenomena". Africa's economic and financial problems were made worse by a combination of:

— an investment in growth and development that failed to earn the expected rewards;

— the international debt crisis, oil price hikes, and rising interest rates, plus the inadequacy of the aid programmes that were meant to provide relief;

— repeated drought, crop failure, and widespread famine;

— the failure of agricultural production to contribute significantly to growth and the increased dependence on imported food.

Poverty, which contributes so much to the environmental degradation of Africa, can in the long run be overcome only by improving economic sustainability, which will be achieved not only through economic reforms but by more appropriate investments, including industrial activities and expanding trade.

2

Environmental Trends

Water Crisis

Water may be the resource that defines the limits of sustainable development. It has no substitute, and the balance between humanity's demands and the quantity available is already precarious. Only about 2.5 per cent of all water on the planet is fresh water—essential for most human purposes—and only about 0.5 per cent is accessible groundwater or surface water. Rainfall quantities vary greatly around the world. Portions of Northern Africa and Western Asia receive very small amounts of rain.

Income is related to the availability of water between and within nations. The more developed regions have on average substantially higher rainfall than those less and least developed. Additionally, richer countries can better afford the investments needed to develop reservoirs, dams and other technologies to capture fresh water run-off and available groundwater.

Global population has tripled over the past 70 years and water use has grown six-fold as the result of industrial development and increased use of irrigation. More recently, per capita use of water has leveled off, so total water consumption is growing at about the same pace as population. Satisfying the water needs of 77 million additional people each year has been estimated as requiring an amount roughly equal to the flow of the Rhine. But the amount of available fresh water has not changed.

Worldwide, 54 per cent of the annual available fresh water is being used. If consumption per person remains steady, by 2025 we could be using 70 per cent of the total because of population growth alone. If per capita consumption everywhere reached the level of more developed countries we could be using 90 per cent of the available water by 2025.

Such extrapolations assume no change in the efficiency of water use. It has been estimated, however, that relatively low-cost technologies could double agricultural productivity per unit of available water. In the past 50 years, industrialized countries have significantly increased efficiencies in industrial and agricultural water use. Many of the same technologies—for example, drip irrigation instead of flood irrigation—are increasingly available in developing countries, but cost and cultural issues (like educational outreach to facilitate behaviour change) must be addressed.

Water Availability

Countries are characterized as water-stressed or -scarce depending on the amount of renewable water available. Water-stressed countries have fewer than 1,700 cubic metres of water available per person per year. In this circumstance, water is often temporarily unavailable at particular locations, and difficult choices must be made among uses of water for personal consumption, agriculture or industry. Water-scarce countries have fewer than 1,000 cubic metres per year. At this level, there may not be enough water to provide adequate food, economic development is hampered and severe environmental difficulties may develop.

In the year 2000, 508 million people lived in 31 water-stressed or -scarce countries. By 2025, 3 billion people will be living in 48 such countries. The number of people living in conditions of scarcity will double, and those living in water stress will increase six-fold.

For some purposes, river basins are a more appropriate unit than countries for analysing water flows. Many of the world's major river basins encompass more than one country. Currently 2.3 billion people live in river basins that are at least water stressed; 1.7 billion live in basins where scarcity conditions prevail. By 2025 these numbers will be 3.5 billion and 2.4 billion, respectively.

Domestic Consumption Needs

According to United Nations Secretary-General Kofi Annan."Access to safe water is a fundamental human need and, therefore, a basic human right." Experts have outlined a basic daily water requirement (BWR)—50 litres per capita per day for the purposes of drinking, sanitation, bathing, cooking and kitchen needs—and urged its recognition as the standard against which to measure the right to safe water.

Countries use different methods for collecting data on domestic water use, and uniform standards for assessing quality have not been set. Available country estimates indicate that 61 countries, with combined populations of 2.1 billion people in 2000, were using less water than the BWR. By 2050, 4.2 billion people (over 45 per cent of the global total) will be living in countries below the BWR standard.

This minimal standard does not take into account other necessary uses of water—for agriculture, ecosystem protection and industry. A consumption standard of 100 litres per person per day would reflect these additional needs; in 2000 there were 3.75 billion people in 80 countries below this level. The population of these countries will increase to 6.4 billion by 2050.

Women in many parts of the world have the primary responsibility for collecting water for their families, and spend up to five times as much time on this as men do. The more distant the water source, the greater the burden on women.

Both distance and the source affect the amount of water used by individual households. For example, when the source is a public standpipe more than a kilometre from home, use is typically less than 10 litres per day; water consumption might be twice as high when the standpipe is closer, and considerably higher in households with running water connections.

Unsustainable Water Use

Many countries use unsustainable means to meet their water needs. If more water is withdrawn than is replenished by natural processes, the excess is essentially "mined" from reserves. These can be recent local aquifers or, in extreme cases, ancient sources of underground "paleo-water". The water tables under some cities in China, Latin America and South Asia are declining at over one metre per year.

Agriculture and industry divert large amounts of water with sometimes-disastrous effects. The best-known example is the Aral Sea, which has been destroyed by diverting its feeder waters for irrigation. The Yellow River in China ran dry from 600 kilometres upstream to the river's mouth every year in the 1990s. In 1997, it ran dry a record 226 days. The Rio Grande River on the U.S.-Mexico border developed a sandbar at its mouth recently, highlighting the loss of its flow.

The construction of large dams has slowed, particularly in more-developed countries, as their disadvantages are appreciated: environmental disruption, displacement of long-settled populations, loss of agricultural land, silting and denial of water to downstream areas, sometimes in other countries. Large dam projects continue in Turkey, China and India.

Water Quality

Quantitative estimates of water availability or consumption do not capture the full challenge of water needs. The quality of the available water is far from adequate. The World Health Organization reports that about 1.1 billion people do not have access to clean water (whatever its quantity). Fully 2.4-3.0 billion people lack access to sanitation. These shortcomings are most pronounced in rural areas, where 29 per cent of residents lack access to clean water and 62 per cent to sanitation systems.

Rapid and unplanned population growth in and around urban areas is overwhelming their capacity to meet water needs. For the first time, official statistics reflect a decline in coverage compared to previous estimates: current estimates are that clean water is not available to at least 6 per cent of urban dwellers and 14 per cent lack sanitation, but this clearly understates the problem.

Water quality is closely related to availability, and to decisions about land use, industrial and agricultural production, and waste disposal. In developing countries, 90-95 per cent of sewage and 70 per cent of industrial wastes are dumped untreated into surface waters where they pollute the usable water supply.

Natural systems purify circulating water when there is enough available. When water becomes progressively scarcer, it is also generally of poorer quality. Intensive land use and industrial development also affect quality. In many industrial countries fertilizer, pesticide and manure run-off from the land and acid rain from atmospheric contamination call for expensive and energy-intensive filtration and treatment to restore acceptable quality. Restoring natural flow patterns to river systems, managing irrigation, chemical use and animal wastes, and curbing industrial air pollution are vital steps towards improving overall sustainability as well as water quality.

New Challenges

Agriculture uses two thirds of the available fresh water. Rising incomes in recent decades have led to an increase in meat consumption in many countries. This requires substantial additional inputs of grain and water. Competition for increasingly scarce water increases the likelihood of international conflict (both economic and military) over water quality and diversion schemes. More than 200 river systems cross national boundaries. Thirteen major rivers and lakes are shared by 100 countries.

There are great uncertainties as to the future impacts of global warming on water availability and thus on the sustainability of human settlement patterns. Rainfall patterns, including the intensity and timing of storms and the rate of evaporation, are likely to change significantly as the climate warms.

Purely technological solutions to water scarcity are likely to have limited effect. Desalinized seawater now accounts for less than 1 per cent of the water people consume. It is likely that this will increase, but it is only feasible in countries wealthy enough to take on the costs—currently oil-producing states of west Asia—with no need to transport the water over long distances. Movement of fresh water in large plastic bags pulled by ships has been of some value in the eastern Mediterranean, but as with desalination, it is of little help to landlocked countries or inland populations and of limited scale.

More ambitious proposals, such as transporting icebergs, have proven unfeasible to date. Collecting large amounts of rainfall that lands on the oceans may become feasible but the effects of reflected light and heat from the plastic sheets required could create problems. Transport of such water to needy populations may very well pose insurmountable problems. As in so many other areas, technology will not ride to the rescue: political and social decisions are needed, which may be difficult now but will certainly be still more difficult as populations grow and their requirements demand more from the same fixed resource.

Trends in Agricultural Production

Environmental degradation, population growth, overstressed agriculture and inadequate international food distribution raise the question: Will there be enough food in the future? Two billion people lack food security as the Food and Agriculture Organization of the United Nations defines it, a "state of affairs where all people at all times have access to safe and nutritious food to maintain a healthy and active life".

In many countries population growth has raced ahead of food production in recent years. The world grain harvest increased about 1 per cent annually between 1990 and 1997, less than the average population growth rate of 1.6 per cent in the developing world. Between 1985 and 1995 food production lagged behind population growth in 64 of 105 developing countries studied by FAO. Africa fared worst among major regions. Food production per person fell in 31 of 46 African countries.

The average amount of grain land per person dropped by almost half between 1950 and 1996—from 0.23 hectares to 0.12 hectares. By 2030, when world population is projected to be at least 8 billion, there would be just 0.08 hectares of grain land per person. As for developing countries, in 1992, there were about 0.2 hectares of arable land per person. By 2050, this figure could fall to about 0.1 hectare per capita.

According to the International Food Policy Research Institute (IFPRI), the world's farmers will have to produce 40 per cent more grain in 2020 than in 1999. Most of this projected increase will have to come from yield increases on existing land, not the cultivation of new land. Countries are not equally affected. Australia, Europe, and North America have large surpluses of food for export. Their populations are growing slowly, if at all, and per capita consumption is not increasing.

These countries are probably capable of expanding food production considerably beyond current levels, though the long-term sustainability of intensive farming practices has been brought into question by recent events. The most widely publicized are outbreaks of "mad cow disease" (bovine spongiform encephalopathy) and foot-and-mouth disease; but there is also considerable concern about salmonella poisoning from eggs and chickens, and mutant, drug-resistant E. coli infections from contaminated meat and water, all of which can be traced in some way to the desire to maximize agricultural output and reduce costs.

There is also considerable controversy over genetic modifications (GM) to food crops and animals. Though GM has not been shown to be directly harmful to humans, the practice carries risks, including social effects, which have yet to be fully evaluated. A British government report has raised fears that GM will threaten biodiversity.

Another group of countries cannot grow enough food on their own land to feed their populations but can make up the shortfall through imports. Such countries include Japan, Singapore, Chile and the oil-producing states of the Arabian Gulf. Over half the world's population, most of the people of the developing world—including nearly all of sub-Saharan Africa—live in "low-income, food-deficit countries", according to FAO.

The low-income, food-deficit countries do not produce enough to feed their people and cannot import sufficient food to close the gap. In these countries just under 800 million people are chronically malnourished, according to a 1999 estimate by FAO.

Problems of Food-Deficit Countries

In many low-income food-deficit countries, food production capacities are deteriorating in the face of soil degradation, chronic water shortages, in appropriate agricultural policies and rapid population growth. The gap between production and market demand for cereals in South Asia is forecast to widen from 1 million metric tons in 1990 to 24 million tons in 2020, and in sub-Saharan Africa from 9 million to 27 million metric tons. The gap between production and need in these grain-short regions will be even greater unless poverty can be significantly reduced. Low-income food-deficit countries face the following constraints to achieving food security:

Limited arable land. Increases in food production will have to come from existing agricultural land. Arable land could in theory be increased by 40 per cent, or 2 billion hectares, but most of the uncultivated land is marginal, with poor soils and either not enough rainfall or too much. Bringing it into production would require costly irrigation and water-management systems and large-scale measures to enrich the soil. Much of this land is now under forest, and clearing it would have unforeseeable consequences for erosion, degradation and local climate change, among others.

Shrinking size of family farms. One effect of rapid population growth is the shrinking size of family farms. In most developing countries, the size of small family farms has been cut in half over the past four decades, as plots are divided into smaller and smaller pieces for each new and larger generation of heirs. For example, in 57 developing countries surveyed by FAO in the early 1990s, over half of all farms were less than one hectare, not enough to feed the average rural family with four to six children. In India three fifths of all farms are less than one hectare.

Land degradation. Moderate to severe soil degradation affects nearly 2 billion hectares of crop and grazing land. This is an area larger than the United States and Mexico combined. When soils are overworked and exposed, they are easily eroded by wind and water, the main agents of soil degradation. Faulty irrigation and drainage can make land useless through waterlogging and salinization. Misuse of fertilizers, herbicides and pesticides also plays a role in soil degradation.

Soil erosion and other forms of land degradation claim 5 million to 7 million hectares of farm land each year. In Kazakhstan, for instance, the Institute of Soil Management has estimated that the country will lose nearly half of its crop-land by 2025 due to soil erosion and degradation. Globally, land degradation threatens the livelihoods of at least 1 billion farmers and ranchers, most of them in poor countries.

Water shortages and degradation. Water for irrigated agriculture accounts for roughly 70 per cent of all water withdrawn for human use annually on a global basis. When water becomes short, rural farmers often find it difficult to maintain food supplies. In the Indian state of Uttar Pradesh, for instance, the number of water-short villages has soared from 17,000 to 70,000 in two decades, suppressing crop production.

Conflicts within countries are also of mounting concern to national governments. In China, for instance, conflicts over water seem to be escalating. In August 2000, six people were killed when officials from Luhe County, in Guangdong Province, blew up a water channel to stop a neighbouring county (Puding) from diverting water from the Yellow River, as agreed to in a court settlement. Farmers in both counties depend on river water to irrigate their crops. Within increasingly limited and polluted supplies, their yields (and incomes) are falling dramatically.

Irrigation problems. Food supply is threatened not only by water shortages themselves but also by ineffective irrigation practices. Although only 17 per cent of all croplands are under irrigation, these lands produce one third of the world's total food supply. Less than half of all water withdrawn for irrigation purposes actually reaches the crops. The rest soaks into unlined canals, leaks out of pipes or evaporates on its way to the fields.

Badly planned and poorly built irrigation systems have reduced yields on one half of all irrigated land, according to a 1995 estimate by FAO. The two main problems are salinization and waterlogging of crops. FAO estimates that salt build-up in soil has severely damaged 25-30 million hectares of the world's 255 million hectares of irrigated land. Another 80 million hectares are affected by a combination of salinization and waterlogging.

Every year, on average, about 1.5 million hectares of irrigated land is taken out of production because of salt build-up alone, half of the amount of land brought into production. With such problems, the world's irrigated croplands may actually be shrinking at a time when they should be expanding to meet growing demand for food, according to the International Irrigation Management Institute.

Waste. Tremendous amounts of food are wasted annually through the effects of rat or insect infestation, spoilage and losses that occur during the transportation process. In China, for instance, an estimated 25 per cent of grain collected is wasted; rats or other pests consume much of it. Similarly, according to the Vietnamese Government, about 13-16 per cent of rice and 20 per cent of vegetables harvested in Viet Nam are wasted because of poor preservation conditions and practices.

Value of Genetic Diversity

After 10,000 years of settled agriculture and the discovery of some 50,000 varieties of edible plants, just 15 food crops provide 90 per cent of the world's food energy intake. Three of them—rice, wheat and maize (corn)—are the staple foods of 4 billion people. Dependence on only a few crops is dangerous because disease can spread rapidly through monocultures, as it did through the Irish potato harvest in the 1840s, starving to death a fifth of the country's population.

Since 1900 about three quarters of the genetic diversity of domestic agricultural crops has been lost, FAO estimates. Without constant infusions of new genes from the wild, geneticists cannot continue to improve staple crops. Cultivars (cultivated plants) need to be reinvigorated every 5 to 15 years in order to give them greater resistance against diseases and insects, as well as to introduce new yield-enhancing traits, such as increased tolerance for drought or saline soils. The most effective way to do this is to interbreed domestic varieties with wild ones.

Plant breeders are alarmed at the continuing genetic erosion of the earth's wild strains of cereals and other cultivars. Tropical deforestation, rapid urbanization, the destruction of vital wetlands and the over-cultivation of dry lands has destroyed countless habitats for wild progenitors of domestic crops. Unless the rate of plant genetic loss is halted or slowed substantially, as many as 60,000 plant species—roughly one quarter of the world's total—could be lost by 2025, according to the International Centre for Agricultural Research in Dry Areas.

Meat Consumption Revolution

For many food deficit low-income countries, feeding a growing population means coaxing more food out of the same amount of land. Canadian geographer Vaclav Smil estimated that the minimum amount of land needed to supply a vegetarian diet for one person without any use of artificial chemical inputs is 0.07 hectare, or slightly less than a quarter of an acre. Based on this, Population Action International estimated that currently some 420 million people live in land-scarce developing countries. If fertility and population growth in developing countries continue to fall, there could be 560 million by 2025. If not, there could be 1.04 billion such people.

According to IFPRI, a "demand-driven livestock revolution is under way in the developing world with profound implications for global agriculture, health, livelihoods and the environment". IFPRI projects that meat demand in the developing world will double between 1995 and 2020 to 190 million metric tons. Demand for meat in the developing world is expected to grow much faster than for cereals—by close to 3 per cent per year for meat compared with 1.8 per cent for cereals. In per capita terms, demand for meat will increase 40 per cent between 1995 and 2020.

What this means is that demand for cereals to feed livestock will double in developing countries over the next generation. By 2020, feed grain demand is projected to reach just under 450 million metric tons. Given this trend, well under way in much of Asia, demand for maize (corn) will increase much faster than any other cereal, growing by 2.35 per cent per year over the next 20 years. Nearly two thirds of this increased demand will go towards feeding livestock. In China, rising incomes and changing diets have resulted in a tremendous demand for meat, particularly poultry and pigs. Over the next two decades total demand for meat will double, increasing pressure on grain producers. It takes 4-5 kilograms of feed to produce 1 kilogram of meat.

Moving Towards Food Security

Achieving food security—assuring that everyone has access to enough food to be healthy—requires action to increase food production, and at the same time protect the environment. Slower population growth in poor countries would allow more time to achieve sustainable food production. Actions that promote slower population growth, especially the empowerment of women, also work towards protecting the natural resource base on which increased food production depends.

Increasing food production. To accommodate the nearly 8 billion people expected on earth by 2025 and improve their diets, the world will have to double food production over current levels. In recent years, there have been some promising developments. These include a new strain of super rice capable of boosting yields by 25 per cent, improved varieties of maize that could increase yields by up to 40 per cent and could be grown on marginal land, and a new blight-resistant potato.

Experience with the Green Revolution of the 1960s indicates that technological advances and market forces can dramatically increase food production, but do not necessarily solve food security problems. New high-yielding varieties, for example, call for specialized fertilizers and pesticides. These inputs increase yields but there is increasing evidence that they disturb the ecological balance, creating new disease and pest problems, which call for further inputs. In low-income areas, these inputs represent a considerable expense, which biases success towards large holdings with considerable cash reserves to invest. Smaller farmers may be less successful and may even be forced to give up their land, becoming casual labourers with an uncertain income.

As Amartya Sen and others have pointed out, the problems of food shortage are often not absolute but related to income. During famines, poor people have often starved while food was plentiful, but beyond their reach. Social mechanisms such as overall responsible governance, local control over food production and supply, and emergency stocks to ensure fair prices are needed to avoid hunger.

Protecting the environment. Protecting the environment enhances a country's food production potential. To achieve food security, countries must reverse the current course of land and water resource degradation. Specific actions include local management, including land ownership reform, and a careful review of land use, especially for cash crops calling for intensive fertilizer application and irrigation. Trade-offs may be sought between different forms of land use, for example, between building dams to increase water supply and losing arable land to reservoirs, or between higher yields and environmental costs. Finding the correct balance calls for careful and responsible discussion among all the parties involved.

One frequent problem is where alternative uses are proposed for land and water resources among remote and scattered communities with little political power. The interests of such communities need protection. In many cases, they represent more than local interests and should be carefully weighed. Such remote areas may be important upland watersheds, or they may be forests that harbour genetic diversity. The simple prospect of increasing food production in the short term may be less important than a more complex long-term calculus taking these factors into account.

Local voices should often be those of women, who have most of the responsibility for finding food, water and fuel for the family. In most of the food deficit countries, women's power to manage local land and water resources does not match their responsibility. Actions to empower women in this area include health care and education, which also give women control over other areas of their lives, including fertility and family size.

Even the poorest countries can safeguard their resource base—particularly topsoil and freshwater sources—improve the productive capacity of land, increase agricultural yields and hope to achieve food security in the future. To do this successfully, however, calls for responsible governance balancing many interests, a commitment to food security, considered action and the cooperation of the international community.

Trends of Climate Change

Carbon dioxide and other "greenhouse gases" trap heat in the atmosphere and raise average global surface temperatures. Emissions of carbon dioxide grew 12-fold between 1900 and 2000, from 534 million metric tons per year in 1900 to 6.59 billion metric tons in 1997. In the same period, human population nearly quadrupled, from 1.6 billion to 6.1 billion, progressively consuming greater quantities of fossil fuels—oil, gas and coal. Expanded agriculture, destruction of forests and increased production of certain chemicals also increase greenhouse gases in the atmosphere.

It is unlikely that the human population could ever have reached its present size without the energy provided by fossil fuels. Conversely, the needs of the growing population have provided an ever-expanding market for exploration and production.

Global CO_2 Emissions

Climate change will have a serious impact. The Intergovernmental Panel on Climate Change (IPCC) estimates that the earth's atmosphere will warm by as much as 5.8 degrees Celsius over the coming century, a rate unmatched over the past 10,000 years. The IPCC's "best estimate" scenario projects a sea-level rise of about half a metre by 2100 (with a range of 15 to 95 centimetres), substantially greater than the increase over the last century.

The human and ecological impacts of rising oceans include increased flooding, coastal erosion, salinization of aquifers, and loss of coastal cropland, wetlands and living space. The intensity and frequency of hurricanes and other hazardous weather may also increase, endangering the growing human population in coastal areas. Rising global surface temperatures and changes in precipitation magnitude, intensity and geographical distribution may well redraw the world renewable resources map.

Whether or not these climatic changes affect net global agricultural production, they are almost certain to shift productivity among regions and countries, and within nations. For example, recent projections suggest that while total U.S. agriculture production may not diminish, certain regions of the country are likely to suffer substantially relative to others, as a result of changes in precipitation and temperature. Climate change policy will have to address changing regional and national fortunes, as well as the global economic and biological impact.

A warming climate also poses a significant public health threat. The redistribution of precipitation would markedly increase the number of people living in regions under extreme water stress—a problem compounded by increasing population. The geographical range of temperature-sensitive tropical diseases, such as malaria and dengue fever, would also expand. Higher average temperatures mean longer and more-intense heat waves, with a corresponding rise in heat-related health problems.

The combined effects of population growth and climate change could produce regional resource shortages, which in turn could result in the exploitation of environmentally sensitive areas such as hillsides, flood plains, coastal areas and wetlands. These conditions may also increase environmental refugees, international economic migration and associated socio-political challenges. Climate and environmental policy should address the geographical distribution and movement of people in the 21st century, as well as their absolute numbers.

Population and Climate Policy

Since 1970, average carbon dioxide emissions per capita have been relatively stable, so that on a worldwide scale the rise in industrial emissions over the last three decades correlates closely with population growth. Population trends and policy have therefore played a major part in the trajectory of emissions in the past, and they could have an even greater role in the future. In 1995, the 20 per cent of the world's population living in countries with the highest per capita fossil-fuel carbon dioxide emissions contributed 63 per cent of the world's total emissions. The 20 per cent with the lowest per capita emissions contributed just 2 per cent of all carbon dioxide emissions.

Almost all additional significant population growth is projected to occur in developing countries (the notable exception being the United States). Developing country emissions will become the major factor early in the 21st century, and a future global climate change treaty will need to respond to this coming demographic reality. Per capita emissions must be reduced, in the developed countries but also in major developing nations such as China and Mexico.

Forests, Habitat and Biodiversity

People now use or appropriate an estimated 39-50 per cent or more of the earth's biological production, through agriculture, forestry and other activities. Half of the world's forests have disappeared since the end of the last Ice Age, and only 22 per cent of the original forest cover remains in large, unbroken areas without substantial human influence. Deforestation rates in the last few decades have reached the highest levels in history, as global population growth has also peaked. In the last 40 years, per capita forest area worldwide has fallen by more than 50 per cent, from a global average of 1.2 hectares to less than 0.6 hectares per person. This is due to both decreasing forest area and increasing population, and it threatens the well-being of both people and the forests they depend on.

The proportional loss of forests (the amount lost relative to the amount remaining) has been greatest in Asia, followed by Africa and Latin America. These ongoing losses have been partially offset (by about 10 per cent) by a relatively small increase in forest plantations and re-growth in some developed countries. Tropical forests contain an estimated 50 per cent of the world's remaining biodiversity (plant and animal species).

At current rapid deforestation rates, and in the absence of any intervention, the last significant primary tropical forest could be harvested within 50 years. Because habitat destruction is the leading cause of species extinction, the loss of tropical forests is likely to lead to a substantial and irreversible decline in global biodiversity. Biomass in tropical forests amounts to a substantial carbon sink within the global ecosystem.

After fossil fuel combustion, tropical deforestation is the second most important source of carbon dioxide, the primary greenhouse gas. Only 8 per cent of the remaining tropical forests are legally well-protected, and often protected status does not confer actual protection. International development and conservation organizations have promoted "integrated conservation and development projects" as a strategy for developing countries where people depend on land and biotic resources within reserves. Tropical parks have been somewhat effective in reducing land clearing (deforestation) relative to surrounding unmanaged areas.

However, their success in slowing tropical deforestation has been mixed or poor, in part because such projects may attract people to the remaining forests. Many of the countries that contain the largest blocks of remaining tropical forest are also those with the highest population growth rates (2-4 per cent per year).

Ongoing human migration, both national and international, is another critical factor that affects forests, habitat and biodiversity. Recent research in Central America has shown that human population density and loss of forest cover are closely correlated at local, district, and national levels and over time, both outside and within protected and managed reserves. Evidence to date suggests that reserves with essentially unbroken forest cover may be successful only where very low human population densities (1-2 persons per square kilometre) can be maintained.

Unfortunately, population growth and fertility rates are often very high in and near developing country forest reserves, while access to reproductive health care and contraceptive prevalence rates are low in these rural and frequently isolated areas. Sustainable forestry and other sustainable development approaches hold some promise for reducing habitat destruction and species loss. However, the projected increases in human population over the next few decades, particularly in the tropics, will inevitably continue to present very difficult choices between the use of land for forests, habitat and biodiversity preservation, and human uses such as the production of food and fuel.

Regional Environmental Trends

The following are highlights of major environmental trends in Asia, Africa, and Latin America, as reported in the United Nations Environment Programme's Global Environment Outlook 2000 report.

Asia and the Pacific

Asia, with 29.5 per cent of the world's land area, supports 60 per cent of its population. High population densities and widespread poverty are putting enormous stress on the environment. Major challenges include:

— *Land degradation:* At least 1.3 billion people (39 per cent of the region's population) live in areas prone to drought and desertification. More than 350 million hectares are already desertified. About 20 per cent (around 550 million hectares) of Asia's vegetated land is affected by soil degradation. In India, Iran and Pakistan, water and wind erosion are major contributors to soil degradation. In India, as much as

27 per cent of the soil has been affected by severe erosion. China, India and Pakistan all suffer from land salinization resulting from excessive groundwater irrigation. Excessive agrochemical inputs are also responsible for land degradation in many countries of this region.

— *Deforestation:* Forest cover has been receding rapidly across Asia, largely due to the unsustainable exploitation of timber reserves and unchecked agricultural expansion. Six countries (China, Indonesia, Malaysia, Myanmar, the Philippines, and Thailand) account for three quarters of recent deforestation in the region. Many forests, such as those in the Mekong Basin, have been logged to the point that they are of critically low quality. Illegal logging amplifies the pressure on forest resources in several Asian countries. Fuelwood harvesting, irrigation schemes, hydroelectric power projects, urbanization, infrastructure development, natural disasters and fires also contribute to deforestation. Wars denuded forest cover in Viet Nam and Laos, while forest fires were a significant factor in Indonesia. The adoption of sustainable forest and agricultural management policies has slowed forest depletion in Thailand, Viet Nam and Cambodia.

— *Water resource depletion:* Agriculture accounts for a larger percentage of freshwater usage in Asia than in any other part of the world and freshwater will be the major limiting factor to producing more food in the future. Dams and groundwater irrigation have disrupted the natural hydrological cycle, reducing river levels, depleting wetlands and aquifers, and salinizing agricultural lands. Dirty water and poor sanitation claim more than 500,000 infant deaths a year. Asia's rivers contain three times as many bacteria from human waste as the world average. One in three Asians has no access to safe drinking water, often as a result of contamination of groundwater and surface water reserves by sewage and industrial waste. A study of 15 Japanese cities, for example, showed that chlorinated solvents from industry contaminate 30 per cent of all groundwater supplies. Agrochemical inputs are a growing source of water contamination as nitrates leach into freshwater bodies. Salt-water intrusion also threatens the water supply in many areas; in Madras, India, for instance, salt water has rendered many irrigation wells useless as far as 10 kilometres inland.

— *Biodiversity depletion:* Indonesia, India, and China are among the countries with the most threatened species of mammals and birds, according to the World Conservation Union (IUCN). Indonesia has the highest number of threatened mammals (135 species), followed by India (80) and China (72). The Philippines has more critically endangered birds than any other country in the world.

— *Air quality and carbon emissions:* Air pollution is now becoming a part of the region's environment, causing deaths. In China, for instance, smoke and small particles from burning coal cause more than 50,000 premature deaths and 400,000 new cases of chronic bronchitis a year. Led by China and Japan, emissions of carbon dioxide increased at twice the average world rate of 2.6 per cent per year during 1975-1995.

— *Urbanization:* Asia has 160 of the world's 369 cities with more than 750,000 residents. Growing populations have frequently outpaced the development of urban infrastructures, and slums and shanty towns are growing in many cities. In Colombo, for example, some

50 per cent of the urban population resides in slums and squatter areas. The urban population of the region, now about 35 per cent of the total population, grew by 3.2 per cent a year between 1990 and 1995, compared with 0.8 per cent a year for the rural population. In most countries, the urban population is likely to grow threefold in the next 40 years. China alone is expected to have 832 million urban residents by 2025.

GEO-2000 reports that "some governments are now taking action to reconcile trade and environmental interests through special policies, agreements on products standards, enforcement of the Polluter Pays Principle, and the enforcement of health and sanitary standards for food exports."

Africa

Africa's population density of 249 people per 1,000 hectares is well below the world average of 442. However, a great deal of the total destruction of the natural environment is occurring in the region. Poverty is a major cause and consequence. Natural disasters such as storms, floods and droughts are common and highly destructive. Global warming may make Africa even dryer in the future; this could seriously disrupt natural ecosystems and make food security a major problem. Widespread poverty, HIV/AIDS and diseases spread by water and insects remain critical challenges for the region. Major environmental issues include:

— *Land degradation:* Soil degradation is a major concern in Africa, where 500 million hectares have been affected, including 65 per cent of the agricultural land. Crop yields could be cut in half in 40 years if degradation continues at the current rate. In Southern

Africa, over-grazing of livestock is a major contributor to soil degradation. Large portions of Northern Africa are facing desertification caused by a combination of over-grazing, rainfall variability and drought conditions. In Western and Central Africa, rising populations and shifting agriculture have damaged large swathes of land.

— *Deforestation*: Although Africa still accounts for 17 per cent of global forest cover, forests are being steadily degraded by population growth, drought, agricultural expansion, fuelwood extraction, commercial exploitation, bush fires, civil wars and political instability. During 1990-1995, Africa lost its forest cover at an annual rate of 0.7 per cent. Unsustainable agricultural practices such as shifting cultivation and slash-and-burn techniques in Southern and Central Africa contributed, as did commercial logging, oil-exploration and mining activities. Ninety per cent of the population depends on firewood and other biomass for energy. Production and consumption of firewood and charcoal doubled between 1970 and 1994 and is expected to rise by another 5 per cent by 2010.

— *Water resource depletion:* While Africa uses only about 4 per cent of its renewable freshwater resources and some countries have abundant lakes and rivers, countries in arid regions depend on limited groundwater reserves. Already, 14 countries in Africa are facing water stress. By 2025, another 11 countries can be expected to face the same conditions. The prospects are particularly bad in northern Africa. The demand for water is expected to grow by at least 3 per cent annually until 2020 as populations increase and economies develop. Surface water contamination is a growing problem with serious implications for public health.

— *Urbanization:* Africa's annual urban growth is now the highest in the world, at more than 4 per cent. In the 1960s about 20 per cent of the population lived in urban areas; the figure rose to 35 per cent in 1995. Urban infrastructure is poorly developed, and periurban areas are expanding, often without planned services and amenities. Much of the urban population lives in medium-sized cities that lack the economic dynamism of larger cities.

— *Biodiversity depletion:* Africa is home to more than 50,000 known plant species, 1,000 mammal species, and 1,500 bird species. This diverse biological heritage is at risk in all subregions.

— *Carbon emissions:* Africa's emissions of greenhouse gases are still low. The region contributes only 3.5 per cent of the world's total carbon dioxide emissions and this figure is expected to increase to only 3.8 per cent by 2010.

Latin America and the Caribbean

Major environmental challenges in Latin America and the Caribbean include:

— *Land degradation:* An estimated 300 million hectares of land have been affected by soil degradation, mostly the result of soil erosion and chemical use. Approximately 100 million hectares are estimated to have been degraded through deforestation and 70 million hectares were overgrazed.

— *Deforestation:* Endowed with the world's most luxuriant tropical forest cover, Latin America is the focus of the global effort to achieve sustainability. Nearly half the region is still covered by natural forest, but 3 per cent of the forest cover was lost during 1990-95. Brazil lost some 15 million hectares of forest area in 1988-97, according to the GEO-2000 report. Agricultural expansion through traditional slash-and-burn practices is considered the prime cause of deforestation. Modern agriculture, logging, mining, infrastructure development, fires and urbanization also contribute.

— *Water resource depletion:* Although Latin America has extensive freshwater systems, nearly two thirds of the region is classified as arid or semi-arid. In some areas, aquifers are being exploited at unsustainable rates as demand for water from domestic, industrial and agricultural users increases. Pollution and sanitation continue to be major issues. The region is also vulnerable to toxic chemical discharge into its water systems from extensive mining and industrial activities.

— *Urbanization:* Nearly 75 per cent of the region's population is already urbanized, many in megacities such as Mexico City (16.5 million people), São Paulo (16 million), Buenos Aires (12 million) and Rio de Janeiro (10 million). Large numbers of city dwellers live in squatter settlements and shantytowns, including 4 million of Rio de Janeiro's 10.6 million residents.

— *Air pollution and carbon emissions:* Air quality in most major cities threatens human health. In São Paulo and Rio de Janeiro, air pollution is estimated to cause 4,000 premature deaths a year. The average ozone concentration in 1995 in Mexico City was about 0.15 parts per million, 10 times the natural atmospheric concentration. The main source of carbon dioxide emissions is deforestation. The region is responsible for 4.3 per cent of the world's total carbon dioxide emissions from industrial processes and 48.3 per cent from land-use changes.

— *Depletion of biodiversity:* The loss of forest cover threatens the region's biological diversity. Already, more than 1,000 vertebrate species are now threatened with extinction. Brazil has the second largest number of threatened bird species (103 species) in the world, and Peru and Colombia occupy fifth place with 64 species each. More than half of the Argentinean mammals and birds are threatened.

Western Asia

Western Asia's population density is well below the world average. However, the scarcity and degradation of water and land resources pose an increasing challenge. Exploitation of the region's oil resources has conferred great benefits to some countries but has also exacted significant costs. Pollution and inadequate waste management are causing degradation of the marine and coastal environment. Major environmental issues include:

— *Land degradation:* Soil degradation has long been a serious problem, increasingly so in the past few decades. Nearly 96 per cent of the land is vulnerable to desertification; nearly four fifths is desert or desertified. Increasing food demand due to population growth has resulted in overgrazing and the extension of cereals onto rangelands in fragile ecosystems; laws and decrees to protect rangeland have not produced significant results. Poor irrigation techniques have also led to soil salinization and nutrient depletion.

— *Deforestation:* Much of the natural forests that once covered much of the north of the region was long ago cleared for settlements, agriculture, grazing and charcoal production. Reforestation programmes have kept forest areas at their current levels over the past two decades, but the high cost of imported timber could increase pressures for further clearing. Clearing of mountain slopes for agriculture has led to severe soil erosion in Jordan, Lebanon, Syria and Yemen.

— *Water resource depletion:* Water is a precious and limited resource in the region, and a potential trigger for serious national conflicts; rainfall is low and erratic and evaporation high. Rapid population growth, relative to water resource development, is reducing per capita use. The Mashriq subregion has rivers that originate outside and short seasonal or perennial rivers.

The Arabian Peninsula is poor in surface water but has larger groundwater reserves than the Mashriq; those reserves are being withdrawn faster than natural recharge rates, however. Conflicts and disputes over water allocations have impeded improvements in the use of surface water. Seawater intrusion and contamination by human and industrial waste and pesticides are affecting water quality. Surface water contamination is a growing problem with serious implications for public health. Costly desalination and wastewater treatment alleviate but do not solve the problems.

Global warming is not expected to reduce, and may worsen, water constraints. Small projected increases in rainfall may be offset by higher temperatures and evaporation.

— *Urbanization:* Urban growth in some countries has been proceeding at twice the rate of overall population growth. More than two thirds of the people live in urban areas (even higher levels obtain in the Gulf countries). Much growth has been concentrated in a small number of cities where opportunities and infrastructure are concentrated. Though land use planning has been attempted, chaotic physical growth and encroachment on agricultural land are common. Peri-urban areas are expanding, often without planned services and amenities.

— *Biodiversity depletion:* The diverse ecosystems of the region are home to many endangered species. Marine ecosystems (mudflats, mangrove swamps, sea grass and coral reefs) are under particular stress. Marine biodiversity has been harmed by over-fishing, pollution and habitat destruction. Protected areas have been established in all parts of the region but depletion of water resources, soil salinization and plant pests are having a large impact on many endemic plant and animal species. Oil and waste spillage into the Persian Gulf is also having a growing impact.

— *Carbon emissions:* The development of the oil industry and rapid industrial and population growth have led some countries to become high energy consumers. Atmospheric emissions of hydrocarbons, carbon dioxide and other pollutants have reached alarming levels, particularly in larger cities. Year-round sunshine and high temperatures help convert primary pollutants to ozone and sulphates, which can be more hazardous to health and the environment.

3

Health and Environment

Environmental conditions contribute significantly to communicable diseases, which account for about 20-25 per cent of deaths annually worldwide. The illnesses most closely related to environmental conditions—infectious and parasitic diseases and respiratory infections and diseases—endanger development prospects, particularly in poor countries and among poor people in any country. Unclean water and associated poor sanitation kill over 12 million people each year. Air pollution kills nearly 3 million more. Changes in land use can create new breeding grounds. Irrigation or dam construction, for example, can encourage waterborne diseases: schistosomiasis established itself in Egypt and Sudan after the building of the Aswan dam. The clearing of tropical forest creates hardpan on which rainwater can collect and mosquitoes can breed. Malaria results in over 1 million deaths each year and accounts for some 300 million new clinical cases each year. Malaria causes 10 per cent of the total deaths in sub-Saharan Africa. It has been estimated that roughly 60 per cent of the global burden of disease from acute respiratory infections, 90 per cent from diarrhoeal disease, 50 per cent from chronic respiratory conditions and 90 per cent from malaria could be avoided by simple environmental interventions.

In more-developed countries, these conditions contribute a lower proportion of the total burden of illness but still are responsible for outbreaks, especially in communities poorly served by sanitation and other clean-water services. Outbreaks of diphtheria in Central and Eastern Europe reflect poorer public health services (including low levels of vaccination) and greater migration of infected and susceptible populations in the wake of political change. Changes in health conditions directly affect development prospects and the chances for eradicating poverty. These are affected by a wide variety of conditions in the human and social environment.

Environmental change can dramatically improve urban health, as in European cities in the 19th century, when piped water and treated sewage eliminated the ancient threat of cholera. In Sri Lanka and other Asian countries in the 1940s a combination of spraying DDT and removing mosquito breeding places temporarily wiped out malaria. Such public health interventions hold down the burden of disease in many developing countries, especially in great cities, but they often fight a losing battle against growing populations, polluting industry, deteriorating infrastructure and housing stock, and shortage of resources.

Crowded living conditions, particularly in urban areas, spread infection. People living in poverty are the most crowded because of the cost of housing and the larger size of their families. Infants in poorer and more crowded portions of cities are at least four times more likely to die than infants in more affluent neighbourhoods. Environmentally related diseases, notably tuberculosis and typhoid, contribute to these differentials.

Trade links between large cities and the surrounding rural areas and smaller cities are accelerating with the integration of economies into the global system. Better transport to centralized markets has helped spread sexually transmitted diseases, including HIV/AIDS.

Infection rates are markedly higher along lorry routes and at border towns where drivers congregate. Ease of transport also allows diseases to travel between regions or continents within human hosts, other animals or cargo. Cholera has travelled from Bangladesh to Chile in the ballast tanks of a freighter. Cholera outbreaks following disasters in India have been spread by infected people leaving the area.

Migration to newly opened lands, sometimes as part of government-approved and -assisted colonization programmes, often removes settlers from the reach of health systems, including reproductive health services. Incentives for doctors and nurses to move to rural locations are generally insufficient and ineffective.

Equipping and re-supply of remote facilities is difficult and their inadequacies deter settlers from using them. Health services in settlements around cities are similarly poor. Mortality rates for the young can be higher than in more-established rural settlements.

Maternal mortality, though difficult to measure, is clearly much higher in rural areas—where fewer births are attended by trained staff and transport in case of pregnancy complications is difficult—than in cities, and higher still in new rural settlements. Large families in new settlements also have a greater effect on their immediate environment than smaller ones. Their needs for food, fuel and water are greater and, with additional resource scavengers, so are their impacts.

HEALTH THREATS

Air Pollution

Air pollution kills an estimated 2.7 million to 3.0 million people every year, about 90 per cent of them in the developing world. The most critical components include: sulphur dioxide (from the burning of oil and high-sulphur coal); particulate matter (from domestic fires, power and industrial plants, and diesel engines); carbon monoxide and nitrogen dioxide (from petrol fumes from motor vehicles); ozone (from the effect of sunlight on vehicle emission-generated smog), and atmospheric lead (from burning leaded petrol or coal).

Outdoor air pollution harms more than 1.1 billion people and kills an estimated half million people per year, mostly in cities. Nearly 30 per cent of these deaths are in developed countries. Fine particulate pollution is responsible for up to 10 per cent of respiratory infections in European children (and twice as much in the most-polluted cities). The situation is particularly serious in the former Soviet Union where, despite reduced levels of industrial output, automobile transport has increased markedly.

Densely populated and rapidly growing megacities in developing countries subject their populations to levels of air pollution exposure far in excess of allowances recommended by the World Health Organization. The one hour per year maximum for specific concentrations (greater than 0.1 parts per million) and 30 days per year limit on generally high ozone exposure are exceeded in Mexico City regularly. The specific limits were exceeded for more than 1,400 hours over only 145 days in 1991.

Asian megacities do better in ozone exposure, but worse with respect to WHO standards for suspended particulate matter and sulphur dioxide (for example in Beijing, Delhi, Jakarta, Kolkata and Mumbai). Cairo, Lagos and Tehran also show high exposure concentrations. Automobile ownership is expanding rapidly in many developing countries.

In Beijing, more than three quarters of survey respondents expect to purchase a car in the near future. India has recognized the growing contribution of automotive exhaust to city pollution. However, efforts in Mumbai to mandate use of liquid propane to power taxis have met strong opposition from drivers and fleet owners. (Similarly, efforts to regulate industrial emissions have generated a counter-response from small businessmen.)

Indoor air pollution—soot from the burning of wood, dung, crop residues and coal for cooking and heating—affects about 2.5 billion people, mostly women and girls, and is estimated to kill more than 2.2 million each year, over 98 per cent of them in developing countries.

Air pollution's impact extends beyond direct health effects. Acid rain results from chemicals dissolved in precipitation. It increases the corrosive effect of rainfall on buildings and structures and makes the lands and waterways that receive it less productive. Alterations in the chemical balance of soils and water have widespread effects on plant and animal life.

Air pollution also reduces food production and timber harvests by impairing photosynthesis. An estimate for Germany suggests that $4.7 billion in agricultural production is lost due to high levels of sulphur, nitrogen oxides and ozone.

Heavy Metals

Heavy metals are released into the environment by metal smelters and other industrial activities, unsafe disposal of industrial wastes, and the use of lead in water pipes and petrol. The most dangerous metals, when concentrated above naturally occurring levels, include lead, mercury, cadmium, arsenic, copper, zinc and chromium. These have diverse effects relating to cancers (arsenic and cadmium), genetic damage (mercury) and brain and bone damage (copper, lead and mercury).

Bangladeshi woman giving birth. Women weakened by environment-related health problems are more vulnerable in pregnancy and childbirth. Lead pollution from leaded petrol (phased out in the United States and the European Community over the past three decades), worsened by use in inefficient or poorly maintained engines, causes widespread health problems in some countries. It contributes to lower levels of intelligence among exposed children and later loss of productivity in adulthood.

Nuclear Contamination

The contaminated areas around the Chernobyl nuclear facility in the Ukraine provide one of the starkest examples of the catastrophic dangers of unsafe nuclear power use. Over 2 million people were immediately affected, including 500,000 children. There has been a great increase in thyroid cancers, in some areas over a 100-fold higher incidence than expected. The full impact in thyroid and other cancers will develop over the coming years. The 600,000 soldiers and civilians who worked to clean up the site over several years will also bear the burden of radiation exposure. The 50,000 who worked on top of the reactor building to put out the fire and build its new concrete containment were most seriously exposed and affected. Research suggests that some 30 per cent suffer from reproductive disorders (including higher levels of infertility and birth defects). Many area residents are afraid to have children from fear of defects, fears that are complicated by the continuing decline in the capacity of the health system. Observed effects are clearly related to proximity and exposure.

Malformations (including cleft palate, Down's syndrome and deformed limbs and organs) increased 83 per cent in severely contaminated areas, 30 per cent in mildly contaminated areas and 24 per cent in "clean" areas. The worst-affected region in neighbouring Belarus has seen increases in childhood cancers (more than 60 per cent), blood diseases (54 per cent) and digestive organ diseases (85 per cent).

Contamination of the land has restricted agricultural production, killed trees and polluted waters. Close attention will be required to monitor and prevent contamination of nearby waterways that supply 35 million people. With growing awareness of the health and climate impacts of oil-, gas- and coal-fuelled power plants, reliance on nuclear power for electrical generation may increase. Many countries still do not have the capacity to run and regulate these facilities properly, or to prepare and implement emergency plans to handle accidents.

Environment and Reproductive Health

Environmental factors have a direct effect on individuals' reproductive health and communities' response to reproductive health conditions. They also affect service access and quality. They have their most serious impacts among the poor, who are more likely to live near sources of pollution and use polluted resources. Impacts start at or before birth. Exposure to some agricultural and industrial chemicals and organic pollutants are associated with pregnancy failures and with infant and childhood developmental difficulties, illness and mortality. Exposure to nuclear radiation and some heavy metals has genetic impacts. Exposure to new interactions, with reproductive risks stretching down the generations, is increasing.

Anaemia is common among ill-nourished girls and women and can affect the age at menarche. Frequent childbearing intensifies the incidence and severity of anaemia. Rural poor women frequently carry large loads of water and household fuel (wood, charcoal and other bio-matter), often for long distances.

In many communities environmental damage has greatly increased the distance women must go for fuel or water. In addition to their general effect on health and the possibility of injury, these heavy loads contribute to low weight and proportions of body fat among women. Below certain levels low body weight contributes to the cessation of menses and reduced fertility.

Women weakened by general ill-health, and by infectious and respiratory diseases, are much more vulnerable in pregnancy and childbirth, especially if they are very young, near the end of their reproductive years, or have had many children. They may also be more vulnerable to HIV infection.

Reproductive Health Service Challenges

Peri-urban and marginal land use. The unplanned development of land around cities and the opening of new, often marginal, rural lands increases the number of people in areas without health delivery infrastructures. The reduced availability of reproductive health services in these areas increases the risks of maternal mortality and unwanted pregnancy.

Water availability: In poor countries and countries in transition with shrinking health budgets, lack of water or clean water at health facilities is a serious problem. Quality health care, including reproductive health care, is impossible without adequate supplies of clean water.

Seasonality burdens: Cases of many diseases increase when seasonal conditions favour their spread. This is true, for example, of water-borne and insect-borne diseases during and after rainy seasons; and infectious diseases in cooler times when more people are indoors or in overcrowded schools. Pregnancies similarly may follow a pattern related to breaks in the agricultural work schedule or certain holidays, for example. These patterns affect the flow of visitors to clinics and hospitals. Improved flow management and staff training are required to maintain appropriate service quality, including sufficient time for counselling and follow-up, throughout the year.

EXPOSURE TO ORGANIC POLLUTANTS

Pollution from emissions, industrial processes, fertilizers, pesticides and waste is exposing people to higher levels and a broader range of chemicals than ever before. Many chemicals that did not exist 50 to 100 years ago are now widely dispersed throughout our environment. People are at the top of their food chain (living on agricultural products and on animals, birds and fish which themselves consume affected organisms, water and prey) and are exposed to concentrated levels of pollutants. Most of these chemicals have not been studied, either individually or in combination, for their health effects. Many questions remain about their possible impacts on early foetal and childhood development in particular.

Developed countries, the major producers of the new substances, vary dramatically in their concern and attention to the issue. The European Community, for example, tends to take a more cautious approach to the regulation of new chemicals than does the United States. Since 1900, industrialization has introduced almost 100,000 previously unknown chemicals into the environment. Many have found their way into the air, water, soil and food—and human beings. One category of these chemicals, endocrine disrupters, is now suspected as an important cause of human reproductive disorders and infertility.

An endocrine disrupter is a synthetic chemical that, when absorbed into the body, interferes with normal hormone function, sometimes altering the amount of hormones inappropriately, sometimes mimicking or blocking their action. This interference can undermine intelligence, decrease disease resistance, or impair reproduction. Virtually every person on earth has been exposed to endocrine disrupters—through direct contact with pesticides and other chemicals or through ingestion of contaminated water, food or air. Many are persistent, accumulating in fat and other tissues, so human exposure may increase from eating fatty foods or contaminated fish.

Assumed endocrine-disrupting chemicals include some of the most commonly used substances in the developed and developing worlds. For example:

— Phthalates—plasticizers found in polyvinyl chloride, used in plastic bags and intravenous equipment, as well as in soaps, hair sprays, nail polishes and cosmetics.

— PCBs—formerly used in electrical equipment and still found in contaminated watersheds, landfills and other disposal sites.

— Dioxins—produced during waste incineration and by industrial processes such as paper production.

At least 84 pesticides—some of the most common are DDT, lindane, vinclozolin, dieldrin, atrazine, 2-4 D (agent orange), 2,4,5-t, some pyrethroids and malathion. Many have been banned in the United States and Europe, but are still exported to and used in the developing world. In fact, pesticide use and human exposure are rapidly growing worldwide. Research about the effects of these ubiquitous chemicals is not conclusive, but mounting evidence links endocrine disrupters to a range of problems, including: infertility among women; miscarriage; declining sperm counts; testicular and prostate cancer; and other reproductive disorders such as hypospadias (malformed penises), cryptochidism (undescended testes) and early puberty in girls; endometriosis; and breast, ovarian and uterine cancers. Children exposed in utero are more likely to suffer development problems and difficulties in learning or cognition.

HIV/AIDS and the Environment

The causes and consequences of the HIV/AIDS crisis are closely linked to wider development issues, including poverty, malnutrition, exposure to other infections, gender inequality and insecure livelihoods. The epidemic, with its direct and devastating impact on health and the family, complicates the problem of environmental protection, intensifies agricultural labour problems and adds to the burdens of women in rural settings. The Food and Agriculture Organization of the United Nations has pointed to the impact of the epidemic on agricultural sustainability. Tenuous land rights and low access to resources already limit rural women's choices. These disadvantages are heightened by the death from AIDS of male heads of farm households. The loss of labour to the epidemic cripples the household. Infection rates are higher among women, who comprise most of the agricultural labour force, produce more than 80 per cent of household food and gather and manage other vital resources for their families.

The impacts are most severe in poorer communities, where farming is labour-intensive with little mechanization and few modern inputs. Land falls out of cultivation; tilling, planting and weeding are delayed; pests become more virulent. A farm may shift to crops needing less labour, and from cash to subsistence production. The loss of experienced farmers and agricultural extension workers deprives the community of their knowledge and management skills. In severely affected areas, the numbers of surviving children and the elderly overload the community's systems of social support. Families are hard put to keep farms afloat, including their share of communal responsibility for land management, to feed and educate the children, or to care for the elderly. Loss of the male landholder may put even the survivors' tenure in question.

Adults and Children Living with HIV/AIDS

The impact of the pandemic in urban centres limits prospects for development, including programmes for environmental protection. By killing workers in mid-life, including employees of productive industries and the public-sector workers such as doctors, nurses and teachers, the pandemic can negate a generation of investment in economic and social development.

Most of the world's most effective pharmaceutical products have been discovered from compounds derived from plants or animals. These are frequently found in tropical climates, where biodiversity is greatest, and often in "biodiversity hotspots" subject to increasing human pressure. Decreased genetic variability in agricultural crops also increases the vulnerability of the food supply to new pathogens. Resistance to pests and climate variation decrease without enough diversity in the strains of common food crops under cultivation.

If crops were adversely affected, widespread hunger and disease would surely follow. Ecologists have also rediscovered what many indigenous cultures and agriculturalists already knew—greater diversity among plants in a field can significantly increase their yields and resistance to pests. Population pressures, increasing consumption and the drive for cheap food have led to the intensification of agriculture. This change has often been achieved at the cost of a greater homogenization of cropping practices. Continuation of this trend could increase the risks to food security.

Great hopes have been placed on the development of genetically engineered crops suited to survive in difficult habitats (whether due to soil conditions, climate or pests). Slower population growth, consistent with the voluntary choices of women and men, could allow more time for the research, distribution and education efforts needed to ensure that such crops are safe and pose no long-term threats to sustainability; relaxing population pressure would also soften the blow of possible failures or reversals of progress.

Effects of Climate Change

There is no certainty about the effects climate change due to global warming might have on health, but what data there are suggest that countries should invest more in public health to meet possible hazards. Environmental change can increase the location, spread and intensity of insect- and water-borne diseases. Epidemics can develop when disease-carrying insects or animals reproduce out of control, or move to new locations where people have not developed immunities. Higher temperatures may encourage insect hosts to breed and to move further up hillsides and mountains. They could also lead to changes in the geographical range of insect hosts as previously cooler areas become more hospitable. Exposure of new populations without prior immunity could lead to virulent outbreaks.

Temperature variation could also shift the timing of seasons and the seasonal transmission of diseases. Changes in the timing of seasonal activities (e.g., harvest or planting times) could interact in complex ways to shift exposures and risks related to disease. Higher rainfall could trigger mosquito-borne disease outbreaks, increase flooding (spreading parasitic diseases), increase the contamination of water supplies with human or animal wastes and increase exposures to run-off of pesticides and other chemicals. Studies in a lake region of Kenya show that malaria, acute respiratory infections and diarrhoeal diseases increase dramatically two or three months after heavy rainfalls.

Geothermal plant in Iceland produces power without contributing to global warming. Climate change could increase outbreaks of various diseases. Global warming will also increase the risks and danger of exposure to heat stress, especially in urban areas, which act as local heat traps because of their interference with air flow patterns, greater reflective surface area and local heat generation. Extreme weather events have a variety of effects on reproductive health, including an immediate short-term decline in fertility. This is largely the result of postponement or cancellation of marriages, decreased frequency of sexual relations and an increase in temporary separations. Fertility may subsequently increase as couples take up postponed or interrupted relationships, or respond to improving conditions and hopes.

Disasters also disrupt health services as infrastructure, equipment and drugs are lost, access becomes more difficult, and other immediate priorities supervene. Reproductive health, including safe motherhood, is an immediate victim, since pregnancy is not regarded as an emergency and contraception is not given priority in relief efforts. Extended settlement in temporary shelters or refugee camps exposes women and girls to sexual abuse, sexually transmitted diseases and unwanted pregnancies.

TOAWRDS SUSTAINABLE DEVELOPMENT

Today, however, the international community recognizes that economic development; the state of the environment; the health of men, women, and children; and the status of women are all intricately intertwined. Development requires improvements in the lives of individuals, usually by their own hand, the status of women powerfully determines the state of development, and women require good reproductive health care for their status to improve. This understanding has been articulated in consensus documents negotiated at a series of global meetings convened in the 1990s. These meetings dealt with environment and development in 1992, with population and development in 1994, and, in 1995, with social development and with women's rights. The consensus agreements are grounded in a series of international human rights treaties, starting with the Universal Declaration of Human Rights.

Countries have entered into over 30 multilateral agreements addressing environment and the natural resource base. Arguably the most successful was the 1987 Montreal Protocol on Substances that Deplete the Ozone Layer, which mandated the phasing out of the manufacture and use of hydrochloroflourocarbon (HCFC) gases. After agreements on further details, two thirds of countries are on track to meet negotiated benchmarks. If current progress continues, the damage HCFC gases have caused to the atmosphere's ozone layer could be reversed within 50 years. Other agreements have addressed hazardous waste management, oil pollution, desertification, endangered species, trade in ivory, fur seals, fisheries, tuna and whaling, among others. The most recent agreement (signed by 127 countries in May 2001 and up for ratification) seeks to stop or regulate the production and use of 12 specific persistent organic pollutants.

Agreements have had some success where technical and financial support has been mobilized, enforcement has been strict, loopholes under-exploited and political will strong. Many of the agreements, however, have not given due consideration to the how demographic trends will affect their implementation or to steps needed to empower and involve local people, particularly women, in finding solutions.

Initiatives Linking Population and the Environment

Around the world, a variety of organizations are engaged in activities that address both population and environmental concerns, by incorporating reproductive health information and services into existing environmental protection efforts, for instance, or including environmental education in reproductive health or population education programmes. Researchers are mapping the connections between a number of variables—environmental stress, fertility, migration, women's health and education status, and the push/ pull effects of economic decisions, for example. Partnerships and collaboration, among governments, international and local NGOs, international development agencies, and in some cases, the private sector, are increasingly important.

In the southern Himalayas of Nepal, the Tamakoshi Sewa Samiti project offers reproductive health counselling and care, environmental services, a micro-credit programme and other income-generating activities, including vegetable cultivation and sale, in 25 villages. Over 100 drinking water systems have been created, and more than 200,000 trees planted. Surveys in 1996 and 1998 found infant mortality in the project area to be 19 deaths for every 1,000 live births, compared to 79 nationally. Under five mortality is also lower: 38 per 1,000 children in the project area and 118 nationally. And contraceptive prevalence is higher: 36.2 per cent in the villages served vs. 26.5 per cent throughout rural Nepal.

In Ecuador, CEMOPLAF, an Ecuadorian NGO, with support from U.S.-based World Neighbors, has joined reproductive health and family planning services with agricultural and resource management efforts in 20 poor, indigenous rural communities where homes are built on steep hillsides, making delivery of services a challenge. As a result, the number of farmers practising soil conservation has doubled, to 50 per cent, and use of modern contraceptive methods has increased from 12 per cent to 41 per cent; 65 per cent of the users of the project's agricultural management services are women.

In the Maya Biosphere Reserve in northern Guatemala, Conservation International is working to meet reproductive health information and care needs in 16 communities where the fertility rate is nearly 40 per cent above the national average. The Remedios project began in 1998 and has trained 45 community-based midwives and 16 rural regional health promoters in reproductive health, including birth attendance, family planning, and prevention of STDs including HIV. Community-based contraceptive distribution programmes are being established in each community. Educational materials incorporate traditions of the region's indigenous and mestizo populations.

In Guanajuato State, Mexico, the Centro Para Los Adolescentes de San Miguel de Allende, an NGO working to improve adolescent reproductive health, runs a maternity and community health care hospital for low-income patients and also provides family planning counselling and contraceptives to rural communities.

Environmental education and management—including construction of fuel-efficient stoves and latrines, reforestation, and preparation of medicinal herbs—have been integrated into in-school peer counselling. In 17 Mexican states, a government health agency, the Instituto Mexicano del Seguro Social, gives demonstrations on herb and vegetable garden cultivation, use of fuel-efficient wood stoves, composting and other environmentally friendly technologies at its comprehensive reproductive health clinics.

The World Wildlife Fund (as WWF is known in the United States) is working to mitigate the impacts of rapid growth around Nashville, Tennessee, and Birmingham, Alabama, on river ecosystems. In the wake of a summer 2000 drought that dried up portions of the Cahaba River, the source of drinking water for Birmingham and its fast-growing suburbs, WWF is sponsoring a study of the river's nutrient levels and how they affect threatened and endangered aquatic life, including fish and mussels.

The drought led to severe water rationing and higher nutrient levels in the Cahaba—devastating to the river's species. These high nutrient levels stemmed from lax state water quality standards and poorly designed sewage treatment plants. Results will be used to encourage Alabama to develop policies and standards on nutrient levels that will minimize the impacts of human population growth on the Cahaba River ecosystem.

WWF is also partnering with a Tennessee-based conservation group to establish voluntary standards and best-management practices that contractors can use to protect aquatic biodiversity by reducing sediment that enters streams from construction of new homes, businesses and roads.

Needed Resources and Technical Assistance

As the 1994 International Conference on Population and Development emphasized, "Efforts to slow down population growth, to reduce poverty, to achieve economic progress, to improve environmental protection, and to reduce unsustainable consumption and production patterns are mutually reinforcing." Mobilizing the resources needed to implement the ICPD Programme of Action is therefore a key action to protect the environment, as well as to promote women's rights and sustainable development.

Ensuring Availability of Reproductive Health Supplies

— The ICPD estimated the annual resources needed to implement a basic package of population and reproductive health programmes in developing countries.

— Reproductive health and family planning programmes were estimated to require $15.2 billion in 2000, rising to $19.9 billion in 2015. Selected HIV/AIDS prevention efforts were estimated to require $1.3 billion in 2000 and $1.5 billion in 2010 and 2015. Basic research, data and policy analysis were estimated to average over $400 million per year between 2000 and 2015 (varying widely in relation to the timing of censuses).

— Total requirements were estimated at $17.0 billion in 2000 and $21.7 billion in 2015. Up to two thirds of these costs were expected to be met by developing countries, with the remainder to come from international development assistance.

These estimates included some HIV/AIDS prevention; it was recognized that additional funds were needed, including funds for treatment and care of people living with HIV. However, the epidemic has advanced faster and farther than the ICPD anticipated, and considerably more resources will be required to ameliorate the impact. Other reproductive health service needs remain substantial as well. Maternal mortality has not declined at the rate proposed at the ICPD. Just under half of all births are still not assisted by a trained birth attendant. Funds are needed for transport in difficult cases and emergency obstetric care. There is also recognition of the need for higher priority to programmes for adolescent sexual and reproductive health, and the incorporation of men as clients and supportive partners in reproductive health care.

Estimates of resources needed to expand reproductive health services reflect projected increases in contraceptive demand. These were based on the growing number of people of reproductive age and continued reductions in unmet need— the number of women and couples who wish to delay or prevent a birth but are not using contraceptives. At the five-year review of ICPD implementation, a new goal was set—elimination of unmet need by 2015. This will require further resources and national and international effort. Eliminating unmet need involves more than physical access to services.

Many women do not practise contraception due to fears of side-effects of available methods, cultural concerns related to specific methods (e.g., changes in menstrual bleeding) or the disapproval of spouses or communities. Addressing these concerns will require investments to make a wide range of method choices universally available, support research to reduce side-effects of existing methods, and provide better training of counsellors.

Assessing the Costs of Inaction

Resources available for reproductive health and population programmes are well below the $17 billion the ICPD said would be needed in 2000. While developing countries are providing most of their share of needed resources, support from international donors is less than half of the $5.7 billion called for in 2000.

Shortfalls in resources for population have also started to affect data collection and research efforts, which are needed to allow countries to assess the impacts of development policies, monitor progress and prioritize programming. The funding shortfall is already showing its effects: fertility declines have been slower than would be expected if more couples and individuals could have the family size they desire. The costs of delaying action will increase rapidly over time.

Programmes addressing population issues, women's empowerment, poverty eradication and environmental protection have important benefits; progress has been made in quantifying some of these. Policy makers need information on the returns to their investments in such programmes to set priorities for resource allocation.

Environmental returns from policies and investments in the social sector cannot be predicted with much precision, because of the difficulty of predicting the demographic, social, and economic consequences of a given policy and its interaction with other factors. For example, better female education is known to be closely linked with a range of social and economic benefits, but it is hard to be specific about how better education might change female labour force participation or economic growth rates.

Research in this area has focused primarily on policies that tend to reduce fertility, where the resulting slowing of population growth is seen as easing human stress on the environment. Some studies have tried to estimate the additional environmental impact of a single birth and its descendants. Others have contrasted the expected environmental impacts associated with diverging demographic scenarios.

Environmental 'Externalities' to Child-bearing

An "externality" is a cost or benefit to society at large of an action taken by an individual. The concept is most commonly applied to economic activity. For example, if a factory pollutes a river and the owner is not held responsible, the environmental cost to society is "external" to the owner's decision about how much to produce, and therefore how much pollution is produced. Externalities can also be positive. For example, investment in research and development in one industry can benefit other industries. If investors cannot capture these benefits, it will lead to under-investment in research and development. Externalities are a useful guide to policy-making; in the examples used here, they might motivate a tax on pollution or public investment in research.

The externality concept can also be applied to child-bearing. The birth of an additional child results in costs and benefits to society, above and beyond those considered by the parents. Possible external benefits include a larger tax base to help pay for public pensions to the elderly or to share the costs of goods like national defence whose costs are relatively insensitive to population size.

External costs might include additional public expenditures on education or health care, or a per capita reduction in the value of national assets like fishing or mineral rights. A number of recent studies have estimated environmental externalities to child-bearing, all using global climate change as an illustrative example. While results vary widely, on balance they indicate that, in addition to other positive development impacts, environmental benefits from policies leading to lower fertility may rival the costs of the policies themselves.

The activities of each person, and their descendants, give rise to greenhouse gas emissions through direct or indirect use of energy and land. Each birth averted—all else being equal—may reduce the cost of climate change to society in two ways. First, total greenhouse gas emissions may fall, reducing the magnitude of future climate change and the resulting damage to society. Second, smaller populations should make it easier to comply with caps on emissions like those envisioned for industrialized countries by the Kyoto Protocol to the Framework Convention on Climate Change.

Estimates of the climate-related costs of child-bearing range from several hundred to several thousand dollars per birth. Their values depend on a wide range of factors. For example, a birth in a developing country where per capita greenhouse gas emissions rates are relatively low has, on average, a smaller impact than a birth in an industrialized country where per capita emissions are higher. For example, a birth in Africa might lead to climate-related costs of about $100, while a birth in the United States might lead to costs of about $4,000.

Since the future costs of an additional birth are spread out over time—decades or even centuries—analysts must decide how much to value future costs relative to costs today. Future costs are generally discounted, but the appropriate discount rate is controversial. One study found that if a typical discount rate of 3 per cent per year were used (which reduces the cost to each succeeding generation by nearly half), the externality associated with a birth in the developing regions would be about $300.

However if costs were valued equally in all years, the total externality would exceed $4,000 by the year 2100. Other assumptions affecting the outcome include future emissions reduction requirements, the cost of reducing emissions, and projected population growth. Despite these uncertainties, it is clear that the costs of an additional birth will be substantial. One reason is that stabilizing the atmospheric concentration of greenhouse gases will eventually require steep and expensive emissions reductions, while a smaller future population size would inevitably reduce the need for the most expensive reductions.

In comparison, the costs of social programmes, when converted into estimated costs per birth averted, are generally in the range of several hundred dollars or less. For example, one estimate puts the cost of education programmes in developing countries at less than $200 per birth averted. Estimates for voluntary family planning programmes range from $30 to $330 per birth averted.

Expressing programme costs in per birth terms does not imply that fertility reduction is, or should be, their main objective. It simply provides a means to compare costs of an easily measurable component of comprehensive reproductive health programmes with potential environmental benefits. While there is considerable uncertainty in such estimates, it appears that costs are, at most, roughly the same as, and possibly less than, their potential climate-related returns.

Climate change lends itself to population externality studies because it is long-term, the impacts of emissions are independent of their geographical origin, and integrated economic-environmental models of the problem have been developed for two decades. Other environmental issues are much more dependent on regional particularities. For example, the effects of air pollution depend very much on local climate conditions, other pollutants in the air, and the characteristics of surrounding ecosystems and human populations.

Alternative Scenarios

A number of studies have analysed the likely impact of population-related policies on climate change by comparing alternative future scenarios. Here again the focus has been on the demographic consequences of population policy rather than broader economic and social consequences. Models of energy use and greenhouse gas emissions have been used to compare likely results under alternative population scenarios. These studies also indicate that policies resulting in more rapid demographic transition are likely to significantly reduce greenhouse gas emissions in the long run.

Mortality Decline and Fertility Decisions

Some analyses start with a set of alternative scenarios for four broad factors which together determine carbon dioxide emissions: population, economic output per person, the amount of energy required to produce a unit of economic output, and the amount of carbon release per unit of energy used.

Central "best guess" assumptions for the last three factors are considered with a range of scenarios for population, to calculate how much difference the variation in population paths makes to total carbon emissions. This result is then compared with similar sensitivity analyses on other variables. Studies of this kind invariably conclude that emissions are most sensitive to assumptions about growth in per capita output, along with factors such as the carbon content of energy in industrialized countries. Population is found to be a major contributor to emissions over time frames of 50 years or more.

The results depend on how different the alternative scenarios are from the central assumptions. If it is assumed that population is unlikely to differ substantially from the central path, then emissions will not appear to be sensitive to population. On the other hand, holding other variables equal when considering alternative population paths may ignore important interactions between demographics, economic conditions and technological development. In particular, slower population growth may stimulate economic growth, leading to increased emissions that would offset reductions predicted by a simple population/emissions analysis.

However, a study examining historical data on population, income, and emissions found that, controlling for economic and technological conditions, population size did in fact appear to have a roughly proportional effect on emissions. Other studies have found that the relationship between population growth and economic growth would have to be implausibly strong to alter the basic conclusions of simpler analyses.

Changes in Age Structure

Few analyses consider the effects of population ageing on future consumption and emissions. As populations grow older, the average household size tends to fall. Smaller households use energy at a higher rate per person than larger households use.

Models based on numbers of households project higher carbon emissions than those based on numbers of people, as much as 30 per cent higher by 2100. But even such studies conclude that a more slowly growing population will lead to a substantial reduction in emissions. Ageing may also influence emissions by affecting economic growth.

There is a general consensus that an ageing population will place considerable strains on public pension and health systems. Researchers have found little evidence, however, that an ageing work force would be less productive than a young one.

Analysis of recent experience in Asia supports the view that changes in age structure can have considerable impacts on economic growth. When the labour force must support many dependants (children and elderly), savings and economic growth rates are depressed. When fertility declines, workers may have fewer dependants to support, leading to a window of opportunity during which savings can increase, stimulating economic growth—if the country has an economic and institutional environment that allows it to take advantage of the opportunity. Over time, as the population grows older, the ratio of dependants to workers will increase again, ending the conditions that can provide an economic bonus.

In East Asia, a rapid decline in the dependency ratio since 1975 is likely to have contributed substantially to the region's rapid growth. Slower falls in fertility and dependency ratios in South and South-east Asia have contributed to more moderate economic growth. In South Asia and South America, economic activity in 2025 could be 25 per cent higher than would-be expected without considering age structure effects. In Sub-Saharan Africa, this "demographic bonus" could be up 50 per cent.

Dependency ratios are likely to begin rising again in East Asia in 2010, and in South and South-east Asia by 2030, leading to slower growth. The fact that policies that tend to lower fertility are also likely to substantially reduce climate change costs does not mean that slowing population growth is the most effective or most equitable means of mitigating climate change.

Reductions in per capita emissions can be made through a variety of means, and are generally considered the most important and direct measures for reducing future emissions. Nonetheless, slower population growth would make the climate problem easier to solve, and capturing these long-term benefits requires investments in population policies in the immediate future.

Agreements on Environment and Health Development

The international consensus agreements of the 1990s, themselves advisory rather than binding, are grounded in legally binding human rights treaties: the Universal Declaration of Human Rights; the International Covenant on Civil and Political Rights; the International Covenant on Economic, Social and Cultural Rights; the Convention on the Elimination of All Forms of Discrimination against Women of; and the Convention on the Rights of the Child. All member states accede to the Universal Declaration of Human Rights, which affirms, "All human beings are born free and equal in dignity and rights." The Declaration also refers to "the dignity and worth of the human person and ... the equal rights of men and women."

About two dozen specific rights are named, from the right to life, liberty, and security of person through legal and judicial rights to the right to education and work. The Declaration also calls for social security and conditions that allow an individual to realize economic, social and cultural rights necessary to dignity and for a standard of living adequate to one's health and well-being. Declaration language also specifies that "everyone is entitled to all the rights and freedoms set forth in this Declaration, without distinction of any kind," including sex. The Covenant on Economic, Social and Cultural Rights states that every human being has the right to "freely determine their political status and freely pursue their economic, social and cultural development", and that states must ensure that men and women enjoy these rights equally.

The Covenant also recognizes people's rights "to be free from hunger," to be educated, and to enjoy "the highest attainable standard of physical and mental health." To achieve the latter, the Covenant lists, in addition to prevention and treatment of disease and the provision of medical services, "improvement in all aspects of environmental and industrial hygiene," an early reference to the link between the environment and health. The International Covenant on Civil and Political Rights states that protection of laws and freedom of expression apply equally to women and men. It states that every citizen, without regard to sex, has the right to take part in public affairs, to vote, to be elected, and to have the opportunity "on general terms of equality to public service".

The Convention on the Elimination of All Forms of Discrimination against Women (CEDAW), which had 168 states parties as of June 2001, constitutes an international bill of rights for women. Referring to pre-existing treaties that call for "the equal rights of men and women to enjoy all economic, social, cultural, civil and political rights," the Convention declares that "the full and complete development of a country, the welfare of the world and the cause of peace require the maximum participation of women on equal terms with men in all fields."

In addition to dealing with unequal treatment of women in law, cultural patterns of discrimination, women's rights to participate in public life, equality of educational and employment opportunities, discrimination against women in the provision of health care, and the special problems of women in rural poverty, CEDAW refers to women's reproductive rights. The education article refers to access to "information and advice on family planning;" articles on health care, rural development, and equality in marriage also mention family planning services. The last states that women are to have "the same rights to decide freely and responsibly on the number and spacing of their children and to have access to the information, education and means to enable them to exercise these rights".

In the article on women in rural areas, CEDAW makes an oblique reference to the environment when it calls on states to ensure that rural women "enjoy adequate living conditions, particularly in relation to housing, sanitation, electricity and water supply, transport and communications."

In December 2000 the "Optional Protocol" to CEDAW went into force. This instrument establishes communication and monitoring procedures to advance implementation of the Convention. As of June 2000 there were 67 signatories and 21 states parties to this mechanism.

UN Conference on Environment and Development

Heads of state met in Rio de Janeiro in 1992 to make a broad inquiry into environmental degradation, which had become increasingly important to the international community since the 1960s both on their own terms and as a constraint on development. The United Nations Conference on Environment and Development (UNCED) was the 20-year follow-up to the first global meeting on the environment, held in Stockholm in 1972. Rio linked environment and development as international agreements had not done before.

The watchword was "sustainable development", economic development to meet the needs of current generations without undermining the environment and compromising future generations' ability to meet their needs. Rio also declared that both poverty and wealth stress the environment, that industrial societies must lessen their environmental impact through "sustainable patterns of production and consumption," and that developing countries need assistance in building their economies to be environmentally benign.

In addition to conventions on forests, climate change, and biological diversity, Rio produced a comprehensive guide to sustainable development, Agenda21. Faced with "worsening poverty, hunger, ill health, illiteracy, and the continuing deterioration of ecosystems," this document asserts, "the only way to assure ourselves of a safer, more prosperous future is to deal with environment and development issues together in a balanced manner." Agenda 21's four main sections deal with social and economic dimensions of sustainable development, conservation and management of resources, strengthening the role of major groups in sustainable development, and implementation.

Nine paragraphs in the first section address "Population and Sustainability". They state that "the world's growing population and production" increasingly stress the earth's resources; urge development strategies that deal with the combined effects of population growth, ecosystem health, technology, and access to resources; urge the development of "population goals" and the integration of population concerns into national strategies for sustainability; call for countries to calculate their "national population carrying capacity;" state that "sustainable development will require reproductive health programmes to reduce maternal and infant mortality, and provide men and women with the information and means to plan family size"; and declare that population programmes require broad support as well as "adequate funding, including support to developing countries".

A chapter on women in the section on "major groups" states that "women have considerable knowledge and experience in managing and conserving natural resources," but "discrimination and lack of access to schooling, land and equal employment" have constrained their role in achieving sustainable development. It calls on governments to:

— Eliminate legal, cultural, social, and other barriers to women's full participation "in sustainable development and public life".

— Increase women's participation in environmental decision-making as officials, scientists, technical advisers and extension workers.

— Improve women's education from illiteracy eradication to post-secondary study in the sciences.

— Create conditions to enable women to play an enhanced role in sustainable development, such as better health care—including maternal and child health care and family planning—a reduced workload, better access to credit, property rights, eliminating violence against women and counting unpaid work in official economic measures.

— Educate women, particularly in the industrialized world, to engage in environmentally sustainable consumption.

While Agenda 21 links population growth and resource use, and recognizes women's role in the environment and their need for education, health care and credit, the population section is mainly demographic in focus and lacks the broader reproductive health and women's rights approach to population adopted at the ICPD two years later.

International Conference on Population and Development

The ICPD Programme of Action, negotiated in Cairo in September 1994, is a far-reaching yet practical roadmap for expanding individual choice, by making critical investments in reproductive health care and education, providing expanded economic opportunities for women, and creating the conditions—legal, political, social and economic—for true gender equality and equity. The Conference recognized that these actions are both just and humane in their own right, and if implemented would also contribute to stabilizing population and advancing environmental security.

The Programme specifies that "reproductive health is a state of complete physical, mental and social well-being and not merely the absence of disease or infirmity, in all matters relating to the reproductive system and to its function and processes." Reproductive rights "embrace certain human rights that are already recognized in national laws, international human rights documents and other consensus documents."

One of the principal goals of the Programme of Action is ensuring universal access to reproductive health care as soon as possible, and by 2015 at the latest. Essential components of reproductive health care include: family planning; maternal health; preventing abortion and managing the complications of unsafe abortion; preventing and treating sexually transmitted diseases, including HIV/AIDS; and eliminating traditional practices like female genital mutilation that harm women's reproductive health and well-being.

Also central to the ICPD approach is the collection of rights, defined in the human rights treaties, that will permit women to realize their dignity—economically, socially, and culturally. "The empowerment and autonomy of women," the Programme states, "is a highly important end in itself. In addition, it is essential for the achievement of sustainable development." It adds, "Experience shows that population and development programmes are most effective when steps have simultaneously been taken to improve the status of women." Thus the Programme of Action calls for education for women and girls, access to "secure livelihoods and economic resources," and full participation in public life. Chapter III of the Programme of Action deals with the interactions among population, economic growth and sustainable development. This chapter reinforces many of the principles articulated at UNCED. "Meeting the basic human needs of growing populations is dependent on a healthy environment," it notes. The document avoids demographic targets or goals, and stresses that poverty and gender inequities affect and are affected by population growth, age structure and distribution. In turn, it states, "unsustainable consumption and production patterns" overuse natural resources, degrade the environment, and reinforce gender inequality and poverty.

"Integrating population into economic and development strategies," the agreement adds, will accelerate progress toward sustainability, alleviating poverty, slowing population growth, and improving quality of life. And it calls for "implementation of effective population policies in the context of sustainable development, including reproductive health and family planning programmes."

Fourth World Conference on Women

The Platform for Action adopted in 1995 at the Fourth World Conference on Women in Beijing built on the progress achieved in Cairo a year earlier. It reaffirmed the international community's commitment to women's rights and equal participation "in all spheres of society" as a prerequisite "for people-centred development".

The Platform for Action strengthened the ICPD's commitment to women's reproductive health. "In most countries," the Platform states, "the neglect of women's reproductive rights severely limits their opportunities in public and private life, including opportunities for education and economic and political empowerment. The ability of women to control their own fertility forms an important basis for the enjoyment of other rights."

The Beijing document, citing Agenda 21, also pointed out that women are disproportionately harmed by environmental degradation and have a powerful, as yet largely untapped, part in protecting and restoring the environment: "Women have an essential role to play in the development of sustainable and ecologically sound consumption and production patterns and approaches to natural resource management."

In June 2000, a General Assembly special session to review implementation of the Beijing Platform for Action adopted a Political Declaration reaffirming the commitments made in Beijing and agreed on priority actions, including the need to address: gender aspects of HIV/AIDS and other sexually-transmitted infections; the disproportionate effect on women and girls of malaria and tuberculosis; the mental health of women and girls; and care for women and girls who experience violence.

World Summit on Social Development

"Economic development, social development and environmental protection are interdependent and mutually reinforcing components of sustainable development," international leaders declared in March 1995 at the World Summit on Social Development, designed to "place people at the centre of development and direct our economies to meet human needs more effectively."

Gender equality was a central goal of the Copenhagen summit. It adopted a Declaration emphasizing that "social and economic development cannot be secured in a sustainable way without the full participation of women" and that "equality and equity between women and men ... must be at the centre of economic and social development."

The Declaration notes that women constitute the majority of people living "in abject poverty" and carry "a disproportionate share of the problems of coping with poverty;" that gender equality is intertwined with continued population growth and poverty; and that "empowering people, particularly women, to strengthen their own capacities is a main objective of development and its principal resource."

The Millennium Declaration

In September 2000, heads of state and government met in New York to negotiate a Millennium Declaration committing the United Nations to achieving "a just and lasting peace all over the world", and rededicating the organization to "respect for the equal rights of all without distinction as to race, sex, language, or religion."

The Declaration affirms that "the equal rights and opportunities of women and men must be assured"; and states that "prudence must be shown in the management of all living species and natural resources, in accordance with the precepts of sustainable development." It calls on states to: "promote gender equality and the empowerment of women as effective ways to combat poverty, hunger and disease and to stimulate development that is truly sustainable;" "combat all forms of violence against women and to implement the Convention on the Elimination of All Forms of Discrimination against Women;" and "adopt in all our environmental actions a new ethic of conservation and stewardship."

4

Impact of Development

More people are using more resources with more intensity than at any point in human history. Fresh water, cropland, forests, fisheries and biodiversity all show signs of stress at local, regional and global levels. Increasing pressure on the environment is the result of, on one hand, increasing affluence—that is, more consumption, pollution and waste, and on the other persistent poverty—that is, lack of resources and the technology to use them, and lack of the power to change these circumstances.

Growing human numbers play a role in both scenarios. Global use of fuel-wood, for example, has doubled over the past 50 years; the Worldwatch Institute attributes this increase largely to population growth. But the six-fold increase in the use of paper since 1950 is ascribed mainly to rising affluence, and the multiple uses for paper products in an increasingly urban environment.

Population size, growth, distribution and movement help determine the relationship between people and their environments. Similar numbers of people can have very different impacts on the environment, depending on for example social institutions, means of production, property rules and forms of governance. Access to education, health and economic opportunity; consumption levels; and gender differentials (the "quality of human capital") all have an influence.

The most basic determinant of impact is scale. Thirty years ago Paul Ehrlich and J. Holdren described this relationship in the now-famous equation:

$$I = PAT,$$

meaning that people's impact on their environment (I) is a product of population size (P), affluence (A, representing output per capita or the level of consumption) and technology (T, representing the per unit output or efficiency in production). This equation has been often used but also often criticized or elaborated.

The main shortcoming is that the factors in the relationship are not independent, but are related in complex ways. Nonetheless, the approach has been useful in demonstrating that population dynamics are central to environmental change. For example, since 1970 global carbon dioxide emissions per capita have been relatively constant, while GDP per capita has increased in both more developed and less developed regions.

This means that improvements in technology have offset the effects of increased consumption. Whether carbon dioxide emissions continue to increase in step with population size will depend on economic and social trends, the institutional response to environmental problems and the pace of technological change.

Poverty and the Environment

Despite soaring global wealth, now estimated at $24 trillion annually, some 1. 2 billion people across the world live on less than $1 a day—a condition classified as "extreme poverty" and characterized by hunger, illiteracy, vulnerability, sickness and premature death. Half the world lives on $2 a day or less. More than a billion people cannot fulfil their basic needs for food, water, sanitation, health care, housing and education. Nearly 60 per cent of the 4. 4 billion people living in developing countries lack basic sanitation, almost one third do not have access to clean water supplies, one quarter lack adequate housing, 20 per cent do not have access to modern health services, and 20 per cent of children do not attend school through grade five.

Worldwide, 1.1 billion people are malnourished, unable to meet minimum standards for dietary energy; and protein and micronutrient deficiencies are widespread. Nearly 2 billion people in developing countries are anaemic. Ending poverty has been an international aim since 1960. After significant advances between 1970 and 1990, the rate of poverty reduction in the 1990s fell to only one third of the pace required to meet the United Nations' commitment to halve poverty levels by 2015.

Although affluence consumes energy and produces waste at far higher rates, the effects of poverty also destroy the environment. Global attention has consequently focused on the complex relationship between environmental degradation, poverty and sustainability. Understanding it may be key to ending poverty and closing the gap between more and less affluent, as well as meeting the objective of sustainable development.

Population pressures are increasing in many poor and ecologically fragile zones in urban as well as rural areas. Fertility in many of these places is already high, and more people are being driven to them by a shortage of land for subsistence farming, by economic policies encouraging large holdings, intensive agriculture and cash crops, and by poverty and high population densities elsewhere.

A breakdown of consumption patterns shows that the "ecological footprint" of the more affluent is far deeper than that of the poor, and in many cases exceeds the regenerative capacity of the earth. In most instances it is the wealthier farmers who engage in large-scale clearing of vegetation, over-use of agricultural chemicals, over-use of groundwater resources for irrigation, over-use of pastoral land for grazing and over-exploitation of soils for export production. Distorted pricing structures perpetuate wasteful input use.

In Gujarat in India, poor tribal farmers pay the full cost of pump irrigation provided through a non-governmental organization while the richer farmers receive subsidized water through state schemes. Higher-income groups consume more energy and produce more waste than the poor, who must extract value from every scrap. Very low-income households in Pakistan spend one 30th as much on fuel as rich households, although they expend much more time and energy on gathering it.

Rural communities will continue to depend heavily on agriculture and natural resources for their livelihood. Environmental degradation will only deepen their poverty, so environmental conservation and poverty alleviation are parallel objectives. In most situations where they enjoy secure tenure, the poor will invest to protect their land and their environment.

Local control may be important: studies indicate that the condition of Nepal's forests has improved since management of forest resource was decentralized to communities. India's Joint Forest Management programme, which also devolves resource management to local people, has had similar environmental benefits in areas such as south-west Bengal. Local control may be more effective than government efforts in limiting illegal logging, fishing, water use and theft, but government participation can help offset the high cost and delayed benefits of investment in conservation. Over the generations poor farmers have accumulated a vast amount of knowledge about sustainable environmental practices. Practices such as shifting cultivation sustained the poor for centuries, until populations grew too large or other factors intervened.

Traditional practices may incorporate an understanding of local conditions not immediately evident to outside observers, however expert. In the mountainous areas of Sumatra, farmers rely on simple stone head-works to create irrigation systems along small streams. Although these structures seem leaky and inefficient, the leakage ensures an equitable distribution of water across the community.

When poor people move to new environments or when the balance of their old environment is altered, for example by rapidly rising populations, there may be a period of relearning in which a certain degree of degradation may occur. But imposing standardized technical solutions that ignore and wipe out indigenous knowledge may have a disastrous ecological impact.

Population growth is not necessarily detrimental to environmental sustainability but it does affect available choices and the prospects of any intervention. Although degradation invariably occurs initially as very low population densities increase, what follows depends on a confluence of factors. If investment needed to improve land is too expensive or the benefits too-long delayed, further degradation will almost certainly result as population rises. In other cases, where a higher population can result in a lower per capita charge for fixed investments (such as water harvesting technology), sustainability and productivity may actually improve in a supportive environment.

If developing countries with rapidly growing populations were encouraged and supported to adopt cleaner technologies, environmental degradation could be mitigated. At current levels of growth, Asia's greenhouse gas emissions are expected to triple in the next 20 years. Effective technology, if it were made affordable, could reduce the growth in emissions.

Globalization and Poverty

In the past 20 years, over 100 developing and transition countries have begun to undertake reform measures to improve the efficiency of their economies. These reform packages typically include fiscal discipline, lower budget deficits, reduced subsidies, tax restructuring, financial liberalization, market-determined interest rates, competitive and stable exchange rates, trade liberalization, encouragement of foreign direct investment, privatization of state enterprises, deregulation of protected industrial sectors and enhanced guarantees of property rights. These reforms have been intended to increase countries' competitiveness in the global marketplace.

International trade has increased dramatically during the period, though a small number of developing countries account for most of the increase outside of the more-advanced market economies. The desire to integrate into the global economy or to offset losses in financial crises has motivated many developing countries to increase their exploitation of natural resources. Globalization has clearly increased overall prosperity and stimulated growth. It has also increased income inequality and environmental degradation.

Although poverty has declined in percentage terms, the number of people living in poverty has steadily increased, and average incomes in many developing countries have remained low. At the same time, environmental degradation is worse than in any comparable period in human history. There is a clear link between environmental degradation and the rising inequality accompanying globalization—increasing poverty is causing many poor people to increase their pressure on fragile natural resources in order to survive.

Some critics have concluded that while globalization has led to significant economic reforms, policy makers have ignored the parallel social, environmental and institutional reforms required to prevent increases in inequality, poverty and environmental degradation.

Measuring Poverty's Dimensions

Traditionally, economists have defined poverty in terms of income, using either a relative standard such as the median income in a country, or an absolute standard such as the cost of a typical basket of goods and services. More recent definitions also encompass measures of health, education, security, political voice and discrimination. The World Development Report 2000-2001 measures poverty across three dimensions: opportunity, empowerment and security. The World Bank includes another dimension: capabilities. These dimensions have multiple determinants, but environmental sustainability runs through each as a common thread.

Opportunity measures an individual's income, consumption and the level of inequality in a society. Opportunity may be enhanced by a stable economic environment, equitable asset distribution, and easy availability of infrastructure. Specific environmental interventions that improve opportunity include improving the productivity of land and fisheries, and environmentally sensitive pricing structures.

Empowerment measures an individual's participation in community decision-making. Empowerment is strengthened by decentralization, transparency and accountability in all aspects of governance, including the management of natural resources. Security is a measure of an individual's protection against economic shocks and personal violence. Environment-focused interventions include disaster prediction and prevention mechanisms, and protection against the illegal exploitation of resources.

Capabilities are the substantive freedoms that allow a person to lead the kind of life he or she values. Reproductive health care, access to safe drinking water, better sanitation, reduction of indoor and urban air pollution, integrated programmes to combat vector-borne diseases, and other environment-focused interventions that reduce poverty are all relevant in this regard. Each of these must be assessed not just in terms of national averages but also in terms of their equitable distribution. Women are often multiply disadvantaged.

Energy and Poverty

Increasing consumption of energy is associated with advanced economies, as well as with longer life expectancies, higher levels of education and other indicators of social development. The correlation is not precise— among industrial economies for example the United States has far higher levels of energy consumption per capita or per dollar of GDP than European countries or Japan. Social development in particular can often be achieved without high levels of energy consumption, as for instance in the state of Kerala in India, or Sri Lanka.

High energy consumption can also fail to produce economic growth if it is misdirected, as in the former Soviet Union, but there are no examples of substantial economic growth without corresponding growth in energy consumption.

This is one of the central riddles of development. All models of development are directed to economic growth—yet if all countries consumed energy at U.S. or even European rates, sources of energy would rapidly be depleted, and the unwanted by-products of energy use would at best tax the ability of the environment to absorb them. The challenge is to find the means for the more affluent to reduce the burdens of consumption, and for poor countries and people to escape poverty without crippling either economies or the ecosphere.

Escaping poverty is not merely a question of finding ways to increase energy consumption, but of changing the kinds of energy used. The energy sources of the poor are inefficient, polluting and unhealthy. Per unit of emitted light or heat, the poor pay higher prices than the rich, including the time they spend obtaining or collecting fuel. Cook stoves burning biomass fuel use only around 15 per cent of its potential energy. Charcoal, coal and kerosene stoves are about 50 per cent efficient. Electricity and liquid propane gas burners convert 65 per cent of their energy.

A study in Pakistan showed that nearly 90 per cent of poor households rely on biomass fuels for cooking and the majority use kerosene rather than electricity for lighting. In contrast more than one third of better-off households use gas for cooking and most use electric light.

Biomass cooking produces soot and other substances linked to acute respiratory infections, chronic obstructive lung diseases, lung cancer and eye problems, as well as low birth weight. Coal in open fires or stoves produces sulphur and toxins such as arsenic, fluoride and lead. The effects of these pollutants are compounded by poor ventilation. Failure to cook food or boil water adequately because of fuel shortage or inefficiency also contributes to malnutrition, intestinal disorders and parasites.

Gathering fuel-wood and related materials takes its toll in time and injury, mostly on women. A study in the United Republic of Tanzania showed that able-bodied women in rural areas carry about 25 metric tons kilometres (combining weight and distance) per year in firewood collection; men expend a very small fraction of this effort. A study in Addis Ababa found that fuel gatherers, who often carry loads nearly equal to their own weights, frequently suffer falls and bone fractures; eye problems; headaches; rheumatism; anaemia; chest, back and internal disorders; and miscarriages.

Poor families spend more than twice as much time gathering fuel as more affluent ones. Wealthier families spend as much as 30 times more on energy but it is cleaner, more efficient and less burdensome—and they buy it at preferential prices. Electricity costs, particularly for urban elites, are often subsidized. The poor pay higher unit prices for energy in small amounts: items such as batteries, battery recharging, candles, kerosene and charcoal. A survey in Uganda showed that rural and peri-urban families spend over $10 per month on candles, lighting, kerosene, dry cell batteries and recharging car batteries. More households in the country derive electricity from car batteries than are connected to the public power grid.

Policy actions to correct these conditions need not be prohibitively expensive and would yield long-term savings. Supplying solar power is often cheaper than extending electrical grids. Subsidies or credit guarantees can put more efficient stoves within reach. Subsidies on electricity prices for the more affluent could be transferred to cleaner fuel for the poor.

IMPACT OF RURAL DEVELOPMENT

The effect of population increase in rural areas can be either positive or negative. A gradual shift from very low to moderate population densities, for example, can encourage new agricultural practices, providing increased yields and supporting larger populations. Such a process may have encouraged the development of intensive settled agriculture. Increasing rural population density increases the labour available for managing fires, working on infrastructure such as irrigation channels and terraces, and improving soils.

But there are many cases where population growth has worked against both people and their environment. Rapid population growth in the last 50 years has doubled and redoubled poor rural populations, faster than their ability to adapt. Their resource base has been sharply reduced by overuse and commercial exploitation. Without a surplus for investment, the technologies available to poor rural populations have also remained unchanged. Continuing improvements in agricultural yields and the quality of life depend on the complex interplay of environmental conditions, availability of technology and social organization, and on choices concerning land use. Higher densities require successive adaptations to new circumstances.

Eventually, further progress may be constrained by natural limits, for example on water for irrigation; by technological consequences, such as soil degradation from repeated use of chemical fertilizers; by political decisions concerning land use and social organization; or by economic factors such as poverty. Communities with access to better technology and social investments such as education and universal health care, including reproductive health, have made good use of them to conserve resources and build viable rural economies—examples can be seen in Kerala and in parts of Sri Lanka. These communities feature less gender inequality, later marriage, lower fertility and slower population growth, despite low incomes.

Intensive agriculture has increased yields in many rural areas, but it has provided cheap food for increasing urban populations, rather than a living for rural populations. Commercial agriculture and timber operations by individuals on common land can be highly profitable as long as inputs are available and resources last, but the benefits rarely go to local communities. The rural poor are often using, and overusing, whatever land, water and timber resources are left over from commercial operations.

The combined results can be seen in bare hillsides, shrinking watercourses, floods, droughts and vanishing wildlife. Recent studies of the Green Revolution in India reveal that increased productivity has led to greater incentive to expand areas under cultivation. Where forests are owned in common, this has led to deforestation, because there is no control over the use of common land. Other studies have shown that the benefits of the Green Revolution have accrued principally to the larger landowners and users of common resources, presumably because they had the most to invest and the most to gain.

Landlessness among former subsistence farmers and impoverishment by loss of common resources have been unlooked-for consequences of the Green Revolution.

Individual property rights may provide a higher motivation for individual protection of the resource base, but do not automatically offset the impact of sheer numbers of people, or of commercial exploitation. Individual property rights may have to be limited by measures to protect the commons: many of the world's prime fisheries have collapsed from commercial overuse, and it remains to be seen whether a public policy of limits on fish catches can bring them back.

IMAPCT OF URBANIZATION

Urbanization has been one of the most striking developments of the past century. In Africa, for example, only 5 per cent of the population lived in urban areas in 1900, about 20 per cent in 1960 and about 38 per cent today. Africa's current annual urban growth is the highest in the world, at more than 4 per cent. The Asia-Pacific region is close behind. The urban population, now about 35 per cent of the total, grew by about 2.6 per cent a year between 1995 and 2000, compared with 0.7 per cent a year for the rural population.

In the less-developed regions, the numbers of city dwellers will double in the next 30 years, from 1.9 billion to 3.9 billion. As dynamos of economic and social development, cities now account for a large and growing portion of demand on resources. Some analyses suggest that urban areas, with just over half the world's people, account for fully 80 per cent of carbon emissions, 75 per cent of all wood use and 60 per cent of freshwater withdrawn for human uses (including water for irrigated crops consumed by urban dwellers).

Today, almost 3 billion people live in urban areas. Over 75 per cent of the population of North America, Europe and Latin America now live in cities, and worldwide 411 cities have populations of more than 1 million, compared with 326 in 1990. In Western Europe and North America, in contrast with most other regions, there is a move out of large cities into suburbs and smaller urban centres.

By 2015, 1.6 billion people will be living in cities of more than 1 million people, 622 million in cities of more than 5 million. In the less-developed regions, the numbers of city dwellers will swell in the next 15 years, from 1.9 billion to 2.9 billion. By 2030, most people in every major region will live in cities. Growth on this scale will have severe consequences for the quality of life and surrounding environments. In the 1970s, the United Nations coined the term "megacities" to describe cities with 10 million or more residents. In 1975, there were five megacities worldwide. Today, there are 19 megacities. By 2015, the number of megacities will grow to 23.

Cities in many parts of the developing world are growing at twice the rate of overall population growth. About 160, 000 people move from rural areas to cities every day. This explosive urban growth is often due as much to the push of collapsing rural environments, poverty, landlessness, and a lack of job opportunities as to the pull of better jobs and social services in the cities.

Migrants often find that their lives become more difficult. Growth is fastest in small cities, which often lack infrastructure, and in shanty towns and squatter settlements around many large cities. In Africa 37 per cent of urban residents live in such "informal" settlements, in Asia 18 per cent, and in Latin America and the Caribbean 9 per cent. In many cities the figure is 25 to 30 per cent. Four million of Rio de Janeiro's 10.6 million residents live in such settlements—some perched precariously on steep hillsides, in flood plains or in areas of high pollution where no one with a choice would live. Dense settlements, particularly if they are badly built, are highly vulnerable to catastrophic events like floods, storms or earthquakes.

Impact of Industrial Growth

Rapid industrial growth and the concentration of urban populations combine to contaminate water and air. Raw sewage is often dumped untreated into local waterways along with industrial wastes. Most developing countries lack the resources to monitor and treat human waste or modern chemical pollutants. As urban population continues to increase, more people must share whatever water is available. The London-based Water Aid reports that the world's biggest cities are already outstripping their water supplies.

Urban centres like New Delhi, Santiago and Mexico City are pumping water from increasingly distant sites. Cities in northern India and China have seriously lowered the water tables in surrounding areas. More people means more air pollution. In India, levels of suspended particles in 10 of the largest cities are three to five times greater than WHO standards. Jakarta is one of many Asian cities polluted by burning garbage and motor vehicle exhaust. Manila has reportedly far higher levels of suspended particulate matter—the tiny solid particles dispersed from pesticides, asbestos and thousands of other products—in its air than New York, London, or Tokyo.

Most cities around the world produce far more garbage and other wastes than they can handle.

Manila's primary sewer network was designed early in the 20th century to serve about 500,000 people. Only 11 per cent of the population of Metropolitan Manila has sewer connections. In underserved areas, sewage flows via road gutters, open ditches and canals to overburdened mains to be pumped untreated into Manila Bay or flow in with the tides.

Around Mexico City, 3 million persons in peripheral areas are not connected to the sewers. Underground aquifers are severely polluted.

In many cities, between 30 and 50 per cent of the garbage goes uncollected. Even more-developed regions find it difficult to keep up with the steady increase in waste that accompanies rising consumption. In the countries of the former Soviet Union, reductions in collection and disposal systems have outstripped consumption declines. In the Russian Federation, of the 130 million cubic metres of municipal solid household waste collected in 1997, only 3 per cent reached processing plants and incinerators.

Urbanization also affects food production by removing agricultural land from cultivation, as cities expand, and by reducing the number of family farms, as more farmers move to the cities. Between 1987 and 1992, for instance, China lost close to 1 million hectares of farmland each year to urbanization and the expansion of roads and industries. In the United States, urban sprawl takes over nearly 400, 000 hectares of farmland each year.

At the same time, people are growing more and more food in urban areas. Worldwide, some 200 million city dwellers are growing food, providing about 1 billion people with at least part of their food supply. In Accra, Ghana, for example, urban gardens supply the city with 90 per cent of its vegetables. In Dar-es-Salaam, United Republic of Tanzania, one adult in every five grows fruits or vegetables.

Garden plots and roof top vegetation can have additional benefits. They reduce light and heat reflection and mitigate the trapping of heat. They can help remove pollutants produced by motor vehicles, industry and energy production.

Urban areas also affect regional and global environments through their production of greenhouse gases and generation of components of acid rain.

Natural conditions like climate, altitude, topography, wind and precipitation patterns affect cities' ability to disperse atmospheric contaminants and determine their impact on their immediate environments. Air pollution episodes in Santiago are as severe and intense as in much larger Sao Paulo even though emissions are only about a tenth as large.

Problems of Growth

Some of the world's largest cities are growing more slowly than in the past, yet their environmental impact increases and their local conditions worsen. Some rapidly growing cities have adopted policies that have improved and protected their environmental conditions. However, most rapidly growing cities face serious environmental health challenges and worsening conditions, particularly in newly settled areas and where institutions to manage and regulate growth are weak.

The growth of small and medium-sized cities in Africa, Asia and Latin America poses special problems, particularly in water provision, sanitation and garbage collection. The planning and regulatory systems of such cities are often rudimentary. They do not receive the government investments and attention that large cities can command, and they are unable to achieve comparable economies of scale—in service provision, land use, transport and water and energy provision.

In most developing countries, rapid urban growth, fuelled by both in-migration and natural population increase, is outstripping capacity to provide health services. Young women are increasingly migrating from rural to urban areas, seeking among other things for better health care, and increasing the pressure on reproductive health services in particular.

United Nations projections suggest that by 2020, there will be more urban than rural women aged 15 to 39. In Kenya, 35 per cent of rural women are aged 15-39; among urban women, 53 per cent are 15-39; similar gaps are found in Bangladesh, Haiti, Indonesia, Nicaragua, and Yemen. Urban women generally want fewer children than rural women, but access to family planning services is failing to meet those desires. Peri-urban areas are often poorly served by reproductive health services. Clinics in central cities may not be open at times convenient to many residents of the wider local area and to workers.

Wasteful Consumption Patterns

Consumption is a critical factor in the relationship between population and environmental stress. Almost all human activities put demands on natural resources: food, housing, clothing and transportation use resources like arable land, water, oil, gas and wood. Most human activities also produce wastes that are released back into air, water and soil, often with little or no treatment to mitigate their environmental impact. While population growth puts increased demands on resources, the environmental impact of a given population depends on a combination of human numbers, levels of consumption and the extractive and regenerative technologies available.

In the 20th century, consumption of goods and services rose to unprecedented levels—powering the expansion of the global economy and changing the realities of billions of people's lives. But vast numbers of people have been left out of the consumption boom. Currently a huge "consumption gap" exists: globally, the 20 per cent of the world's people who live in the highest-income countries account for 86 per cent of total private consumption expenditures; the poorest 20 per cent, by contrast, account for just 1.3 per cent.

A child born today in an industrialized country will add more to consumption and pollution over his or her lifetime than 30 to 50 children born in developing countries. Currently, the fifth of the world's people who live in industrialized nations produce over half of the carbon dioxide emitted into the atmosphere, while the poorest fifth produce only 3 per cent. The United States alone, with only 4. 6 per cent of the global population, emits nearly 25 per cent of global greenhouse gases.

Consumption in industrialized nations directly impacts the developing world. For example, almost a billion people in 40 developing countries risk losing access to their primary source of protein, fish, as over-fishing driven by demand for animal feed and oils in industrialized nations adds pressure to already declining fish stocks. And the estimated 111 million people who will be added to the U.S. population over the next 50 years will expand energy demands by more than the current energy consumption of Africa and Latin America combined.

Vast amounts of natural resources are required to produce the goods used in industrialized countries. The impacts are often felt in regions far from home where metals are mined, oil is extracted, timber harvested and food grown. Transporting these goods also consumes substantial amounts of energy resources.

As individuals and countries grow more affluent, their demands move beyond basic needs—magnifying the impact of population growth even in poor regions. And with the globalization of Western consumer culture, demands for a range of products, including cars, computers and air conditioners will only increase—adding pressure on natural resources and ecosystems' capacity to absorb waste.

Despite the linked challenges of rapidly taming excess consumption and ending the privation of under-consumption, there are some signs of positive change. Governments and industries are increasing their use of renewable resources and less- or non-polluting technologies and are exploring future potentials. Sustainable management programmes are being attempted in a growing share of forest lands. Public debate about the various environmental topics (including energy and land use policies) is intensifying, and international agreements are under discussion.

Still, what the economist Herman Daly wrote nearly 30 years ago seems relevant today: a sustainable economy "would make fewer demands on our environmental resources but much greater demands on our moral resources".

HUMANITY'S ECOLOGICAL FOOTPRINT

To measure people's impact on the environment, some scientists have devised an "ecological footprint" indicator. It shows which regions are the heaviest consumers of specific resources, on a per capita basis as well as in absolute terms. The footprint estimates a population's consumption of food, materials and energy in terms of the area of biologically productive land or sea required to produce those natural resources or, in the case of energy, to absorb the corresponding carbon dioxide emissions. Measurement is in "area units".

One area unit is equivalent to one hectare of world average productivity. Each region is represented by a rectangle in which the width is proportional to the population, the height represents per capita resource consumption, and the area represents the region's total consumption. Thus, Asia, which has a population over ten times the size of North America's but a per capita resource consumption level only one sixth as large, has a footprint only slightly bigger than North America.

Such an analysis captures the two most important dimensions of the challenge of sustainability—per capita resource consumption and population growth. This indicator also identifies areas of high and low natural biological capacity and regions responsible for "ecological deficits", where resource consumption exceeds sustainable use levels. According to the Living Planet 2000 report, global consumption in 1996 stood at 2.85 area units per person, 30 per cent more than biological availability (2.18 units).

The wealthy countries in the Organization for Economic Cooperation and Development (OECD) had a total ecological footprint of 7. 22 area units per person in 1996, more than twice the biological capacity of 3.42 units. Non-OECD countries had a total ecologic footprint of 1.81 area units per person, slightly less than the biological capacity of 1.82 units.

Africa had an ecological surplus in 1996 of 0. 40 area units per person (a footprint of 1.33 units and an available biological capacity of 1.73 area units). Many African countries enjoyed large ecological surpluses and very few countries had deficits in excess of 1 area unit per person. However these surpluses result from extensive poverty rather than beneficial management.

Latin America and the Caribbean had the world's highest ecological surplus, 3.93 area units per person, due to its high natural biological availability (6.39 units) and relatively low resource consumption (2.46 units). The highest per capita surpluses were found in Bolivia, Brazil and Peru.

The Middle East and Central Asia had an ecological deficit of 1.82 area units per person, largely due to its low biological capacity (0. 91 units). The total ecological footprint of the area was 2.73 area units per person. Wealthy oil economies such as the United Arab Emirates and Kuwait had the highest deficits.

Asia and the Pacific's ecological deficit of 0. 67 area units per person is partly attributable to its high population, which reduces biological capacity to 1.11 units. The total ecological footprint of the area was 1.78 area units per person in 1996. Singapore, Japan and South Korea had the highest deficits.

North America had the world's highest ecological deficit (5.64 area units per person) in 1996, despite having the second highest biological capacity (6.13 units). The United States registered an ecological deficit of 6.66 area units per person.

Western Europe had an ecological deficit of 3.35 area units per person, the second highest in the world. The ecological footprint was 6.28 units against a biological capacity of 2.93 units. The United Kingdom, Switzerland and Denmark registered the highest deficits.

Central and Eastern Europe had an ecological footprint of 4.89 area units per person, a biological capacity of 3.14 area units and a deficit of 1.75 units in 1996. The Czech Republic and Estonia had the highest deficits.

Living Planet 2000 also reports five components of the ecological footprint: cropland, grazing land, forest (fuel-wood and wood products, including paper), fishing ground (marine fish and seafood products including fish-meal and oils fed to animals) and carbon dioxide (fossil fuel consumption plus the net energy required to make imported manufactured products). These also show a big consumption gap between developed and developing regions.

For example, North America's cropland footprint (1.44 area units per person) was more than twice the world average (0.69 units). The fishing ground footprint of consumers in OECD countries was three times that in non-OECD countries. The OECD consumer's average carbon dioxide footprint in 1996 was more than five times that of the non-OECD consumer. North America's carbon dioxide footprint, 7 area units per person, was five times the global average and more than seven times the averages of Latin America and the Caribbean, Asia and the Pacific, and Africa.

Environmental Refugees

Population displacement due to environmental degradation (due to natural disasters, war or over-exploitation) is not a recent phenomenon. What is recent is the potential for large movements of people resulting from a combination of resource depletion, the irreversible destruction of the environment and population growth, among other factors. When a tidal wave hit the shores of Papua New Guinea in 1998, the death toll was in the thousands because human settlements dotted the coastline and the banks of lagoons.

When the Yangtze caused massive flooding in China, the disaster was exacerbated by deforestation and erosion due to overpopulation along the riverbanks. In January and February of 2001, thousands of people were uprooted when powerful earthquakes struck El Salvador, causing deadly landslides on mountain slopes cleared for subsistence agriculture.

The World Bank estimates that in 1998 there were 25 million people displaced by environmental degradation, outnumbering war-related refugees for the first time in history.

Displaced refugees often threaten the areas where they are staying. The 1994 crisis in Rwanda led to the influx of more than 600, 000 people into north-west United Republic of Tanzania, where they caused considerable environmental damage by harvesting firewood and building poles, poaching in game reserves, and putting land under cultivation. Environmental refugees have significant economic, sociocultural and political consequences. Currently, developed nations pay $8 billion each year to accommodate refugees, one seventh of the foreign aid supplied to developing countries.

WOMEN'S ROLE IN ENVIRONMENTAL DEVELOPMENT

The direct and critical relationship between women and natural resources draws its strength not from biology—that is, not because women are born female—but from gender, and the socially created roles and responsibilities that continue to fall to women in households, communities and ecosystems throughout the world. Women have primary responsibility for rearing children, and for ensuring sufficient resources to meet children's needs for nutrition, health care and schooling.

In the rural areas of developing countries, they are also the main managers of essential household resources like clean water, fuel for cooking and heating and fodder for domestic animals. Women grow vegetables, fruit and grain for home consumption and also for sale—often, as in much of Africa, producing most of the staple crops. In South-east Asia, women provide 90 per cent of the labour for rice cultivation.

Women are more than half (51 per cent) of the world's agricultural work force. As economic opportunities open up, women in developing countries are growing, processing and marketing non-food products made from natural resources, for consumption at home and, increasingly, overseas. In Burkina Faso, for example, women are producing hundreds of tons of shea butter each year, selling much of it to European cosmetic markets.

In Colombia, thousands of female workers are tending flowers for sale in the United States. But such livelihoods can also present new environmental and health risks: it is estimated that flower workers in Colombia are exposed to 127 different types of chemicals, many of which have been banned in the United States and the United Kingdom. Many of these activities take place in the interstices of men's use of resources. Women occupy niches allowed by traditional gender structures or opened up by economic and social change.

In coastal Mozambique, women are not allowed to come close to the boats men use for ocean fishing, or to do such fishing themselves, although they process and market the men's catch. Their aquatic space is close to the shore, where they harvest and sell shellfish, crabs and other small sea creatures—women's work that provides about 20 per cent of average monthly household income according to a recent study.

As poverty persists and, in many parts of the world, deepens, women's income from such activities becomes critical to family survival—reinforcing the importance of the environment in women's lives (and increasing the dangers posed by degraded environments). In the growing number of female-headed households, this work is essential, particularly for children; women already head almost a quarter of rural households in the world's poorest countries. Women's income can also create the conditions for expanded opportunities, choices and autonomy—all of which advance the larger goal of gender equity and equality.

Effects of Environmental degradation on Women

Women have the responsibility for managing household resources, but they typically do not have managerial control. Given the variety of women's daily interactions with the environment, they are the most keenly affected by its degradation.

Deforestation or contamination increases the time women must spend seeking fuelwood or safe, clean water, and increase women's risk of water-borne disease. In the state of Gujurat, India, women now spend four or five hours a day collecting fuelwood, where previously they would have done so once every four to five days. Soil erosion, water shortage and crop failures reduce harvest yields; soil exhausted from over-use reduces the productivity of household gardens.

Toxic chemicals and pesticides in air, water and earth are responsible for a variety of women's health risks. They enter body tissues and breast milk, through which they are passed on to infants. In a village in China's Gansu province, discharges from a state-run fertilizer factory have been linked to a high number of stillbirths and miscarriages. Water pollution in three Russian rivers is a factor in the doubling of bladder and kidney disorders in pregnant women, and in Sudan a link has been established between exposure to pesticides and perinatal mortality—with the risk higher among women farmers.

In urban settings in particular, air and water pollution can be extreme, and sanitation and waste treatment poor or non-existent, presenting new threats to health, particularly for women, who have the highest levels of exposure. In the Indian cities of Delhi and Agra, for example, drinking water comes from rivers heavily polluted by DDT and other pesticides.

Degraded environments mean that women must spend more time and effort to find fuel or produce food, but their other responsibilities, for meeting household needs and ensuring family health, do not diminish. Gendered divisions of labour have so far resisted real change. In many countries, women already work 12 hours or more a day in and out of the home; in Africa and Asia, women work an average of 13 hours more each week than do men.

At the same time, women have little **power over the** conditions of their lives. Decision makers often overlook this reality, even though women's use and management of local environmental resources is fundamental to household and community well-being. Agricultural extension services are heavily biased towards men. Education and outreach efforts in support of sustainable farming and land management methods often pass them by.

National law or local customs often effectively deny women the right to secure title or inherit land, which means they have no collateral on which to raise credit. Poverty, precarious land tenure and lack of expert support discourage women from investing in newer technologies or long-term strategies such as crop rotation, fallow periods, sustainable levels of cultivation or reforestation. On the contrary, these factors encourage fast-growing cash crops such as cotton, which quickly exhaust the land, and woodland clearance for short-term income.

Such pressures on limited land resources deplete nutrients and degrade soils. Land degradation reduces yields, leading to a spiral of more intensive use, further degradation and still lower yields. Farmers may seek new land, but often find it only in frontier or marginal areas, especially if they are women and cannot close a sale or negotiate a loan.

In the worst-affected countries, HIV/AIDS has increased poverty and decreased choices, forcing people to fall back on natural resources to meet basic needs. In South Africa, large numbers of poor people, particularly women, are trying to produce food and fuel on marginal lands, increasing the pressure on fragile ecosystems. Unsustainable land use can often be traced to denial of technical and financial resources. Given the opportunity, women may well have a predisposition to practice sustainable agriculture and maintain overall land quality—precisely because of their strong reliance on natural resources. A World Bank study in Ghana found that women's plots had a lower rate of decline in soil fertility than men's—even in the same household.

In India, women are leading rural movements to promote sustainable farming practices and resist large-scale agricultural operations that rely on intensive chemical fertilizers and pesticides. And in the United Kingdom, where farming is male-dominated, half of all organic farmers are women—10 times the proportion in the farming industry overall. Women who lack rights to own and manage natural resources often lack rights in other aspects of their lives, reinforcing gender inequalities. Like millions of women throughout the world, women in the strongly patriarchal rural communities of south-east Madagascar have no access to the resources that bring status—property, cattle and farmland.

As a result, they have little part in community or household decisions. This includes decisions about reproduction (fertility is high), marriage (early marriage is common) and education for themselves and their children (education rates for boys are low and for girls lower still). In the past, large families were common in rural communities: children were important to agricultural productivity (especially on large land tracts), often joining their mothers (and at times fathers) in fields or household gardens, tending domestic animals and assisting with household resource needs—fetching water, and foraging for fuelwood and edible and medicinal plants. Rural women married young and had many pregnancies.

One legacy of high fertility, lower infant mortality and a limited supply of land is fragmentation. As they passed from one generation of sons to another, plots were divided again and again. Eventually the plots were simply not big enough to provide enough food for family or market. Pressures to increase yields have intensified, and men have left in search of non-farm employment. Without them, women's family burdens and responsibilities have increased, though urban relatives often send money to improve the remaining land, as well as for housing, education and health care.

Urbanization offers a series of risks and opportunities to women. Urban growth and poverty produces new environmental threats that increase health risks. Again, those most exposed are women and their children. On the other hand, pregnancy and childbirth are generally safer in urban areas, where health care is more likely to be accessible. City life also offers women a broader range of choices for education, employment and marriage, but it also carries heightened risk of sexual violence, abuse and exploitation. For poor women, urbanization means less physical labour to find fuel, food and water, but they often lose direct control over quality or quantity. For the very poor, these basic resources are more expensive—in absolute as well as relative terms—than for better-off groups.

In environmental terms, what urbanization offers the poor with one hand, it takes away with the other. The very poor in urban areas, for example those who live on and off garbage dumps, are arguably the most deprived on the planet, in human as well as economic terms. As women join the migration from rural to urban areas, they are vulnerable to economic and sexual exploitation—sweatshop labour, trafficking, abuse or violence; factory workers face possible exposure to chemicals, dust or other forms of pollution.

Along with the risks, however, go new economic opportunities. Freedom from the social and gender hierarchies of rural communities may also open up chances to go to school, college or university, to acquire marketable skills and to choose whether, when and whom to marry. Urban women are more likely to be able to decide when, if and how many children to bear, both because of changing gender relations and because they have easier access to reproductive health information and services.

To be effective managers of household and other resources, both rural and urban women need a range of options: choices over family size and spacing; health care, including reproductive health; education; and partnership with men. There are many examples of programmes to empower women that reinforce both their management of resources and their reproductive health. Extension programmes can typically provide aspects of reproductive health care together with information and assistance for resources management.

Involving Women in Environmental and Health Decisions

Sustainable development demands recognition and value for the multitude of ways in which women's lives intertwine with environmental realities. Women's right to own and inherit land should be enforced; individual and communal security of land tenure should be guaranteed; women should have access to credit, and to agricultural extension and resource management services, and they should be included in decisions about the services' organization and content.

Women's involvement must extend to information, education and services for reproductive health and rights. Choice about fertility is a step towards equality: women thus empowered can intervene in other decisions in the household and the community, for example, education and health care for girl children; the use of common resources and the development of economic opportunities. Women's involvement in health and environmental decisions works to the benefit of individuals, society and the environment itself.

In fact, as a growing body of experience shows, reproductive health and environmental services can work very profitably together, if they are designed to meet communities' own priorities. Integration eliminates the need to duplicate outreach, and responds to women's interrelated needs.

Trust is key in such efforts: in one Latin American project, a female staff member of an environmental organization who developed considerable rapport with local village residents was inundated with requests for reproductive health information and care. At the same time, a government health worker without similar rapport received few such requests. Not surprisingly, studies have also found that the most critical element of the success of integrated reproductive health and environmental services is the active engagement of women. Shifting environmental conditions can begin new and more intense gender conflicts, but can also bring opportunities for women and men to negotiate gender equality.

For example, in Newfoundland, Canada, the collapse of North Atlantic fish stocks has brought mass unemployment to communities that once relied almost wholly on fish. Before the crisis, men did the fishing and women worked in fish processing plants. But with men and women both at home during the day, domestic conflict increased. Women wanted more help in the house, but also felt invaded; men often felt emasculated by their demands. Alcohol use and conflict with men outside the home also increased. Young women began to see husbands and boyfriends as undesirable, the number of female-headed households rose, and levels of migration for both women and men, especially those with more education, increased significantly.

A more positive response to a changed environment can be seen among salt miners in Bilma, Niger. For hundreds of years, large numbers of men crisscrossed the Sahara for months at a time, transporting and trading salt for fruit, grain and gold. In recent years, the value of salt has fallen and lorries have taken over much of the trade from camels, forcing most men into a more sedentary existence. In response, men and women have created new forms of partnership.

Many women now work alongside their husbands scooping salt from pits—something not possible a generation ago. In those days, when a father died his daughters could not maintain his pits; boys or men were required. But today, when a woman marries she can join her new husband in the mine. Several couples also mine together, and the salt miners even include unmarried women.

Environmental change imposes new stresses and choices on women's and men's lives. Evolution in gender roles induced by environmental change can mean better communication and shared decision-making; but negotiating new roles and responsibilities can be a painful process. It is important to maximize social flexibility and the resources women and men can bring to negotiations with each other and with the natural world.

Forging New Relationships

Successful negotiation between women and men will be helped by having access to information and education, and to agricultural and reproductive health services. The support of laws and policies on women's rights and equality and on the sustainable use and protection of natural resources are also essential. With such support women and men can create a virtuous circle of sustainability and equity. Without it they are trapped in a vicious spiral of continuing environmental degradation, poverty, high fertility and limited opportunity, leading to environmental and social collapse.

Women's groups are organizing to integrate women fully into the political process, so they can take their full part in making policy decisions affecting their lives, including policies on: the use of land and water resources for agriculture; power, drinking water and energy supply; health and education services; and economic opportunities. In many countries, they are succeeding.

A successful outcome will depend on forging new relationships between women and the environment, and between women and the world at large. Wangari Maathai is a Kenyan environmentalist and founder of the Green Belt Movement, which works with women in 20 countries to plant trees. As she suggests, such social and ecological transformations are well under way: "Implicit in the action of planting trees," she says," is a civic education, a strategy to empower people and to give them a sense of taking their destiny into their own hands, removing their fear so they can stand up for their environmental rights. So that they [women] can control the direction of their own lives."

5

Ecological Restructuring

Before the beginning of the industrial revolution, some two centuries ago, human activities - on the average - were not really incompatible with a healthy and sustainable biosphere. The vast majority of humans lived and worked on farms. Land was the primary source of wealth. Horses and other animals, supplemented by windmills, sails, and waterwheels, provided virtually all power for ploughing, milling, mining, and transport. The sun, either directly or through products of photosynthesis, provided virtually all energy except in a few coal mining regions.

Metals were mined and smelted (primarily by means of charcoal), but their uses were almost exclusively metallic rather than chemical. Recycling was normal. Precisely because wealth was derived exclusively from the land, Thomas Malthus worried at the end of the eighteenth century about the propensity of human population to grow exponentially, in view of the limited amount of potentially arable land available for human cultivation. As we approach the end of the twentieth century, humans are far more numerous and also wealthier (on average) than they were two centuries ago when Malthus wrote.

In particular, those countries that industrialized first are now comparatively rich. In the rich countries most people live in cities. Land is no longer the primary source of wealth. Energy (except food) is largely derived from the combustion of fossil fuels (coal, oil, gas). Power for machines is obtained mainly from engines driven by heat from (internal or external) combustion of fossil fuels. (Nuclear and hydroelectric power, together, account for a relatively small percentage of the total.)

However, one key attribute of this recent rise to wealth is critical for the future of humankind: what we have achieved so far has been done by exploiting an endowment of natural capital, especially topsoil and minerals. For some material resources technology can offer viable substitutes. For other resources in the natural endowment - notably the biosphere and its functions - no substitute is likely. The report of the United Nations' World Commission on Environment and Development (WCED) - known as the Brundtland Commission - was published in 1987 under the title Our Common Future. This triggered the Global Environmental Summit at Rio de Janeiro in June 1992 and its major product, Agenda 21.

Since that time it has been widely recognized that there is a very real conflict between meeting the needs and desires of the 5 billion people now alive and the possibility of satisfying the 10 billion or so people expected by the middle of the twenty-first century. It will be exceedingly difficult simultaneously to satisfy the objectives of environmental preservation, on the one hand, and accelerated economic development of the third world, based on current population trends and energy/material-intensive technologies, on the other. The implications of this conflict have been delineated eloquently in the Commission's report.

Experts can and do disagree on the probabilities and timing of environmental threats relative to other problems facing the human race. Some ideologues have even argued that the threats are figments of the fevered imaginations of the "Greens." Arguments on these matters will probably continue for some time to come. But there is increasing evidence to suggest that major changes in the global economic and industrial system may be needed if the world is to achieve a sustainable state before the middle of the twenty-first century.

Even though there is not yet a scientific consensus on the extent of the needed changes, it is clear that they will involve significant technological elements, as well as major investments. The population problem comes to mind first, especially in the context of the 1994 Cairo Conference on Population and the Status of Women. It is unlikely that the other problems of the global environment can be solved if the world's population is not stabilized. Experts now generally agree that education and the status of women are central issues here. This implies that a world of relatively stable population must be one in which social patterns are significantly different from those now encountered in many parts of the world.

The kinds of techno-economic changes envisaged as necessary conditions for long-term sustainability also include a sharp reduction in the use of fossil fuels (especially coal) to minimize the danger of global "greenhouse warming." Alternatives to increasing use of fossil fuels include a return to nuclear power, large-scale use of photovoltaics, intensive biomass cultivation, large-scale hydroelectric projects (in some regions), and major changes in patterns of energy consumption and conservation. Again, there are disputes over which of these energy alternatives is the most (least) desirable, feasible, etc. However, the future of energy, from both the supply (technology) and the demand perspective, is a critical topic.

Since the early 1970s, the environmental movement has become increasingly professionalized and bureaucratized. As a consequence, largely, of the latter development, the "environment" is seen no longer in a holistic sense but in terms of a number of specific, essentially independent issues. Nowadays, the "causes" of pollution are attributed, for the most part, to narrowly defined actions of equally narrowly defined "polluters." The responsibilities for abatement or clean-up are correspondingly narrow.

Solid wastes, hazardous or toxic wastes, liquid wastes, and airborne wastes are likely to be allocated to different government departments, ranging from public health agencies to water/sewerage authorities, whose regulatory powers are controlled by different kinds of legislation framed in different circumstances, sometimes based on quite different regulatory philosophies. "The right hand does not know what the left hand is doing," and vice versa. Activities of different arms of the same agency can interfere with each other. For instance, incineration can reduce the solid waste disposal problem, and even produce useful energy as a by-product, but it creates an air pollution problem.

On the other hand, to reduce the emissions of particulates and sulphur oxides from power plants creates solid wastes that must be disposed of somewhere on land. There is nobody with a global view of the problem to mediate among the parochial interests. There is nobody with the responsibility or the authority to induce competing offices, departments, and bureaux to cooperate. Yet the environment is, by its very nature, unsuited to incremental control strategies. It is equally unsuited for reductionist "bottom-up" modes of analysis.

The problem is that scientific insights are now, and will continue to be, insufficient for predicting the detailed environmental consequences of any change or perturbation. To take a concrete instance, nobody can predict the exact physiological effects of ingesting any chemical from knowledge of its structure. Still less can the genetic or ecological consequences of its dispersion be predicted. This uncertainty is multiplied by the enormous number of different chemicals, materials, and mixtures simultaneously manufactured and used by man (natural and synthetic alike), not to mention the variety (type and intensity) of possible reaction modes and interaction effects.

Setting aside carcinogens and highly toxic or radioactive substances, one important environmental problem has as yet been predicted in advance from the creation or displacement of any particular material stream. This single exception was Rowland's chance recognition of the reactive potential of chlorofluorocarbons (CFCs) in the stratosphere, and the resulting possibility of stratospheric ozone depletion. This potential hazard, derided by chemical industry spokesmen in the 1970s as "speculative," has turned out to be real. In speaking of the environment it is literally true that "everything depends upon everything else."

A holistic "top-down" perspective is essential to identifying the most important underlying factors and relationships. It is equally important to adopt a very broad perspective for seeking and - it is hoped - finding effective global strategies to save the planet.

Environmental Threats and Sustainability

There has been a good deal of academic debate in recent years on the exact meaning that should be ascribed to the term "sustainability." For instance, Repetto states that "current decisions should not impair the prospects for maintaining or improving future living standards". The WCED paraphrased the same general idea; sustainable development "meets the needs of the present without compromising the ability of future generations to meet their own needs". Tietenberg phrases it in utility terms, and defines sustainability as non-declining utility.

Pezzey goes further and insists that it is the discounted present value of utility that should not decline. Mainstream economists have concerned themselves with replacing depleted natural resource stocks. For instance, Nobel Laureate Robert Solow proposed that "an appropriate stock of capital - including the initial endowment of resources - [be] maintained intact". More recently Solow has said: "If 'sustainability' is anything more than a slogan or an expression of emotion, it must amount to an injunction to preserve productive capacity for the indefinite future. That is compatible with the use of non-renewable resources only if society as a whole replaces used-up resources with something else".

All of these definitions (and others) essentially agree on a single economic measure of welfare (GNP). They fundamentally assume unlimited substitutability between conventional economic goods and services that are traded in the market-place and unpriced environmental services, from stratospheric ozone to the carbon cycle. However, virtually all environmentalists and an increasing number of economists explicitly reject the unlimited substitutability view as simplistic. Similar critiques have been articulated by David Pearce and his colleagues.

The "ecological" criterion for sustainability admits the likelihood that some of the important functions of the natural world cannot be replaced within any realistic timeframe - if ever - by human technology, however sophisticated. The need for arable land, water, and a benign climate for agriculture is an example; the role of reducing bacteria in recycling nutrient elements in the biosphere is another; the ozone layer of the stratosphere is a third. The ecological criterion for long-run sustainability implicitly allows for some technological intervention: for example, methods of artificially accelerating tree growth may compensate for some net decrease in the area devoted to forests.

But, absent any plausible technological "fixes," this definition does not admit the acceptability of major climate changes, widespread desertification, deforestation of the tropics, accumulation of toxic heavy metals and non-biodegradable halogenated organics in soils and sediments, or sharp reductions in biodiversity, for instance. Having said this, it is obviously easier to find indicators of unsustainability than of sustainability. In work for the Advisory Council for Research on Nature and the Environment (Netherlands), preparing for the UNCED Conference in Rio de Janeiro, 1992, Dutch researchers proposed a taxonomy of sustainability indicators. Their taxonomy has three dimensions:

1. Pollution of natural systems with xenobiotic substances or natural substances in unnatural concentrations. The results include acidification and "toxification" of the environment.

2. Depletion of natural resources: renewable, non-renewable, and semi-renewable. In fact, biodiversity can be regarded as a depletable resource, though not one that is commonly thought of as such. Of course, it also differs from other depletable resources that are exchanged in (and priced by) well-developed markets.

There is no such market for biodiversity, or for its complement, genetic information.

3. Encroachment (human intervention) affecting natural systems, e.g. loss of groundwater or soil erosion.

The notion of "sustainable level" in regard to pollution, toxification, acidification, greenhouse gas build-up, and so on is predicated on the idea that natural processes will compensate for some of the damage. For instance, natural weathering of rocks generates some alkaline materials that can neutralize acid. (Increased acidity will, however, increase the rate of weathering.) Similarly, it is assumed that some of the excess carbon dioxide produced by combustion processes may be absorbed in the oceans or taken up by accelerated photosynthetic activity in northern forests (this process is called "CO_2 fertilization").

Regarding depletion, it is assumed that some minerals (such as aluminum) can be mined more or less indefinitely, even though the highest-quality ores will be exhausted first. Other depletable ores could in effect be exhausted, in the sense that recovery from minable ores would be too expensive to be worthwhile except for very specialized and limited uses. Copper might be an example of this kind (though many geologists are more optimistic than Weterings and Opschoor). As regards renewable resources such as fisheries and groundwater, it has long been known that there is a level of exploitation that can be sustained indefinitely by scientific management, but that beyond that level harvesting pressures can drive populations down to the point where recovery may take decades, or may never occur at all.

Many fisheries appear to be in this situation at present, notwithstanding the fact that sustainable levels are not very precisely known. Granted some uncertainty, it is nevertheless clear that, in all three dimensions, "sustainability" would require significant reductions in current levels of impact. In recognition of the fact that both soil erosion and groundwater loss overlap considerably with the "depletion" category, the later version of their work substituted "loss of naturalness," namely loss of integrity, diversity, absence of disturbance. What remains in category (3) is the notion of "disturbance of natural systems" as such.

Most environmentalists think of "systems" in terms of ecosystems and biomes. The sum total of such disturbances is indeed a significant environmental problem, though individual cases tend to be geographically localized. However there are also global systems that are being dangerously disturbed by anthropogenic activity. Examples of global systems include the hydrological cycle, ocean currents, the climate, the global radiation balance (including the ozone layer that protects the earth's surface from lethal ultraviolet radiation), the carbon/-oxygen cycle, the nitrogen cycle, and the sulphur cycle.Holistic analysis presupposes that it is possible to classify variables by degree of importance and derive significant and defensible results by judicious simplification. A universal measure to estimate and compare the relative environmental impact of different activities, goods, services, and regulatory policies would be of great value.

Such a measure should satisfy the following conditions:

— it should be based on measurable quantities;

— it should relate to the most significant environmental impact potentials of human activities;

— it should allow transparent, cost-efficient, and reproducible estimates of the environmental impact potentials of all kinds of plans, processes, goods, and services;

— it must be applicable on the global level as well as regional and local levels.

Choosing a single indicator to compare the environmental impact intensities of all kinds of present and future processes, goods, and services might seem to be a daring step, precisely because it constitutes a vast reduction of complexity. Simplification cannot be proven to be "correct" in scientific terms. Only its plausibility in a variety of circumstances can be established. For several reasons it can be argued that aggregate resource productivity, the ratio of GNP (or a better unit of economic welfare) to an index of total renewable-but-unrenowned or non-renewable resource inputs, in physical units, might be a plausible measure of sustainability.

At least the two are correlated: the greater the resource productivity, the nearer to long-term sustainability. Obviously, the inverse of resource productivity - non-renewable or non-renewed resource use per unit of welfare output - is a measure of unsustainability. Regrettably, neither this measure nor anything similar is currently computed at the national level by statistical agencies, and the required data are not readily available even to them, still less to non government organizations.

Non-controversial Issues

There has been, and still is, great controversy as regards the essentiality (non-substitutability) of certain environmental resources. However, the controversy is largely over definitions and details, not fundamentals. Possibly this confusion has arisen because the issues were not formulated sharply enough, until recently. The existence of "critical" environmental resources is not seriously doubted by most people. The doubters are mostly conservative libertarians with a deep faith in the ability of markets to allocate scarce resources and to call forth technological (or other) substitutes in response to any perceived scarcity.

The weakness of this position is that markets for environmental services are virtually non-existent. Markets must function through price signals. Clearly we need food, sunshine, clean air, and fresh water. We also need the waste disposal services of bacteria, fungi, and insects. All are, at bottom, gifts of nature. Because they are not "commodities" that can be owned and possessed or physically exchanged, they have no prices.

Moreover, since these services are not produced by human activity, price signals could not induce an increase in the supply. What is still doubted by many scientists, on the other hand, is the answer to the second half of the question: whether or not these essential environmental resources are truly vulnerable to human interference and possibly subject to irreversible damage.

One example of an essential environmental resource that appears to be subject to irreversible damage is the ozone layer of the stratosphere. The cause of damage, it is now agreed, is atomic chlorine, which originates from the inert chlorofluorocarbons (CFCs) that do not break down in the lower atmosphere and gradually diffuse into the stratosphere where they are broken up by high-energy ultraviolet radiation (UV-B). The chlorine atoms, in turn, react with and destroy ozone molecules, thus depleting the protective ozone layer. This phenomenon was very controversial 20 years ago, but the controversy has largely subsided, thanks to the discovery of annual "ozone holes" in the polar stratosphere, which were first seen in the mid-1980s.

Another example of increasing consensus concerns climate change. The climate is certainly an environmental resource. Even a decade ago there were still a number of scientists expressing serious doubts about whether the problem was "real." The major source of doubt had to do with the reliability of the large-scale general circulation models of the atmosphere that had to be used to forecast the temperature effects of a build-up of greenhouse gases (e.g. carbon dioxide, methane, nitrous oxide, CFCs).

Since then, the models have been improved significantly and it has been established fairly definitely that climate warming has been "masked" up to now by a parallel build-up in the atmosphere of sulphate aerosol particles (due to sulphur dioxide emissions), which reflect solar heat and cool the earth. The two effects have tended to compensate for each other. However, the greenhouse gases are accumulating (they have long lifetimes) whereas the sulphate aerosols are quickly washed out by rain.

In other words, the greenhouse gas concentration will continue to increase geometrically, whereas the sulphate problem may increase only arithmetically or not at all (if sulphur dioxide emissions are controlled). In any case, the Intergovernmental Panel on Climate Change (IPCC) has now agreed that the greenhouse problem is indeed "real." The controversy continues, however, with regard to likely economic damage and optimal policy responses.

There is already a near-consensus among experts that continued human population growth is not consistent with long-run sustainability and that some natural resources must eventually be depleted. On the other hand, there is less agreement about whether or not increasing waste and pollution would constitute a limit on growth or whether or not the balanced natural systems such as the carbon, nitrogen, and sulphur cycles are at risk.

The unacceptability of continued population growth is a matter on which there is reasonably wide consensus. Malthus foresaw that population growth would eventually outrun the carrying capacity of the earth. Colonization of new lands in the western hemisphere, together with dramatic improvements in agricultural technology, forestalled the crisis for two centuries. Some conservative economists regard this as sufficient evidence that "Malthus was wrong" and that today's neo-Malthusians are unnecessarily alarmist.

Nevertheless, the alarm has been raised once again, perhaps on better grounds: there are no more "new lands" waiting for cultivation, and the potential increases in yield available from fertilizers and plant breeding have already been largely exhausted. Technological optimists - notably Herman Kahn and his colleagues - have unhesitatingly projected that early twentieth-century rates of increase in agricultural productivity can and will continue into the indefinite future. However, agricultural experts are much less sanguine. The potential gains from further uses of chemicals by traditional methods are definitely limited.

Ground water is already becoming seriously depleted and/or contaminated in many regions of the United States and Western Europe, where intensive irrigation cum chemical agriculture have been practiced for a few decades. Such problems are now also becoming acute in places such as northern China. Over a decade ago Bernard Gilland wrote:

Since the onset of the rapid rise in the world population growth rate over 30 years ago, there has been speculation on the human carrying capacity of the planet. Most writers on the problem either hold, on technological grounds, that the Earth can support several (or even many) times its present population, or warn, on ecological grounds, that the Earth is already overpopulated and that human numbers should be reduced. Gilland went on to conclude: Estimates for global carrying capacity and long-range demographic projections are admittedly subject to wide margins of error, but the consequences of relying on an excessively optimistic assessment of the future population food supply balance would be so serious that a conservative assessment is justified.

Admittedly, Gilland's assessment was based on conventional agriculture using land now classified as "arable." Julian Simon argued that this is not a fixed quantity, and that so-called arable land had actually been increasing at a rate of about 0.7 per cent per annum (from 1960 to 1974). This is one of the reasons food shortages projected earlier did not occur. But most of the "new" cropland was formerly tropical forest (the rest was grassland, such as, for instance, the vast and ill-conceived "new lands" projects of Soviet central Asia).

Deforestation has now become an acute problem throughout the tropics, and most tropical forest soils are not very fertile to begin with and are rapidly exhausted of their nutrients by cropping. There is no basis for supposing that the amount of arable land can continue to increase much longer, if indeed it has not begun to decrease already for the reasons noted above. In any case, erosion and salination are taking a constant toll of the lands already in production. With regard to the possibility of continuing to increase the productivity (yield) of existing arable land, there is a continuing push to develop improved varieties and higher photosynthetic efficiencies.

Biotechnology is now beginning to be harnessed to increase food production. There is optimistic talk of a "second green revolution." For some years past, global grain production per capita has actually been declining. Thus, incremental improvements will be needed just to keep up with population growth. Gilland also did not take into account several theoretical possibilities, including such "high-tech" schemes as genetically engineered bacteria capable of digestion of cellulose or crude oil, large-scale hydroponics, and massive irrigation of tropical deserts such as the Sahara using desalinated sea water.

Certainly, these possibilities must be taken seriously, and some of them may play an important role before the end of the twenty-first century. On the other hand, there is no chance that any of them could make a difference within the next 20 or 30 years. In short, there are strong indications that agricultural technology cannot continue to outpace population growth in the third world for more than another few decades.

For these reasons, the majority of demographers, and most economists, now take it for granted that population growth must be brought to an end as soon as possible if sustainability is to be achieved. As regards concerns about resource exhaustion, the "neo-Malthusian" position was taken very seriously by some alarmists, such as Paul Ehrlich, in the 1970s. The argument was made that economic growth is inherently restricted by the limited availability of exhaustible natural resources.

However, it is now widely agreed among both economists and physical scientists that energy or mineral resource scarcity is not likely to be a growth limiting factor, at least for the next half-century or so. The Malthusian "limits to growth" position adopted by some environmentalists in the 1960s and 1970s has been largely discredited, both by empirical research and by many theorists.

The main reason for the change of perspective is that the neo-Malthusian view was naive in two respects. First, the neo-Malthusians neglected the fact (well known to the fuel and mineral industries) that there is no incentive for a mining or drilling enterprise to search for new resources as long as it has reserves for 30 years or so. This is a simple consequence of discounting behaviour. It explains why "known reserves" of many resources tend to hover around 20-30 years of current demand, despite continuously rising demand. Secondly, they gave too little credit to the power of market-driven economies to call forth technological alternatives to emergent scarcities.

However, as it turns out, it is overused "renewable" resources, such as arable land, fish, fresh water, forests, biodiversity, and climate, that are more likely to be limiting factors. The existence of feasible strategies to achieve population stability is now generally accepted. The subsidiary question of the most appropriate means remains murky. This optimism is based partly on evidence of a slow-down in global population growth in recent decades.

However it is admittedly unclear whether the observed slow-down (mostly in China, so far) can be extrapolated to other countries, particularly in the Muslim world. Still, the majority of experts seem to believe that the required "demographic transition" is economically and institutionally feasible, in principle.

Here the central problem is seen to be to achieve near-universal literacy, equal rights and legal standing for women, a social security net for the poor, and real economic growth to finance all of this, at a rate fast enough to reach that "middle-class" standard within a few generations. Demographers and social scientists generally agree that these are the preconditions for radically reduced birth rates.

BIOSPHERIC STABILITY

The existence of plausible threats to biospheric stability, even survival, is by no means obvious. The question about whether or not pollution constitutes a possible limiting factor for economic growth is perhaps the one most debated at present. It is highly controversial. If there is any consensus on this issue it is merely that "toxification" is unacceptable. But the extent to which pollution constitutes a limitation on growth itself, or on the welfare generated by economic activity, remains an open question.

The issue of environmental acidification and/or toxification has never been considered seriously as a global threat to human survival. However, concerns are beginning to arise, especially in regard to cancer and human reproductive capacity. The link between various chemical agents and biological impacts none the less remains largely speculative, and is likely to remain so for many years. Damage mechanisms and thresholds are known in some cases, but not in others. However, it is fairly easy to construct a simple catalogue of measures of materials flux and consequent waste generation that self-evidently cannot continue to increase indefinitely.

The issue of whether or not there is a threat to biospheric stability itself is rather deep. There are two aspects: the first has to do with phenomenology; the second has to do with the essential indeterminacy of the risk. Not only is there no consensus on either of these points, there has been almost no discussion up to now.

Exposure to Toxicity

There is no doubt that widespread fear of exposure to toxic chemicals is one of the major driving forces behind the environmental movement. The near-hysterical media coverage of the "Love Canal" episode and the proliferation of "Superfund" sites certainly support this contention. Yet, as a basis for discussing environmental threats half a century hence, one needs a different kind of evidence. Unfortunately, methodological problems proliferate even faster than superfund sites. First, the number of industrial chemicals produced in annual quantities greater than 1 metric ton is estimated at 60,000. The number grows by thousands each year.

Only a tiny percentage of these has been tested for the whole range of toxic effects. In fact, it could be argued that none has, since new effects are being discovered all the time, often by accident or from epidemiological evidence long after the fact. For instance, mercury was not known to be harmful in the environment until the mysterious outbreak of "Minamata disease," a severe and sometimes lethal neurological disorder among cats, seabirds, and fishermen living near Minamata Bay, in Japan. It took several years before public health workers were able to trace the problem to organic mercury compounds (mainly methyl mercury) in fish from the bay.

The ultimate source turned out to be inorganic mercury from spent catalysts discharged by a nearby chemical plant. The toxic effects of cadmium ("itai-itai disease") were discovered in a similar way. Second, quantitative production and consumption data for chemicals are not published consistently even on a national basis, still less on a worldwide basis. Data can be obtained only with great difficulty, from indirect sources (such as market studies), and for only the top 200 or so chemicals.

In the United States and virtually all countries with a central statistical office (or census), production and shipments data are collected, but the data are withheld for "proprietary" reasons if the number of producers is three or fewer. In Europe, the largest producer of most chemicals, all quantitative production and trade data are suppressed. Data are published in terms only of "ranges" so wide that the official published numbers are useless for analysis.

Data on toxic chemical emissions are extremely scarce. The US Environmental Protection Agency's Office of Toxic Wastes is the only official primary source of such data in the world, and its major tool is the so-called Toxic Release Inventory (TRI). The survey must be filled out by US manufacturing firms (Standard Industrial Classification 20-39) with 10 or more employees and that produce, import, process, or use more than a threshold amount of any of 300 listed chemicals.

The reporting threshold as regards production or processing for each chemical was initially 75,000 lb; since 1989 it has been 25,000 lb (roughly 12 metric tons), while for use the reporting threshold is now set at 10,000 lb (roughly 4.5 metric tons) per year. Releases are reported by medium (air, water, land) and transfers for disposal purposes to other sites are also reported. There is serious doubt about both the completeness and the accuracy of the TRI reports, because published data are very difficult to reconcile with materials balance estimates.

Third, a large number of manufactured chemicals - probably the vast majority in terms of numbers, if not tonnage's - are produced not because they are really needed as such, but because they are available as by-products of other chemical processes. This is particularly true of products of chlorination and ammonylation reactions, which require repeated separation (e.g. distillation) and recycling stages to obtain reasonably pure final products.

For instance, it has been estimated that 400 chlorinated compounds are used for their own sake, but at least 4,000 are listed in the directories. This is because it is easier to treat them as "products" than as wastes. Many such chemicals are found in products such as pesticides, paint thinners and paint removers, dry-cleaning agents, and plasticizing agents. Fourth, many of the most dangerous toxic chemicals are known to be produced by side reactions in the manufacturing process, or "downstream" reactions in the environment.

Perhaps the most infamous toxic/carcinogenic chemicals are the so-called "dioxins," which are not produced for their own sake but appear to be minor contaminants of some chlorinated benzene compounds that are used for herbicide manufacturing. Thus dioxins were accidental contaminants in the well-known herbicide 2-4-D, which became known as "Agent Orange" during the Viet Nam war. They are also probably produced by incinerators and other non-industrial combustion processes, depending on what is burned.

As regards downstream processes, the example of methyl mercury - produced by anaerobic bacteria in sediments - was mentioned earlier. Exactly the same problem arises in the case of dimethyl and trimethyl arsine, extremely toxic volatile compounds that are generated by bacterial action on arsenical pesticide (or other) residues left in the soil. Still other examples would be the dangerous carcinogens such as Benz(a)pyrene (BAP) and peracyl nitrate (PAN) produced by reactions between unburned hydrocarbons, especially aromatics, nitrogen oxides (NOx), and ozone. (This occurs in Los Angeles "smog", for instance.)

In fact, oxides of nitrogen are themselves toxic. NO_x is produced not only by most high-temperature combustion processes but also by atmospheric electrical discharges. An even more indirect downstream effect is exemplified by the Waldsterben (forest die-back) in central Europe. The conifer trees of the Black Forest and much of the Alps are now being weakened and many are dying. This appears to be the result of a complex sequence of effects starting with increased acidity of the soil.

As the pH drops below 6 there is a sharply increased mobilization of aluminium ions, which are toxic to plants. There is also an increased mobilization of heavy metals hitherto fixed in insoluble complexes with clay particles. Many toxic heavy metals - from pesticides, or from deposition of fly ash from coal burning - have long been immobilized by adherence to clay particles at relatively high pH levels (thanks, in part, to liming of agricultural soils). However, as the topsoil erodes as a result of intensive agriculture, it is being washed into streams and rivers and, eventually, into estuaries, bays such as the Chesapeake, or enclosed seas (such as the Baltic, the Adriatic, the Aegean, or the Black Sea), where it accumulates.

This sedimentary material is "relatively" harmless as long as the local environment is anaerobic, except for the localized risk of bacterial methylation of mercury, arsenic, and cadmium mentioned earlier. But this accumulated sedimentary stock of heavy metals (and other persistent toxic chemicals too) would become much more dangerous in the event of a sudden exposure to oxygen. For instance, sediments dredged from rivers and harbours may be rapidly acidified and could become "toxic time bombs".

Fifth, many toxic compounds are produced naturally by plants and animals, largely as protection against predators or as means of immobilizing prey. Nicotine, rotenone (from pyrethrum), heroin and morphine (from opium), cocaine, curare, digitalis, belladonna, and other alkaloids are well-known examples from the plant world. Recent research suggests that natural (i.e. biologically produced) compounds have about the same probability of being toxic or carcinogenic as synthetic compounds. The widespread idea that "natural" products are ipso facto safer than synthetic ones is apparently false.

In fact, Bruce Ames (inventor of the "Ames test") has argued with considerable force that the use of synthetic pesticides is less dangerous, to humans, than reliance on "non-chemical" methods of agricultural production, because plants produce greater quantities of natural toxins when they are under stress. However, probably even less is known about the range of toxic effects from natural chemicals than from industrial chemicals. In fact, there is no general theory of toxicity. It comes in many colours and varieties.

The notion includes mutagenic effects visible only after generations, effects on the reproductive cycle, and carcinogenic effects (e.g. asbestos, dioxins, vinyl chloride), or chronic but minor degradation of physiological function. At the other extreme are acute effects resulting in rapid or even instantaneous death. Methyl isocyanate (MIC), the cause of the Bhopal disaster, is an example of the latter. Chlorinated pesticides and polychlorinated biphenyls (PCBs) were not even thought to be dangerous to humans until long after they had been in widespread use. It was belatedly discovered that these chemicals tend to accumulate in fatty animal tissues and to be concentrated as they move higher in the food chain.

Eagles, falcons, and ospreys were nearly wiped out in some areas by DDT because their eggshells were weakened to the point of non-viability. As noted above, soil acidification resulting from anthropogenic emissions of SO_2 and NO_x to the atmosphere is also releasing toxic metals (and other compounds) that were formerly immobilized in the soil. Large accumulations of toxic metals reside in the soils and sediments in some areas. For many decades lead arsenate was used as an insecticide, especially in apple orchards. Copper sulphate and mercury compounds (among others) were widely used to control fungal diseases of plants.

Mercury was also used to prevent felt hats from being attacked by decay organisms. Chromium was, and still is, used for the same purpose to protect leather from decay. Copper, lead, nickel, and zinc ores were roasted in air to drive off the sulphur (and the arsenic and cadmium). Lead paint was used for more than a century, for both exterior and interior surfaces. For half a century tetraethyl lead and tetramethyl lead were used as gasoline octane additives (they still are so used in much of the world). Soft coal has been burned profusely in urban areas; usually the bottom ash was used as landfill for airports and roads.

Coal ash contains trace quantities of virtually every toxic metal, from arsenic to mercury to vanadium. For decades, phosphate fertilizers have been spread on farmland without removing the cadmium contaminants. In all of these cases, increasing acidity means increased mobilization of toxic metals. These metals eventually enter the human food chain, via crops or cows' milk. It is clear that toxicity is not simply a problem associated with the production and use of industrial chemicals or heavy metals. It is intimately linked to a number of other anthropogenic processes, not least of which is global acidification.

To take another example, it is well known that CFCs emitted to the atmosphere are responsible for depleting the ozone layer in the stratosphere. The major consequence on the earth's surface is an increase in the intensity of harmful UV radiation reaching the surface. Spawning zooplankton and fish in shallow surface waters are likely to be adversely affected. This is, in effect, a form of eco-toxicity. Is there any common factor among all these types of toxicity? It can be argued that all human toxins are, in effect, causes of physiological disturbance. All interfere with some biological process.

Mutagens interfere with the replication of the DNA molecule itself. Carcinogens interfere with the immune system; neurotoxins (e.g. cyanide) interfere with the ability of the nerves to convey messages. Many toxins cause problems for the organism because they closely resemble other compounds that perform an essential function. Thus carbon monoxide causes suffocation because it binds to the haemoglobin in the blood, as oxygen does. But, when the haemoglobin carrier arrives at a cell in need of oxygen, the potential recipient "sees" only a carbon atom where an oxygen atom should be. The point of this example is that toxicity, to an organism, is just another word for imbalance or disturbance.

A toxin is an agent that causes some metabolic or biological process to go awry. Every organism has a metabolism. Metabolic processes are cyclic self-organizing systems far away from thermodynamic equilibrium. The same statement can be made of the metabolic processes - the "grand nutrient cycles" such as the carbon and nitrogen cycles - that regulate the whole biosphere. Any disturbance to the biosphere is "toxic," in principle. The stability of the biosphere: The impossibility of computing the odds The fundamental question about whether or not the stability of the biosphere is at risk was deferred. This is a very deep question indeed.

First, a quick review of the case for believing there may be a real threat to survival. Most people who have never thought deeply about the matter tend to assume that life is a passive "free rider" on the earth. In other words, most people suppose (or were taught) that life exists on earth simply because earth happened to offer a suitable environment for life to evolve. They imagine that earth was much like it is now (except for more volcanic activity) before life came along, and that if life were to be snuffed out by some cosmic accident-- say a massive solar flare - the animals and plants would disappear but the inanimate rivers, lakes, oceans, and oxygen-nitrogen atmosphere would remain much as they are today.

The above quasi-biblical vision is not in accord with the scientific evidence. It is true that life probably originated on earth (though some scientists speculate that the basic chemical components of all living systems may actually have originated in a cold interstellar cloud - Hoyle and Wickramasinghe 1978). Life certainly evolved on earth. The earliest living organisms appear to have been capable of metabolizing organic compounds (such as sugars) by fermentation, to yield energy and waste products such as alcohol's.

The organic (but non-living) "food" for these simple organisms was created by still unknown processes in a reducing environment. The composition of the atmosphere of the early earth cannot be reconstructed with great accuracy, but it undoubtedly contained ammonia, hydrogen sulphide, and carbon dioxide, plus water vapour. There was certainly no free oxygen. It is less certain, but possible, that no free nitrogen was present. Life would have disappeared as soon as the supply of "food" was exhausted, if it had not been for the evolutionary "invention" of photosynthesis.

The first photosynthetic organisms converted carbon dioxide and water vapour into sugars, thus replenishing the food supply. But they also generated free oxygen as a waste product. For a billion years or so, the free oxygen produced by photosynthesis was immediately combined with soluble ferrous iron ions dissolved in the oceans, yielding insoluble ferric iron. Similarly hydrogen sulphide and soluble sulphites were oxidized to insoluble sulphates. These were deposited on the ocean floors. Thanks to tectonic activity, some of them eventually rose above sealevel and became land. (Virtually all commercial iron ores and gypsum now being mined by humans are of biological origin.) When the dissolved oxygen acceptors were used up, oxygen began to build up in the atmosphere.

As a metabolic waste product, oxygen was toxic to the anaerobic organisms that produced it. Again, there was a threat of self-extinction. Once again, an evolutionary "invention" came to the rescue. This was the advent of aerobic respiration, which utilized the former waste product (oxygen) and also increased the efficiency of energy production sevenfold over the earlier fermentation process. Aerobic photosynthesis followed, thus closing the carbon cycle (more or less) for the first time. This occurred less than 1 billion years ago, though life has existed on the earth for at least 3.5 billion years. But the carbon cycle and the earth's atmosphere did not stabilize for several hundred million more years.

The free oxygen in the atmosphere exists only because large quantities of carbon, with which it was originally combined, have been sequestered in two forms:

1. as calcium carbonate, in the shells of tiny marine organisms (which later reappear as chalk, diatomaceous earth, or limestone), or

2. as coal or shale.

The carbon sequestering process took place over several hundred million years a period culminating in the so-called carboniferous era during which the carbon dioxide content of the atmosphere declined to its present very low level. In addition, sulphur has been sequestered, primarily as sulphates. Similarly, though somewhat less certainly, the free nitrogen in the earth's atmosphere was probably originally combined with hydrogen, in the form of ammonia of volcanic origin. Whereas the carbon has mostly been buried, the missing hydrogen has probably recombined with oxygen as water vapour.

The early atmosphere and hydrosphere of the earth were quite alkaline compared with the present, because of the ammonia. The hydrogen-rich reducing atmosphere of the early earth has been replaced by an oxygenating atmosphere; the hydrosphere is correspondingly more acid than it once was before life appeared. The biosphere has stabilized the atmosphere (and the climate), at least for the last several hundred million years.

If all life disappeared suddenly today, the oxygen in the atmosphere would gradually but inexorably recombine with atmospheric nitrogen and buried hydrocarbons and sulphides (converting them eventually to carbon dioxide, nitric acid, nitrates, sulphuric acid, and sulphates). Water would be mostly bound into solid minerals, such as gypsum (hydrated calcium sulphate). This oxygenation process would also further increase the acidity of the environment. Suppose all possible chemical reactions among carbon, nitrogen, and sulphur compounds - including those currently sequestered in sediments and sedimentary rocks - proceed to thermodynamic equilibrium.

The atmosphere would consist mainly of carbon dioxide. The final state of thermodynamic equilibrium would be totally inhospitable to life. (For one thing, the temperature would rise to around 300°C.) Once dead, the planet could never be revived.

Complex systems stabilized by feedback loops are essentially nonlinear. An important characteristic of the dynamic behaviour of some non-linear systems is the phenomenon known as chaos. Such systems are characterized by trajectories that move unpredictably around regions of phase-space known as strange attractors. "Stability" for such a system means that the trajectory tends to remain within a relatively well-defined envelope. However, a further characteristic of non-linear multi-stable dynamic systems is that they can "jump" also unpredictably - from one attractor to another. (Such jumps have been called "catastrophes" by the French mathematician René Thom, who has classified the various theoretical possibilities for continuous systems.)

The resilience of a non-linear dynamic system - its tendency to remain within the domain of its original attractor - is not determinable by any known scientific theory or measurement. In fact, since the motion of a non-linear system along its trajectory is inherently unpredictable (though deterministic), the resilience of the earth system is probably unknowable with any degree of confidence. It is like a rubber band whose strength and elasticity we have no way of measuring.

The climate of the earth, with its feedback linkages to the biosphere, is a non-linear complex system. It has been stable for a long time. However, there is no scientific way to predict just how far the system can be driven away from its stable quasi-equilibrium by anthropogenic perturbing forces before it will jump suddenly to another stable quasi-equilibrium. Nor is there any way to predict how far the equilibrium will move if it does jump. The earth's climate, and the environment as a whole, may indeed be very resilient and capable of absorbing a lot of punishment. Then again, they may not.

What can be gained by more research? Probably we can learn a lot about the nature of the earth-climate-biosphere interaction. We will learn a lot about the specific mechanisms. We will learn how to model the behaviour of the system, at least in simplified form. We will learn something about the stability of the models. We may, or may not, learn something definitive about the stability of the real system. The real system is too complex, and too nonlinear, for exact calculations. There is no prospect at all of "knowing the odds" and making a rational calculation of risk. The problem we face is that the odds cannot be calculated, even in principle. In the circumstances, prudence would seem to dictate buying some insurance. The question on which reasonable people can still differ is: how much insurance is it worthwhile to buy? The answer depends, in part, on the technological alternatives.

One can identify the following hypothetical necessary (but not sufficient) conditions for long-term sustainability:

— no increase in the atmospheric concentration of "greenhouse gases" (beyond some limit yet to be determined);

— no increase in environmental acidification (hydrogen ion concentration) in surface waters and soils (beyond some limit);

— no increase in toxic heavy metal concentrations in soils and sediments (beyond some limit);

— no further topsoil erosion, beyond the rate of natural soil formation;

— no further degradation of groundwater with nitrates and nitrites; no further draw-down of "fossil" (non-replaceable) groundwater;

— preservation of (most of) the remaining tropical rain forests, estuarine zones, coral reefs, and other ecologically important habitats; no further disappearance of species.

A shorter list that is substantially equivalent to the above has been set forth by Holmberg, Robèrt, and Erikkson. Their list (paraphrased) is as follows:

— no accumulation of substances taken from the earth's crust in "nature," i.e. the biosphere or its supporting physical systems (atmosphere, oceans, topsoil);

— no accumulation of synthetic materials produced by man in natural systems;

— no interference by man in the conditions for biospheric diversity and stability;

— natural resources should be utilized as efficiently as possible.

To satisfy these conditions, several straightforward implications can be drawn. Among them are the following:

— use of fossil fuels must stop increasing and must drop to very low (and declining) levels by the middle of the twenty-first century;

— agricultural, forestry, and fishery practices must be radically overhauled and improved, with much less dependence on chemicals and mechanization;

— net emissions to the environment of long-lived toxic chemical compounds (especially compounds of the toxic heavy metals and halogenated organics) must drop to near zero levels by the middle of the twenty-first century, or so.

To simplify even further, one can argue that the average materials intensity per unit of service (MIPS) must be decreased radically for society as a whole. Although such a radical productivity increase may seem utopian at first, it is well to recall that labour productivity in the Western world has increased by much larger factors, perhaps a hundredfold or more, since the beginning of the industrial revolution, largely by substituting capital goods and energy from fossil fuels for human and animal labour.

To attempt an "existence proof" of at least one plausible long-run solution (setting aside the question of cost for the moment), the technical implications of eco-sustainability must be spelled out more precisely. As noted already, agricultural and industrial activity today is almost entirely dependent on fossil fuels (and also on dissipative uses of toxic chemicals and heavy metals) whose extraction and use harm the environment. This pattern is clearly incompatible with long term sustainability. It is obviously not possible to describe, in detail, technology based on discoveries and inventions that still lie in the future, perhaps a century hence.

However, the constraints imposed by the definition of sustainability limit the range of possibilities worth exploring considerably. In addition, it is possible to carry out a major part of the analysis in terms of macro-scale indicators of technological performance that could be achieved in many different ways. For example, it is clear that sustainability requires much more efficient use of energy in the future than we observe today. Some improvement will occur as a direct consequence of the fact that electricity is displacing other energy carriers, because of its convenience and cleanliness at the point of use.

Electric space heating can be quite economical (using heat pumps), especially in properly insulated buildings. (However, effective means of recycling refrigerant fluids will be necessary.) Microwave cooking is so much faster and more efficient than its competitors (gas or electric cooking) that it is rapidly spreading anyhow. Substitution of electric power for other fuels for space heating, hot water, and cooking can and will occur more or less quickly, assuming appropriate price incentives. There are no technological barriers. Most energy needs, except for transportation, can be supplied by electricity.

Very long distance high voltage lines - or possibly super-conducting lines - could distribute power around the globe, and even under the sea. Orbiting solar satellites or lunar photovoltaic (PV) farms transmitting energy to earth via satellite are a possible variant. Of course, there is little or no environmental advantage in using electricity if it is generated by burning fossil fuels. Fortunately, there are viable long-term alternatives on the supply side, including biomass and wind (near term), PV-electric and PV-hydrogen (longer term). Also, efficiency gains can reduce the need for more energy.

Nuclear power (fission or fusion) cannot be ruled out of consideration. However both variants involve long-term storage of radioactive wastes, not to mention other major costs that continue to escalate. Thus, nuclear options are less attractive in the very long run than the solar option. Most mobile power sources at present (except for the few electric trams or trains) depend on liquid fuels derived from hydrocarbons. Up until the present time, centrally generated and wire-distributed electric power has not been economically attractive for mobile power, although it is technically feasible for local deliveries and commuting.

Middle East petroleum will finally approach exhaustion around the middle of the twenty-first century (or sooner). It seems probable that electric vehicles (for short distances) will finally become economically competitive with any coal-based synthetic fuel, especially if coal is made to bear anything like its real environmental costs. There seems little doubt today that, sooner or later, the electric car will play a bigger role. The fact that gasoline-burning vehicles are becoming increasingly intolerable in large cities suggests a plausible mechanism for this to come about: large cities plagued by traffic congestion, noise, and smoggy air may begin to create "car-free" zones in their centres, permitting only small electric cars (as some lakes already permit only electric boats).

At first, the electric cars will be found largely in these zones. But, these same central zones will also be accessed by high speed electric (probably "mag-lev") intercity trains, which will finally begin to reverse the auto-induced suburban sprawl of recent decades. As time passes, the electric vehicles will get better and cheaper, the "electric" zones will spread to the suburbs, and eventually gasoline (or synfuel) powered ground vehicles will be essentially limited to rural use. By the second half of the twenty-first century electric vehicles may be able to extend their range by using automated mag-lev pallets along major intercity routes. Electrification is only part of the solution.

As suggested above, sustainability implies reliance mainly - if not entirely - on renewable sources of energy. In principle, the energy could easily be supplied by the sun, as combustible biomass, as direct heat for buildings, as heat to operate engines, or via photovoltaic cells. The latter, in turn, could generate hydrogen by electrolysis. (There are other possibilities too, including geothermal heat and nuclear fusion.) The most likely solution seems to be a combination of wind power for irrigation water pumps, direct solar heating or "district heat pumping" using waste heat from high-temperature industrial processes to supply warm water for many buildings, and electrolytic hydrogen as a fuel for aircraft.

To reduce waste and pollution by converting them into raw materials is another technological and economic challenge of the next half-century. To accomplish this structural change we need to create a whole new class of economic activities - the equivalent of decay organisms in an ecosystem - to capture useful components, compounds, and elements and re-use them. In other words, the linear raw material-process-product chains characteristic of the present system must ultimately (within the next century or so) be converted into closed cycles analogous to the nutrient cycles in the biosphere. This new class of activities, called "industrial ecology," will gradually replace some of the extractive activities and associated waste disposal activities that are characteristic of the current system.

The existence question can also be addressed theoretically by putting it in the negative sense: are there any fixed minimum materials/ energy requirements to produce useful goods and services for humans? Or are there fundamental limits to the amount of service (or welfare) that can be generated from a given energy and/or material input? If there is no such limit, then energy intensities and materials intensities can be reduced indefinitely; there can be no fixed relationship between primary energy or materials requirements and GNP.

In fact, if this condition is met there is, in principle, no theoretical maximum to the quantity of final services - i.e. economic welfare in the traditional sense - that can be produced within the market framework from a given physical resource input. It follows, too, that, there is no physical limit (except that imposed by the second law of thermodynamics) to the theoretical potential for energy conservation and materials recycling. This restatement is actually critical to the fundamental case for optimism today. However, it is not a "mainstream" view among engineers and "men of affairs," or even economists, at present.

In common with the World Commission on Environment and Development (WCED), virtually all economists would regard continuing economic growth as both necessary and possible. However, the implication that economic growth can and must be permanently "delinked" from energy and materials use is far from universally accepted. (In short, most economists and business leaders have not thought through the consequences of their assumptions.) In fact, something like an "existence proof" is needed, to demonstrate that there are feasible technologies that, if adopted, could end our current dependence on fossil fuels and substantially close the materials cycle.

This is still an area of sharp disagreement. The politically powerful extractive industry argues strongly for linkage: No doubt about it, we all need to be careful of the amount of energy we use. But as long as this nation's economy needs to grow, we are going to need energy to fuel that growth.... For the foreseeable future, there are no viable alternatives to petroleum as the major source of energy... Simply put, America is going to need more energy for all its people. (Mobil Corp "Public Service" advertisement in the New York Times, April 1991)

In other words, the conventional position is that economic growth cannot occur without more energy - i.e. a fixed relationship does exist. In principle, any such fixed relationship between energy/materials use and economic activity would be quite inconsistent with fundamental axioms of economic theory, which assume general substitutability of all factors of production. Economists who are quick to attack neo-Malthusians for unjustified worry about natural resource scarcity should be equally optimistic about the potential for energy savings by increased conservation. Unfortunately, this is not the case, for reasons discussed later.

Optimism in regard to the potential for energy/ materials conservation - or increasing energy/materials productivity - is also justified by recent history. The energy/ GNP ratio has been declining more or less continuously for many decades in the case of the advanced industrialized countries. Past experience suggests that this ratio tends to increase for countries that are in the early stages of industrialization, only to decrease later; this is the so-called "inverted U" phenomenon. Moreover, countries industrializing later have lower peaks than countries that industrialized earlier. Lower energy intensity reflects the shift from heavy industry to "high tech" and services. The trend would almost certainly continue in any case. It can probably be accelerated significantly by appropriate policy changes.

The energy/GNP ratio is closely related to the thermodynamic efficiency with which the economy uses energy. For this purpose, it is convenient to define the so-called "second-law" efficiency - or, in European parlance, the "exergy efficiency" - with which energy is converted from primary sources to final services.10 Electricity is currently generated and delivered to homes with an overall efficiency of about 34 per cent in the United States. This figure has increased only slightly in recent years. Efficiency in less developed countries (LDCs) is significantly lower, implying greater room for improvement.

Energy experts generally agree that by the year 2050 efficiency might increase to something like 55-60 per cent for steam-electric plants, taking advantage of higher temperature (ceramic) turbines, combined cycles, co-generation, etc. Energy is currently used very inefficiently to create final services, as compared with the first stage of energy conversion and distribution. The problem is that energy is lost and wasted at each step of the chain of successive conversions, from crude fuels to intermediates, to finished goods, to final services.

For instance, incandescent lights (converting electricity to white light) are only 7 per cent efficient (fluorescent lights are better). Moreover, lighting fixtures are typically deployed very inefficiently (c.10 per cent) so that the final service (illumination where it is actually needed) is probably less than 1 per cent. Electricity may be used less wastefully than fuel, although this is doubtful because many end-uses of electricity are extremely inefficient from a second-law perspective.

Second-law (exergy) end-use efficiency has been estimated at 2.5 per cent for the United States as a whole. This means that, in principle, the same final services (heat, light, transport, cooking, entertainment, etc.) could have been obtained by the expenditure of only 1/40 as much energy as was actually used. Western Europe and Japan are significantly more efficient (in the second-law sense defined above) than the United States. Both regions are in the 4 per cent range, while Eastern Europe, the former Soviet Union, and the rest of the world are even less efficient than the

United States perhaps 1.5-2.0 per cent. For the world as a whole, it is likely that the overall efficiency with which fuel energy is used is currently no greater than 3.0-3.5 per cent. But there is no fundamental technical reason why end-use efficiency could not be increased by several-fold (perhaps as much as a factor of 5) in the course of the next half century or so.

There are three technical elements to a programme leading to long-term sustainability. The first is to reduce, and eventually eliminate, inherently dissipative uses of non-biodegradable materials, especially toxic ones (such as heavy metals). This involves process change and what has come to be known as "clean technology." The second is to design products for easier disassembly and re-use, and for reduced environmental impact, known as "design for environment" (DFE). The third is to develop much more efficient technologies for recycling consumption waste materials, so as to eliminate the need to extract "virgin" materials that only make the problem worse in time.

There is also an important socio-economic and political dimension to the problem. To state it very briefly, the strategies that maximize profits for an individual firm in the manufacturing sector of our competitive economic system tend to be the ones that exploit economies of scale and do so by maximizing sales and production. The downstream consequences, in terms of energy consumption, pollution, and final disposal of worn out goods, are not the responsibility of the producer and are, there fore, not taken account of in either product design or pricing. Thus, competitive markets, as they currently function, tend to over-produce both goods and pollution, while simultaneously over-consuming natural resources.

In short, there is an inherent dissonance - economists call it an externality - in the economic system that must be eliminated or compensated. It does not follow that the resolution of this fundamental dissonance is to be found in public ownership. That "solution" clearly does not work. The next most obvious solution seems to be regulation. But the regulatory approach works well only when the regulations are simple and easy to enforce. It has worked well mainly in the case of outright bans on the production of certain products, such as DDT, PCBs, and tetraethyl lead. But this strategy is also limited. It does not work well, for instance, when applied to widely used consumer products such as cigarettes, liquor, drugs, hand-guns, or pornographic literature.

"Green" taxes on resource consumption, or on pollution per se, are another possibility. But, there are at least two major drawbacks. One is that taxes on resource consumption - or pollution - tend to be regressive (hitting low-income consumers most heavily). The .other drawback is that they would be complex to administer, because of the need to provide exceptions and exemptions, e.g. for farmers, health workers, exporters, et al. In practice, green taxes are probably not feasible at the national level. There would have to be major efforts at cross-border "harmonization" in order to maintain international competitiveness. Still other approaches are currently being explored, such as tradable permits and quotas.

However, there is very little experience of actual implementation for these newer ideas. It is not easy to discern a long-term trend toward increasing recycling/ reuse. Indeed, anecdotal evidence would suggest the contrary: poor societies recycle and re-use far more efficiently than rich ones do. Also, the increasing complexity of both materials and products has made recycling and re-use more difficult in many cases. For instance, old wool clothes were once routinely collected by rag-merchants and recycled (after a complicated process of washing, unpicking, bleaching, re-spinning, re-weaving, and readying) into blankets and pea jackets.

Today, because of the prevalence of blends of natural and synthetic fibres, recycling is almost impossible. Much the same problem occurs in many other cases. To increase re-use and recycling, it may be necessary to induce manufacturers to sell services, rather than products, and/ or to take back products they have previously made. Remanufacturing avoids many of the problems of recycling. It is not an important economic activity at present. However, it may grow, especially as the shortage of landfill sites induces municipal authorities (or, perhaps, original equipment manufacturers forced by law to accept trade-ins) to offer subsidies.

Remanufactured refrigerators, cars (or engines), and other large appliances can offer a good low priced alternative to low-income workers in the rich countries, or they could fill an important economic niche in the developing countries. Actually, since remanufacturing will always be more labour intensive than original equipment manufacturing, it is inherently a suitable activity for border regions such as Mexico, Eastern Europe, or North Africa. (As these countries develop, of course, the "border regions" will shift too.) In the case of municipal waste (mostly paper products and containers), recycling is already increasing in importance. Again, the shortage of land for disposal is mainly responsible.

More efficient technologies for separating materials will certainly be developed in coming decades. In any case, there is no technical reason why the recycling/re-use rate for most types of materials should not be dramatically increased from the low levels of today. This will happen, eventually, when material prices better reflect the true environmental costs of both extraction and use. It is not really necessary to know in detail how this will be accomplished. It is sufficient to know that it is technically and economically feasible. (It remains, still, for policy makers to create the appropriate incentives to harness market forces. But this is a separate topic.) Of course, specific "scenarios" might be helpful in making such a conclusion more credible to doubters.

However this would serve a communications purpose rather than an analytic one. Assuming the existence of a collection of potential technological "fixes," the last question follows: is there a feasible political/institutional pathway to get from "here" to "there"? What, in particular, is the role of economics? This question can be rephrased to make the underlying problem clearer. Assuming technical and economic feasibility, it is reasonable to assume political feasibility if (and only if) there exists a painless (or near-painless) development trajectory, such that each incremental socio-economic change leaves every politically powerful interested party better off- or at least no worse off than before. Along such a path there must be very few or no losers.

Everybody gets richer more or less automatically. This is called a "win-win" strategy, in the language of game theory. In more literary terms, it might be termed a "Panglossian" path. To restate the question then: is there a Panglossian path? The fundamental problem is that an affirmative answer (i.e. that low-cost "win-win" solutions, or "free lunches," do exist) is essentially inconsistent with most economists' fundamental belief in profit-maximizing behaviour and perfect information. Given these assumptions, the economy would always be in (or close to) equilibrium and this equilibrium would reflect the most efficient (i.e. least cost) choices of technology.

If this were true, energy and natural resource conservation should cost a lot more money ("there is no free lunch"). This view seems to be supported by econometric data, based on historical responses of energy demand to price changes. These data indicate that higher prices encourage lower consumption, and vice versa. Reduced physical consumption is commonly interpreted by economists as "anti-growth." It happens to be convenient to incorporate this set of assumptions in long-term forecasting models based on the assumption of a quasi-general equilibrium varying slowly along an optimal path over time.

However, such models do not - and cannot reflect the endogenous nature of technological change. How can an optimal path be determined that takes into account unpredictable technological change? Nor do these models reflect the distortions due to institutional barriers and "wrong" prices. To explain the dilemma in non-economic terms, if a lot of "win win" opportunities really do exist, then somehow these opportunities must have been overlooked by entrepreneurs. Assuming entrepreneurs always do what is in their own best (economic) interest, any real opportunities to make profits would be instantly snapped up; consequently no more such opportunities can exist.

The obvious flaw in this reasoning is that entrepreneurs are constantly finding opportunities for making extraordinary profits. If no profitable opportunities existed, there would be no entrepreneurs. Since there are many entrepreneurs, it follows logically that many more such profit opportunities must exist. In recent years, since environmental concerns have become more pressing, surprisingly many profitable opportunities have been found to reduce environmental pollution. To explain this, it must be assumed that industry and consumers have not always chosen the optimal energy technologies, even at present (too low) prices.

Entrenched oligopolies or monopolies, established regulatory bodies, institutional separation between technological decision makers and final consumers who pay the costs, and lack of technical information are the most likely reasons. Inappropriately low prices due to subsidies (e.g. to coal mining and nuclear power) compound the problem. Fortunately, there is a potential link between increasing resource productivity and reducing unemployment.

Unemployment is becoming a very serious political issue in Europe. Conservative (business oriented) economists tend to blame the problem equally on high wages and benefits and "labour market rigidity" (i.e. the network of taxpayer-supported measures known as the "social safety net"). But there is growing recognition that the tax system itself may be more to blame than the size of the public sector.

The problem is that the "safety net" in Europe is financed almost exclusively by taxes on labour, whereas the use of energy and materials by industry is virtually untaxed (except for motor fuel) and, in many countries, fossil energy is heavily subsidized. Up to now, environmentalists have approached the issue of environmental protection largely as a regulatory problem.

Regulations in this field are now numerous, burdensome, and - in many cases inefficient. As an alternative, environmental economists have recommended schemes such as effluent taxes, but this approach has not been strongly supported by the business community (which, surprisingly, is less opposed to regulation than its rhetoric would suggest).

Environmental economists argue that revenue from effluent taxes and resource-based taxes could be used to reduce other unpopular taxes, such as taxes on savings or investment. Conservatives fear that "revenue neutrality" would not be adhered to in practice, and that any increase in government revenue would be used to finance more "spending." In recent years another scheme ("tradable permits") has received some support. The idea here is that "rights to pollute" would be issued, but in limited amounts corresponding to the total target level for a given pollutant. The initial allocation system could be either "free" to current polluters or based on an auction (as with offshore oil rights).

Once allocated, these rights would be tradable. Those firms able to reduce their emissions below their entitlements could sell the excess entitlement. This possibility would induce firms to innovate. The revenues would remain in the private sector and government revenues (after the initial auction, at least) would not be increased by such a system. The tradable permit is opposed by many environmentalists on moral grounds. It is argued that there should be no "right to pollute," and certainly it is repugnant that such a right should be purchased for money. But, to some extent, this issue is a matter of perception.

For instance, consumers now have an implicit "right" to pollute by virtue of the fact that they have a right to consume. Thus, the right to consume gasoline, for instance, could be rationed equally. Those able and willing to consume less than their "share" could be allowed to sell the excess. This would actually provide a kind of minimum income for the poor and elderly (if they do not drive cars) and could serve as a partial substitute for existing and increasingly unaffordable social services provided by the government from taxes.

The main alternative to regulation is to use emission-based or resource based taxes or exchangeable permits as a method of internalization of environmental damage costs. For both regulation or standard-setting and for the use of emissions taxes or permits, there is still a problem of enforcement and a role for government. On the one hand, bureaucrats must determine the standards; on the other hand, they must set the scale of fees or fix the allocation of permits, and regulate the operation of the market mechanism to minimize opportunities for fraud. In any case, government must also monitor the effects of the policy.

Unfortunately, a "win-win" path is not necessarily painless. Those now receiving subsidies will experience pain. Those who cannot reduce their pollution levels by innovation will have to pay more. This being acknowledged, the obvious implication is that a truly painless pathway to an ecologically sustainable future may not exist! If a painless path does not exist, or cannot be found, it means that to get from our present techno-economic state to one capable of permanent sustainability - even by the "least-pain" route - significant short-term adjustment costs must eventually be borne by some groups or institutions. This means, in turn, that some very hard decisions will have to be taken, and soon.

Unfortunately, experience suggests reason to doubt that our chaotic world of nearly 200 sovereign nation-states can make such a transition successfully. Nevertheless, if the human race is to have a long-term future, we must make the attempt. High unemployment (together with increasing associated costs of social security) is one of the most persistent socio-economic problems in the West, it seems only logical to explore possibilities for solving both the sustainability problem and the unemployment problem with a single common policy approach. It may not be too much to hope that this approach will also be beneficial to the less developed countries and the developing countries.

At first glance, increasing employment seems to imply decreasing labour productivity, which is not consistent with continuing economic growth. In the short run, some measures to increase resource productivity - especially by using less energy - may temporarily have this effect. Recycling tends to be more labour intensive than manufacturing with virgin materials, for instance. However, in the longer run, the object is to increase total factor productivity while using a lot fewer resources and a little more labour. At any rate, it seems clear that there are some promising possibilities to be explored. This exploration is critically important.

Some will say that society must seek pathways to long-run eco-sustainability regardless of what the cost in conventional economic terms turns out to be, whether high or negative (i.e. profitable). If the latter turns out to be the case, so much the better. However, society will be much slower to adopt a high-cost path than a profitable one. Indeed, there is good reason to fear that, if the cost (or pain) appears too high, the difficult decisions will be delayed too long - perhaps until it is too late.

6

Eco-restructuring due to Technological Transformation

Technologies cannot be assessed in isolation. Sustainable technologies must satisfy a number of requirements and constraints. These include

— the limited capacity of the biosphere to absorb wastes and recover from injury, both globally and on a regional level,

— the limits of cultural and social acceptance,

— economic feasibility, and

— technical feasibility.

In addition, it is obvious that technological "fixes" alone will not suffice to assure long-term sustainability, although technology plays an essential role. Four main fields of technical application (apart from food and beverages) are well known. These are health care, agriculture, environmental remediation, and industrial materials processing.

The health-care field of biotechnology includes the production of vaccines, hormones (such as insulin), therapeutics, diagnostics, and antibiotics via conventional process routes, such as cell cultures, using natural organisms. Antibiotics are normally made in this way. For instance, penicillin, the first antibiotic, is produced by a fungus. Increasingly, however, "modern" pathways are being exploited, based on genetically engineered organisms (GEOs). These GEOs either lack certain genes or contain genes from other organism. As a result they have properties not found in the natural versions of those organisms.

Agriculture and Foodtechnology

Older agriculture shaped natural plants and animals to human uses by means of breeding techniques. The modern branch of agriculture uses chemicals derived from biological materials (such as hormones and plant growth regulators, single cell protein, vaccines), microbial cultures, and new plants and animals created deliberately by genetic engineering modifications of existing organisms by recombinant DNA methods. Potential and obviously desirable future applications of genetic engineering are to introduce nitrogen fixation capability and/or disease resistance into important crops, such as potatoes, corn, or rice.

Environmental biotechnology is understood in a broad sense as the application of biotechnologies - mainly micro-organisms - to the solution of existing environmental problems, including the treatment of sewage, waste water, and even soil decontamination. Early applications include biogas systems. Genetically engineered organisms are also increasingly used in this field, resulting in the same public concerns about safety mentioned above.

Industrial biotechnology is an established field, including cheese-making, winemaking, the brewing of beer, and the production of baker's yeast, vinegar, alcohol, acetone, acetic acid, citric acid, etc. from carbohydrates and sugars, mainly by fermentation. GEOs are not yet being applied in this area, although it would seem to be an inevitable evolutionary development. It is quite important for the evaluation of biotechnologies to consider the normal life cycle of technologies.

The different stages of development are marked by the production of molecules of increasing complexity (e.g. bulk chemicals, single cell protein, drugs). A rather visionary, more distant future stage can be denoted "eco-technology," or simply "eco-tech." The name is intended to convey the idea that biotechnology eventually begins to substitute for more conventional technologies in a wide range of applications, resulting in significant environmental benefits and a much closer approach to long-term sustainability. Scientifically the advantages of bio-processing over chemical processing can generally be characterized as follows:

— big-catalysts are highly active, specific, and selective; their regeneration is easier than in the case of chemical catalysts; there are no environmental problems as with heavy metals;

— reaction conditions are mild (temperature, pressure, and also concentrations);

— internal energy is supplied by energy-enriched compounds, e.g. ATP, which are formed during metabolism;

— impure, diluted, and inactive raw materials can be used, owing to the high specificity and selectivity of big-catalysts;

— big-products are biodegradable in natural cycles.

The most competitive opportunities for biotechnology, at present, lie in the domain of high-price/low volume "specialty" products. However, increasing success in this domain, together with rising prices for petroleum and other fossil hydrocarbons, suggests that opportunities will gradually increase over coming decades in the domain of low-price/high-volume "commodity" products. Two observations apply to biotechnologies in general. In the first place, to produce highly complex and specific products such as pharmaceuticals, or to degrade toxic substances in the environment, the biological path is already clearly superior to the chemical path in many cases.

A similar competitive break-point can be expected in the near future in several other cases, where bio-processing becomes yearly more competitive. To be more specific, the most successful current applications of big-processes are as follows:

— the production of foods (e.g. cheese, yogurt, soya sauce) and beverages (wine, beer);

— the production of complex molecules on the industrial scale for use in health care for humans, animals, and plants (pharmaceuticals and therapeutics, antibiotics, proteins, steroids, etc.);

— the degradation/purification of wastes and toxic substances in the environment (sewage, industrial wastes, water treatment, etc.);

— sequential reactions in one-step processes (e.g. the production of steroids), highly selective stereo-specific conversions, etc.

There are other domains where the advantages of "biologicals" compared with "chemicals" are likely to be established soon. These include the reclamation of soil, the recycling or sequestration of carbon dioxide, the production of biofuels from waste agricultural or forest biomass, the creation of new and more productive plants capable of surviving in different climates, resisting diseases, etc. The beneficial products of bio-processing will surely increase in the next decade. A second observation is that process economics for biotechnological products (thus far) suffer generally from the fact that they depend on growth cultures.

The latter involve lower concentrations, higher water content, and, consequently, higher energy requirements for separation and purification than does chemical processing, in general. The need for more sophisticated equipment, and more highly educated technicians, also contributes to the current competitive disadvantage of biotechnologies as compared with chemical processing. Thus, despite their potential benefits in terms of long-term sustainability, most big-processes are not yet economically competitive. Biotechnology is not expected to become competitive on a wide range of fronts before the year 2030 (OECD 1989).

Even this forecast will prove overoptimistic unless efforts toward commercialization are accelerated, especially by strengthening process engineering sciences. Research programmes in big process engineering have been recently stepped up in Japan, the United States, and Europe.

The near-term opportunities for bio-processing can be summarized briefly as follows:

— the production of organic chemicals with the aid of big-catalysts, e.g. enzyme technology (fine chemicals, starch and cellulose, bio-polymers), fermentation products (ethanol, single cell protein, antibiotics, nitrogen fixation for fertilizers), and animal and plant cell cultures;

— the use of biomass for fuel and energy production;

— food production and processing;

— the production of industrial materials (e.g. vegetable oils, pulp, and paper) from biomass.

Enzymic conversions, as a consequence of the potential advantages mentioned, are in an excellent position to contribute to a cleaner environment. The use of enzymes offers industry an opportunity to replace processes using aggressive chemicals with mild big-processes exhibiting minimal impact on the environment. The raw materials come from agriculture. Also the effluents are non-toxic, although they contain nitrogen, phosphorus, and organic matter. This leads to high amounts of wastes in the water. The major part of the spent dry matter is collected as a sludge and then spread on nearby farmland. The sludge consists of dead biomass, filter aid, nutrient surplus, and an insoluble residue.

In 1990, Novo Nordisk, a Danish pharmaceutical manufacturer, reused 500,000 m3 of sludge containing 5 per cent dry solids including 800 metric tons of nitrogen and 285 metric tons of phosphorus. The sludge instead acts as an efficient slow-releasing N-P fertilizer: more than 90 per cent of N is bound in organic matter, which means that the evaporation of ammonia is minimal.

Biological control agents

A big-pesticide is a living organism or a product derived from microorganisms or plant sources that kills the pest in order to sustain its own growth cycle. The characteristics of a big-pesticide are pest specificity, environmental stability, safety, and low cost. Bio-control agents, despite being new entrants in the field, have already made substantial contributions in preserving the fertility of the soil, maintaining an ecological balance, and preventing resurgence of pests. This has been achieved with little harm to non-target animals and plants and with few side-effects. The potential of big-toxins being active as insecticides, herbicides, and fungicides is basically known. However, widespread practical application is still in the wings, mainly owing to high costs.

A good example of application is in India, where the big-pesticide market is around 100,000 tons per year, representing 3 per cent of the total market. Biologicals have a market share of 0.5 per cent of global chemical pesticides, as of 1995, while in the year 2000 a penetration rate of about 10 per cent is expected by some experts, out of a total global pesticide market of US$40-45 billion. At the moment the biotoxins produced from Bacillus thuringiensis (Bt) dominate, with nearly 70 per cent of the market.

Bio-pesticides can already substitute effectively for some chemical pesticides in agriculture (e.g. protection of cotton, sugar cane, oil seeds such as groundout, rapeseed) as well as floriculture and horticulture. They have uses too in public health. Bio-pesticides can be broadly classified into the following categories, indicating a broad diversity in species as well as in specific actions:

— predators pathogens

— parasites/parasitoids

— pheromones

— kairomones

— neem oil

Predators : Commonly used predacious species are Cryplolaemus nontrouzuri, Chrysopa, Scymnus, Coccivera, and Nephus spp. against mealy bugs and Cerilocorus nigritus and Pharoscymnus houri against scale insects. Ladybird beetles are used to protect rice (against brown plant hopper), fruits such as citrus and grapes, and plantation crops such as coffee.

Pathogens (viral, fungal, bacterial): Among the different entomopathogens, referred to as "biorational pesticides" as viral pathogens, the most important are the bacillo viruses. More than 10 types of such viruses have been isolated and extensively studied for their potential in pest management. Of these, nuclear polyhedrosis viruses (NPV) and granulosis virus (GV) are found to have good potential for pest control. The use of fungi to control pathogens that incite plant disease is another concept that has been in existence for some time. Insects infected with fungus exhibit general lethargy, slow growth, cessation of feeding, and changes in colour.

The difference between fungi and other pathogens is that fungi do not have to be consumed by the insect to cause disease; instead they grow through the insect's skin. Many fungi are found to be pathogenic to a number of pests such as Metarhizium anisopilae, Beauveria brongniartii, Anopheles stephensi, and Trichoderma. The most prominent bacteria in biological control are in the genus Bacillus, the group of Gram positive, rod-shaped bacterium. Bacillus thuringiensis (Bt) is the most widely known and researched aerobic spore-forming bacterium within this group for insecticides properties and is differentiated from other spore-forming bacilli by the presence of a parasporal body that is formed within the sporangium during sporogenesis.

The parasporal body is a high molecular mass protein crystal that is referred to as crystalline protein deltaendotoxin. The insecticidal activity of B. thuringiensis products is based on the deltaendotoxin. Bacillus thuringiensis is primarily a pathogen of lepidopterous pests. Being a natural protein, Bt endotoxin is highly biodegradable. It is also degradable by ultraviolet radiation. As a result, it is environmentally safe, because it cannot leave behind any residues to contaminate the soil, water, or food. Naturally occurring Bt are spore forming bacteria. The spores are resistant to desiccation, high temperature, UV, and biodegradation.

Parasites/parasitoids: The families Mermithidae, Steinernematidae, Romanomernis culicivoran, Goniazas nephantidis, Bracon brevicormis, Sturmiopsis inferens, and Trichogramma are of special importance as examples of insect parasitic forms. The parasporal body is a high molecular mass protein crystal that is referred to as crystalline protein delta-endotoxin. The insecticidal activity of B. thuringiensis products is based on the deltaendotoxin. Bacillus thuringiensis is primarily a pathogen of lepidopterous pests. Being a natural protein, Bt endotoxin is highly biodegradable. It is also degradable by ultraviolet radiation. As a result, it is environmentally safe, because it cannot leave behind any residues to contaminate the soil, water, or food. Naturally occurring Bt are spore forming bacteria. The spores are resistant to desiccation, high temperature, UV, and biodegradation.

Pheromones: Insects rely on a sense of smell and communicate with each other by releasing specific chemicals (odours) to indicate their selection of food plants, sites to lay eggs, location of prey, defence and offense, mate attraction, and courtship. These specific chemicals that deliver intra-specific communications between individuals of single species are called pheromones. Between 600 and

1,000 pheromones have been isolated, identified, and synthesized, many for insects.

Kairomones: Kairomones are compounds emitted by an insect to convey a behavioral response to a member of a different species. They carry an advantage to the receiver (e.g. compounds used by parasites to locate a host). They are utilized in conjunction with Trichogramma to improve their efficiency in parasitization.

Neem oil: Extracts of Neem seed provide various crops with resistance to insect pests. Neem oil contains several chemicals of which the most potent one, "Azadirachtin," interacts with the reproductive and digestive processes of insects. Neem oil acts in a number of subtle ways, especially as a repellent and anti-feedant. It also has a growth regulatory effect by disturbing the insect's metabolism during various phases of development.

Another interesting field of research is allelopathy, where the metabolic substances produced by one plant inhibit the growth of another plant. This can be regarded as a potential alternative to the use of chemical herbicides and the evolution of herbicide-resistant crops. Plants also offer quite innovative chances for new applications in the area of removal of heavy metals from the environment, e.g. "phytoremediation", especially from soil, e.g. "phytoextraction", and from aqueous media, e.g. "rhizofiltration".

Bio-leaching

Bio-leaching utilizes sulphur-loving bacteria that live in the ore itself. Examples include Thiabacillus ferroxidans, Thiobacillus thiooxidans, and Leptospirillum ferroxidans. When exposed to oxygen and carbon dioxide they obtain metabolic energy by reacting oxygen with sulphur, producing sulphuric acid as a metabolic waste. Compared with conventional heap leaching methods (using sulphuric acid recovered from ore roasting), big-leaching can offer real economic advantages. Typically the economic feasibility differs for several plants on several site-specific factors such as concentrations, leaching rates, and residence times.

Bio-leaching is commercially applied for the recovery of copper and uranium in the United States and for gold in South Africa and Brazil. The main obstacle is the investment in conventional plants (TME1992). The Biox(r) Genmin process for gold leaching involves the oxidation of a sulphitic concentrate slurry in a series of stirred tanks. Large volumes of compressed air are sparged into the tanks to fulfil the oxygen and carbon dioxide demand of the bacteria. A retention time of 3-5 days results in more than 90 per cent conversion of gold.

The oxidized slurry then flows into a series of counter-current decantation thickeners to separate solids from acidic solutions. After neutralization to a pH of 11, cyanide is added and the gold is dissolved. Bio-oxidation currently offers real economic advantages over roasting and pressure oxidation for production plants with a capacity of less than 1,200 tons per day.

In the denitrification of drinking water, denitrifying bacteria reduce nitrates and nitrites to harmless nitrogen gas and oxygen, which they use for metabolic purposes. A full-scale denitrifying plant is in operation in Austria, using a 2 m3 fixed-bed big-reactor system, operating with a natural population of microbes as denitrifiers. Because it is based on a naturally existing strain of bacteria, which accumulates during the start-up phase itself, sterile process operation is unnecessary.

Nowadays a large number of synthetic polymers are produced from petroleum derivatives because they are cheap, are available, can be prepared and processed easily, and are subject to few fluctuations of quality. Moreover, synthetic polymers offer a wider range of characteristics than natural polymers. However, genetic engineering offers at least the possibility of producing natural polymers with equivalent properties without the need for large-scale chemical processing. There are two different ways to obtain polymeric materials from plants that are useful for engineering purposes:

1. making use of the original polymeric structure of the plant material by conserving most of it and chemically modifying only side chains;
2. degrading the plant material chemically, or having it degraded by animals or micro-organisms, and subsequently synthesizing new polymers by means of chemistry or biotechnology.

Quite a few classes of plant polymers can be used as engineering materials without degrading the polymer backbone. Cellulose is one. The biosphere is abundant in cellulose, from timber, cotton, flax, and hemp. (Cellulose is the basis of rayon, cellophane, and celluloid.) Other natural polymers include natural rubber (a cis-polyisoprene), gutta-percha, lignin, polyphenols, and gums. Technologically useful polymers derived from animals also include proteins, such as wool, silk, leather, horn, gelatin, casein, chitin, and chitosan.

Some polymers with possible industrial application are produced by microorganisms. Biopolymers (e.g. polysaccharides), with properties and applications similar to those of plant gums, are secreted by certain bacteria and can be obtained by means of biotechnology. In the 1980s processes were developed to produce polyhydroxy-alkanoates (PHAs) as thermoplastics on an industrial scale. PHAs are polyesters that are produced by a great variety of micro-organisms as a cellular storage material. The most widespread type of PHA is PHB (polyhydroxybutyrate). However, its properties are not quite suitable to serve as a thermoplastic. This is why methods to produce similar substances with improved processing and application properties are sought.

Genetic Engineering

"Modern biotechnology" consists of new techniques, based on recombinant DNA technology, monoclonal antibodies, hybridoma techniques, cell fusion, vector-initiated gene techniques, and novel methods of cell and tissue cultures, resulting in genetically engineered organisms (GEOs). The complexity, as well as the costs of development, increase in the following sequence : biological nitrogen fixation, plant tissue culture, embryo transfer, monoclonal antibody production, plant protoplasm fusion, rDNA for disease diagnosis, biocontrol agents, animal vaccine development, rhizobia improvement, plants, animals.

Regardless of the high costs, there is no debate over the question of whether or not developing countries should begin genetic species engineering. Even the poorest should be thinking about a "survival kit" based in modern techniques; for example, a country with root crops as a staple food should initiate a tissue culture laboratory to facilitate the importation of tissue cultures of virus-free clones developed abroad. This would also allow rapid propagation if the plants proved adaptable to local conditions and acceptable to local producers and consumers.

It is generally agreed that the potential use of genetic techniques is very promising. Their application can further promote sustainability by, e.g., diversification of agricultural, forest, and fishery production systems, supplementation of genetic resources, and development of life forms appropriate to formerly impossible agricultural situations. A major consequence is considered to be the reduction of economic risk, but environmental risk is also likely to be reduced. Current technologies can modify a single gene or chromosome.

Major future breakthroughs will require more complex transfers. For example, at least six gene modifications would be involved in transferring nitrogen-fixing ability to cereals. Longer-term progress thus depends on further advances in basic science, notably in such areas as genome mapping. Bio-engineering applications are still extremely limited. The potentials have barely begun to be exploited. They are currently being held in check by the need for still more research to identify more useful genes plus more research to avoid harmful effects and big-safety hazard.

Ancient knowledge is a source of inspiration for sustainable technology development. Meso-American cultures had wide technological activities resulting from the combination of cultural, biological, and ecological diversities. A famous example in agriculture comes from the Incas, who were able to grow cereals at an altitude of 4,000 m with extraordinarily high productivity (10 tons/ha), although modern techniques (with chemical fertilizers) yield only 4 tons/ha. This 3,000year-old "waru-waru" process is completely natural, having a renaissance in Bolivia under the name of "socca collos."

The plants are grown on platforms 1 m in height, 4-10 m wide and 10-100 m long, made from soil dug from the canals. Water absorbs the sun's heat by day and radiates it back by night, protecting the crops against frost by creating a layer at +4°C. By capillary effects water ascends to the roots of the plants. Sediments from nitrogen-rich algae and plant and animal remains serve as fertilizer.

When Europeans arrived, the Incas had domesticated between 60 and 80 edible plants after centuries of interaction with ecosystems and species. In addition, more than 600 non-cultivated plants with adequate nutritional value, 300 species of fish, and 101 species of insects were used as food. Although much of this knowledge has evidently been lost, some of it may be recoverable. Surely the effort would be worth while. Meanwhile, the simple fact that such knowledge did exist at one time constitutes a powerful argument for preserving biodiversity.

Indigenous technologies are also very rich sources for human health care (big-drugs). Some international firms have initiated joint ventures with tropical countries to identify active compounds from roots and plants.

Bio-fertilizers

The growing need for fertilizers to enable a relatively fixed amount of arable land to support a growing human population is clear. Are chemical or biological fertilizers the best choice? A strong argument for replacing water-soluble chemical fertilizers such as urea, used in quantities up to 250 kg/ha, is that as much as about half of it goes directly into the groundwater and much of the remainder is lost to denitrifying bacteria. Bio-fertilizers such as Rhizobium can be applied in lesser amounts - as little as 0.5 kg/ha potentially resulting in reduced costs.

Genetic manipulation is possible, in the case of Rhizobium species, for further improvement. Some plants depend symbiotically on other microbes for nitrogen fixation. Recently it has been found that such microbes live not only in the roots but sometimes also on the surface of the plant. There are also non-symbiotic N-fixing bacteria (e.g. azobacter, cyanobacteria, blue and green algae).

There is a renaissance of plant-derived bulk raw materials in the United States. In the past decade, technological advances have lowered the cost of producing high-quality products from plant matter, while environmental regulations have raised the cost of using petroleum-derived products. Another potential source of renewable materials is the large amount of waste organic material from agriculture and forestry, especially paper pulping, municipal solid wastes, and food processing. The total is nearly 350 million metric tons/year in the United States alone. The potential of using plants as industrial raw materials, instead of crude oil, has been neglected up to now owing to the low cost of petroleum. Consequently petrochemicals are the primary source of several categories of industrial materials.

In effect, oil has replaced plant-derived matter not only for most textiles but also for significant uses of glass, metals, wood, and even paper. Practically all products can, in principle, be produced from plant materials. The basic technologies exist; only cost considerations, and sometimes quality differences, are preventing introduction to the market.

The processing of plant matter into final industrial products or consumer products is potentially much less environmentally burdensome than the processing of fossil fuels. The latter requires additional chemicals, resulting in a serious disposal problem. In particular, the pyrolysis process applied to plant materials generates no harmful wastes. A decade age, virtually the only plant-matter-derived products on the market were adhesives and lubricating oils and a handful of intermediate chemicals.

Today, plant-derived products compete in just about every major product category. They enter the market by displacing some petroleum-derived product in a portion of its market, and then gradually increase their market share. Fourteen product categories represent over 90 million of the 108 million metric ton (m.t.) commodity petrochemical market. In all cases, the prices of competitive big-products have dropped since 1985; for example, in the case of inks this drop was over 30 per cent.

Admittedly, most plant-derived consumer products are not yet competitive with their petrochemical counterparts. But the price premium for plant-derived products has dramatically diminished. Even when their costs are higher, plant-based products are gaining market share as a result of a combination of "green" consumerism and government regulation. A number of plant-based products have established their reliability and quality, not to mention environmental value. The cost of big-products should continue to drop and their market share should continue to expand.

The interplay of public regulation, consumer sophistication, and private entrepreneurship has brought "biologicals" produced from renewable raw material into almost every major product category. Much larger markets can be achieved through concerted marketing and commercialization. Spurred by the surplus of agricultural crops, governments and some trade associations have targeted new market developments, focusing on those new markets as alternative crops that impact directly on the consumption of fossil fuels. Currently, the best return to biomass is available by displacing petroleum from high value specialty chemical markets. These markets tend to be very small except for half a dozen chemicals.

About 90 per cent of all petroleum products are presently used as fuels, the fuel market is the most interesting long-term prospect. Active research continues to develop processes for the conversion of lignocellulose to ethanol. Although potential margins in this area appear to be greater than in starch-based ethanol conversion, they are realized only if markets can be found for carbon by-products such as lignin or furfural. Unfortunately, given the disparity between fuel requirements and chemical markets, these by-products would saturate existing chemical markets even at relatively modest levels of ethanol production.

Stricter environmental regulations may provide attractive alternatives for stimulating the biomass industry by targeting environmentally friendly products. The costs involved can sometimes be internalized in the producer's economics. But, more often, they entail external social costs, which allows government to make the cost benefit analysis and provide incentive programmes.

Restructuring of Infrastructures

The transport sector is a major contributor to environmental change. Apart from the land-take and materials-use implications of building transport infrastructures and machinery, which are considerable, environmental stress is imposed by the pollution implications of transport energy use. Part of the eco-restructuring agenda must therefore be to reduce the environmental disturbance caused per unit of transport, which is mostly a function of the characteristics of different transport modes and of modal splits, and to reduce the volume of transport. The issues involved are complex partly because of the systemic interlinkages between production and consumption patterns, the characteristics of transportation technologies, the characteristics of other technologies that can substitute for physical transportation, and the prevailing incentive structures that give rise to patterns of land use and technological, logistical, and transportation choices. Geographical differences between countries in size, shape, topography, resource endowment, state of development, and socio-economic conditions also complicate analysis. So do differences in the structure of different firms and industries and the locations of different types of manufacturing activities.

The dynamics of freight transportation, at the factors affecting developments, and at how these might be influenced. Because much of the scope for reducing freight volumes hinges on changing the nature of existing relationships and trends between freight transport, logistics (the ways in which companies organize the movement and storage of goods in the supply chain to consumers), and patterns of industrial and economic space use. Patterns of land use and freight transport in Western industrialized societies have co-evolved under market conditions where natural resource productivity has never been a priority, where road-building has been publicly financed, and where levels of (demand-led) road provision have been economically and environmentally excessive. Under these conditions, current (profit-maximizing) land-use and transport patterns represent an excessive use of transport. Although there is no necessary link between market liberalization and transport volumes, deregulation and shifts toward free trade have contributed to an internationalization - in some cases a globalization - of economic activities, which, in practice, has added significantly to freight tonne-kilometers. For this reason, developments affecting international trade and/or the relationship between internationalized economic activities and freight transport volumes are of interest because they may help or hinder progress toward eco-restructuring.

The choices made over the substance and coverage of the chapter in respect to the wider debate on transport and sustainability are due to my view of the importance of the transportation sector generally as regards policies and measures to usher in a restructuring of our economies and societies. Certainly, it is conceivable that much of the concern over the sustainability of current transport arrangements would be reduced were a competitively priced transportation technology based upon a renewable energy source to become available; for example, a technology based upon the solar-derived. However, such technologies are unlikely to become available within the next 50 years.

More importantly, their development will come about only in the context of appropriate incentives. In the near term, then, reducing the environmental impact of transport will depend mostly upon reducing transport volumes and increasing transport efficiency; i.e. cutting out or substituting for transport that can be avoided, undertaking remaining movement so that this does least environmental damage, and making most productive use of this remaining movement. This suggests that the preference should be for policy instruments that will stimulate these changes and simultaneously provide incentives for the longer-term development of fundamentally more sustainable transportation technologies. A lead taken along these lines within the industrialized countries would also signal an important message for caution over the extent of public road provision to countries now rapidly building their transportation infrastructures.

Significance of Freight Transport

Although the transport sector as a whole is receiving attention in the environment-development and eco-restructuring discussion - in particular, in respect to the future of private passenger transport the discussion has tended to focus on the central role of the car and on urban settings. It is true that Western industrial societies and their cities can be characterized as autocentric. It is also true that in terms of perhaps the most topical environmental policy concern on the international agenda - climatic change - the contribution of the automobile to carbon emissions and the build-up of atmospheric concentrations of greenhouse gases is greater than that of freight transport.

None the less, the relative importance of the two - cars and trucks - must be considered in terms of the significance of the sector as a whole in commercial energy use and its overall contribution to anthropogenic carbon emissions. Transport energy use accounts for more than one-quarter of worldwide commercial energy consumption. Moreover, with an average growth rate of 2.7 per cent per annum between 1971 and 1990, transportation energy demand is the fastest-growing energy end-use category. Passenger travel accounts for 60 per cent of transport energy use, and freight movement for the remaining 40 per cent. Transport energy use accounts for almost 30 per cent of all energy end-use-related anthropogenic carbon dioxide (CO_2) emissions.

Since anthropogenic CO_2 emissions currently amount to 26 billion tonnes annually, of which 80 per cent are energy related, transport is responsible for around 7.5 billion tonnes of CO_2 per annum. Passenger cars account for just less than half of this (around 3.6 billion tonnes) and goods vehicles for about one third (c. 2.4 billion tonnes). Other vehicles account for the rest. Although the freight share of CO_2 emissions is less than the passenger car share, the freight share is increasing. Moreover, at least in respect to most OECD countries, the energy intensity of goods transport is increasing owing to shifts to faster modes.

The Second Assessment Report of the Intergovernmental Panel on Climate Change (IPCC) has discussed this development in some detail and has analysed the reasons for it in respect to geographical differences between countries and to the types of trucks involved. "In countries where services and light industry are growing faster than heavy industry, the share of small trucks and vans in road freight is increasing. The energy intensity of light trucks is high compared with large trucks.

Along with general increase in the power-to-weight ratios of goods vehicles, these developments offset and in some cases outweigh the benefits of improving engine and vehicle technology". The two noteworthy points are that transportation energy intensity tends to be lower in countries where a high proportion of goods traffic is made up of bulk materials or primary commodities than in more industrialized and diversified economies, and that improvements in vehicle technology have partly been used to increase vehicle performance rather than to reduce energy use. Both contribute to the increasing energy intensity of goods transportation within the OECD countries.

Freight transport is therefore absolutely significant in its own right as a source of pollution and a target for eco-restructuring attention. Perhaps most important is to compare freight CO_2 emissions with those of industry. Industrial activity as a whole accounts for just less than 35 per cent of all anthropogenic carbon emissions; i.e. around 9 billion tonnes of CO_2 per annum. The contribution by freight transport is therefore equivalent to more than a quarter of all industrial CO_2 emissions.

Moreover, the freight contribution is greater than that of any single industrial sector and is increasing. It is responsible for 10 times the energy-related CO_2 emissions of the cement industry (although only just over twice that industry's overall CO_2 emissions), eight times those of the pulp and paper industry, and twice those of the steel industry. As well as contributing to carbon emissions, freight transport is associated with other pollutants. These include nitrogen dioxide (NO_2) and sulphur dioxide (SO_2). NO_2, like CO_2, is a greenhouse gas - though more than 200 times more potent than CO_2 in terms of radiative forcing. Both NO_2 and SO_2 contribute to environmental acidification.

Carbon monoxide (CO) and nitrogen oxides (NO_x), both of which are also emitted, have reaction products that add to these effects. The quantities of these emissions have recently been estimated as 2.1 g of CO and 1.85 g of NO_x per tonne-kilometre. Noise pollution and accident fatalities were also included in the ECMT study and are important because, although not directly relevant to globally or regionally threatening environmental change, they, too, represent costs that remain to be fully internalized within fuel, road, and transport prices.

Another cost of transportation is the time cost of delays caused by congestion. Internalization of the costs associated with these externalities would contribute to reducing freight transport volumes and so, also, to eco-restructuring. Viewed against the backdrop of the role that freight transport currently plays in environmental change, its relative neglect within the eco-restructuring discussion is surprising.

Transport is usually considered in terms of passenger transport and car use, in respect to which discussions have focused heavily on technological opportunities for reducing unit impacts.

These have centred around the need for energy efficiency improvements and for low-carbon or carbon-free energy carriers as replacements for fossil fuels. Work has also looked at public alternatives to private transport (train, metro, bus, tram, light railway, etc.) and at how modal shifts might be encouraged. In terms of demand management, there has been some discussion of the technological opportunities to substitute for passenger travel; for example, by using telecommunications for remote working, teleshopping, and home entertainment.

Relatively little has been done, however, to examine the relationships between patterns of space use and passenger transport demand; for example, the links between a greater mixing of land uses (residential, recreational, retail, office, etc.) or between the scale of provision of services (large centralized schools, hospitals, and shops versus small-scale facilities serving local neighborhoods) and auto use.

This omission is significant in respect to the parallels that exist between passenger transport and freight transport (which is not), because considerable potential for demand reduction in the freight sector could lie in reorganizing spatial divisions of labour and logistics to reduce transport intensities at the product level. Several important issues in respect to past and future trends in the development of freight transport are, thus, raised:

— What factors and trends have been important in the past patterns of freight transport growth and development?

— What is the current level and structure of production of freight transport?

— What factors and trends are shaping future developments in freight transport volumes and patterns?

— How much scope is there for reducing freight volumes?

— How might this scope be taken up?

— How would the space-use, logistics, transport, and trade patterns of a sustainable society and economy differ from today's patterns?

Many of the examples and data given reflect European Union (KU) experience. None the less, these are believed to be representative for other industrialized countries. Inferences can be drawn for developing countries, especially in respect to opportunities for avoiding heavy investments in infrastructures that imply long-term commitments of environmental (and also economic) resources to potentially unproductive or low-productivity uses.

Patterns of freight transport development

Present-day patterns of transport, logistics, and land use are the still evolving outcome of a century-long - and still ongoing - process of industrial development. Consistent features of the trajectory have been its exploitation of:

— volume production and consumption as a metric and target for economic growth,

— cost reduction via productivity improvements as an engine for growth,

— scale economies and comparative advantage for total factor productivity gains,

— energy/materials/capital to substitute for labour (for labour productivity gains).

Development has followed an energy- and materials-intensive production regime based heavily upon the one-time conversion of natural (environmental) capital stock to current income. The generated income has been used to develop different forms of "man-made" capital appropriate to the continuation of the trajectory and to provide for high levels of current consumption.

Within this trajectory, the most important factors in shaping the evolving geography of economic activities have been: deregulation and the liberalization of markets; improvements in transport infrastructures/technology; the maintenance of low transport and energy prices; and developments in logistics and in information technologies. Competition and the search for profits have been the major dynamic forces. The major constraints have been some (usually weak) restrictions on land development and land use.

Market liberalization and deregulation

Liberalization has taken place within countries, between pairs or groups of countries, and at the global level, affecting both tariff and non-tariff barriers in respect to markets in factors, goods, and services. All factors (save labour) have been affected. The freeing-up of capital markets has been particularly comprehensive. The process began immediately after the end of World War II in an attempt to stimulate economic growth and prosperity at the world level and avoid a repeat of the depression that had accompanied inter-war protectionism. Some changes were agreed bilaterally among major trading partners, but the major multilateral mechanism for liberalizing world trade has been the General Agreement on Tariffs and Trade (GATT) process, which started in 1947 and culminated in the Uruguay Round of negotiations and Marrakesh agreements. The development of regional trading blocs has also been a significant - in the case of West European countries, perhaps the most significant development in the post-war liberalization process. Blocs now include the European Union, the North American Free Trade Area, the Association of South-East Asian Nations, and Mercosul.

By way of illustrating the removal of tariff barriers, there is no better example than the passenger car. The contrast between tariff levels during the highly protectionist period of the 1920s and 1930s and those of the 1970s and 1980s is stark. During the inter-war period each European country separately determined its tariff level. The average across the major European carproducing nations in the 1930s was around 45 per cent of customs value. In the case of France and Italy, tariffs were in the range 47-74 per cent and 101-111 per cent, respectively. Japan also had a highly protected market. Its tariff level in 1940 was 70 per cent. By the early 1980s, the situation was completely different.

The EU countries had harmonized on a tariff structure within a range to 10.5 per cent of customs value. Tariffs in the United States and Japan were minimal to non-existent. The impact of deregulation and trade liberalization on transport demand arises through three principal effects: the exploitation of comparative advantage; the exploitation of scale economies; and the expansion of markets. In respect to the first two, the removal of barriers increases geographical specialization and concentration of production. Comparative advantage is particularly important for inter-industry trade, whereas exploitation of scale economies or experience is particularly important for intra-industry trade. In respect to the third, falling import barriers, lower product prices, higher per capita consumption, and access to wider markets lead to increases in the average distance between points of production and points of consumption.

As barriers to factor mobility have been reduced or removed, the world economy has become steadily internationalized. Together with accompanying technological, institutional, and organizational innovations, this has allowed economic activities to be restructured through a series of "spatial fixes". As the spatial framework has expanded, entrepreneurs have been free to engineer the most profitable business arrangements under the prevailing new conditions. Some argues that, through these, a long-threatened growth crisis has been repeatedly postponed. Each new spatial fix has brought higher factor productivities and has permitted growth to continue within the context of the same mass production/mass-consumption model.

Governments have taken responsibility for infrastructure provision and have used infrastructure development in macroeconomic policy, employment creation, regional development, and defence strategy as well as in transport policy. Governments have typically taken a supply expansion rather than a demand-side management approach to balancing demand and supply. More important, they have catered for "anticipated" demands. A result has been the considerable extension and improvement of road infrastructures.

Meanwhile, markets in respect to energy, land, and transport have been so constructed as to externalize many costs. The environmental costs of energy use in terms of depletion and pollution have not been factored into energy prices, which have in any case been low and either stagnating or reducing in real terms over the past decade. Diesel and petrol prices to consumers were lower in 1993 than in 1985 in several countries (e.g. the United States). This reflects depressed oil prices, which have only partly been offset by increases in the percentage share of taxes in consumer prices. Neither are the environmental and social costs of land-take factored into user charges for roads, ports, or airports.

As with all public subsidies, the benefits are available to be privatized while the costs are socialized. This has provided strong incentives for businesses to increase the use of transport and to make logistics a key aspect of technological choice in respect to strategies for rationalization, marketing, and competitiveness. Part of the low cost of transport has been passed on to consumers in the form of transport-intensive goods and services with prices lower than would have been possible without the subsidies.

Positive feedback mean that many of these distortions are self reinforcing. Subsidy has favoured high levels of mobility and low density land-use patterns. High dependence on mobility has been important, in turn, as a justification for further infrastructure provision, particularly because of the inherent biases toward provision within the benefit-cost and discounting methodologies used by government agencies for investment appraisal.

Developments in logistics

Particularly since the 1980s the function of logistics within business operations and competitive strategy has changed. Key drivers have been shifts in consumer markets, with less brand loyalty and greater competition among producers. This has elevated the importance of customer service - including product availability, delivery lead-times, reliability of deliveries, etc. - within the competitive process and led to shifts in approaches to business management and logistics. A related development has seen logistics reorganization being used to secure reductions in inventory and warehousing costs. Facilitating developments have been deregulation and privatization and rapid advances in information technologies. Change has followed a three-stage development.

In the 1970s, companies began to bring together transport, warehousing, and inventory management at the firm level (integrated distribution). The concept was then extended beyond the boundaries of the firm so that the whole materials chain from the sourcing of raw materials to the final consumption of finished products was integrated (channel integration).

By the early 1990s, a third phase has seen operations becoming integrated across national boundaries (geographical integration), which, as well as enabling the promotion of new product strategies, offers companies the opportunity to reap scale economies in purchasing, manufacturing, warehousing, and transport. By regionalizing warehouses, firms are able to rationalize and reduce inventory. A parallel development upstream in the supply chain has been a growing emphasis on "focused factories," where companies select factories to specialize in producing parts of the product range rather than its entirety. Focused factories invariably serve more than one country.

An equally important development, from the perspective of truck traffic generation, has been the growing importance of information technology in logistics management. Whereas inventory holding levels used to be greater than strictly necessary to compensate for deficiencies of information, transparency in the supply chain by virtue of information technology means that it is increasingly possible to reduce levels of inventory.

Accurate and timely information on stock holdings and whereabouts increasingly encompasses stock on trucks. Together with a more responsive transport service, remaining inventory can be concentrated at a smaller number of strategic locations. Firms have been able profitably to trade off higher transport operating costs against (much) lower warehousing costs. Within Europe, the lead companies in the integration process are those in the automotive and business equipment sectors together with some retailers.

Spatial and Transport Outcomes

The most important spatial-economic outcomes of these developments and their implications for transport have been:

— increasing geographical specialization and concentration in production,

— growing separation of points in value-adding chains,

— increasing distance between points of production and points of consumption,

— internationalization of economic activities and of transport, growing transport volumes,

— increasing average haulage distances, shifts to faster modes.

In terms of the transport implications, the most significant effect has been rapid growth in the volume of truck-kilometres. In 1993, the OECD truck fleet travelled a total of 1,823 billion kilometres. This represents a 68 per cent increase over the 1980 kilometrage. Truck movements on important international corridor routes such as the Rhine and Danube valleys and through sensitive Alpine passes have become particularly problematic. Part of the overall growth in truck-kilometres is attributable to increases in average haulage length. Within the KU, the average haulage length of goods (all commodities) transported by road grew by more than 20 per cent in the 10 years to 1990. Some of the growth has also come from mode shifts.

Competition favours the use of flexible, direct, and fast modes of transport. Truck and air have gained relative to slower and less direct modes. Rail, in particular, has lost out. Not only is the rail share of total tonne-kilometrage reducing, but rail has experienced absolute reductions in freight-tonne kilometres. Studies of German freight transport have shown that the threshold of substitution between slower modes and truck occurs at value densities of little more than DM 1-2/kg. Truck dominates the value range from this to the DM 100/kg level, which encompasses most consumer products including autos and domestic electrical (white) goods. Above DM 100/kg, air freight becomes dominant.

International trade has grown consistently and has outpaced the growth in real world product. No EU country now imports less than 30 per cent of its total GNP. Competition and profit-maximizing behaviours have been the critical driving force behind these impacts. Together, these have constituted a powerful imperative to cut costs, expand market presence, and respond quickly to demand. Evidence is rife of bizarre transportation consequences. Freight transport surveys have shown that, to take advantage of cost differences between countries, some products are shipped long distances in the process of adding value, ultimately only to arrive back at their point of origin. Prawns landed in Hamburg and destined to be sold in the German market have been found in transport to and from Poland, where they are cooked and peeled.

Most West European household pot plants, wherever grown, are sold at auctions held in the Netherlands from where they are trucked to final market, sometimes even to places where they were originally grown. In both these cases, it is the same (not just an equivalent) product that is being transported in both directions. Even low value-density commodities and products have to be transported into foreign markets at risk of their producers losing overall market share. At the high value density end of the market, there are even more questionable, but apparently profitable and cost-effective, goods movements. An example is the case of the Cadillac Allante. The car body is manufactured in Italy. But the car is assembled and sold in the United States. The body is transported over 5,000 km by air from Turin to Detroit.

There is evidence that transport intensities at the national level (measured as tonne-kilometres per unit GNP) may now have peaked in some OECD countries and even have begun to decline. This is the result of higher average specific values (value/kg) of cargo and is likely to reflect changes in the structure of economic activity within countries - including the offloading of environmentally damaging aspects of production to other countries. It is unlikely, therefore, to be a reliable indicator of shifts to or away from transport dependence. Time-series of product-specific transport intensities would be better indicators but these are not routinely calculated. In an exceptional (and exemplary) study aimed at establishing transport intensity at the product level, Böge has used lifecycle methods to trace all the inputs used in the manufacture of a single pot of strawberry yoghurt emanating from a production plant in southern Germany.

The transport requirement associated with producing the inputs, bringing these to the production plant in southern Germany, and distributing the final product to consumers is summarized over the life cycle on a unit product basis. Böge expresses the transport intensity in terms that enable it to be considered - and possibly listed like any other "ingredient" on the label of the product. Each 150g strawberry yoghurt was found to have required the equivalent of more than 9 metres of truck movement. Every tonne of yoghurt sold accounts for more than 600 truck-kilometres. In respect to overall sales of yoghurt - a seemingly simple, healthy, and "natural" product marketed in massive quantities - the implied daily, weekly, or annual transport requirement is enormous. Production from the single plant studied, which serves mostly local markets, gives rise to 24,000 truck-kilometres annually.

Future developments affecting freight patterns

As concerns reducing the environmental impact of the freight transport sector, virtually all present trends point in entirely the wrong direction. Freight volumes (measured in tonne-kilometres) are increasing not decreasing. Moreover, the growth in freight volumes is now attributable almost entirely to increases in the distance that goods are transported - reflecting greater separation between points in the value-adding chain - rather than to increases in the quantity of goods transported. What is worse, transport volume per capita tends to increase as societies become more affluent and, even though transport intensity (measured per unit of GDP) is beginning to fall in the most affluent societies, the decrease is more than offset by increases in GDP per capita. What matters from an environmental standpoint is that freight transport volumes and energy intensities are increasing in absolute terms.

The trends at international level are also bad. Most developing countries assisted by Western advisers and consultants, by various international agencies, and by development banks - have development strategies that are heavily based upon providing physical infrastructures to facilitate industrialization on the Western model. If successful, these would lead to their joining the industrialized West in having economies and societies that are transport intensive and fossil fuel dependent.

Shachar points out that this convergence of industrialized and developing countries on the same mobility patterns and fossil-energy-based economies is one of the main reasons - if not the main reason - for our moving away from sustainability at the global level. There is also reason for concern over the effects of further liberalization of world markets as a result of the Marrakesh agreements that concluded the final, Uruguay Round of the General Agreement on Tariffs and Trade negotiations in April 1994. Although, in principle, trade liberalization is not inconsistent with environmental protection (because measures in respect to both have a common goal in securing efficient resource allocations), the sequencing of measures is important.

Although it has been pointed out that both liberalization and environmental protection policies have broadly equal claims to priority - in that barriers to free trade and environmental externalities are both alleged to cause similar allocation distortions - progress toward free trade is being made more rapidly than progress toward internalizing environmental externalities. Moreover, the nature of the two distortions is fundamentally different in that tariff and non-tariff restrictions have the effect of restricting the spatial range of economic operations, both production related and marketing. In so doing, they act to limit the distortions in resource allocations - especially the excessive use of transport - that arise from market imperfections and subsidies.

Liberalization within the transport sector itself will increase competition and lower the prices charged by operators. Liberalization within other sectors - specifically agricultural commodities, chemicals, petroleum, coal, steel, metals, and automobiles presents considerable scope for trade expansion because these have traditionally been tightly protected at national level and are transport intensive.

Liberalization of the transport equipment and energy industries will likely lead to reductions in the costs of inputs relevant to the supply of transport services and therefore to reductions in transport costs. Increased geographical specialization and concentration of production will increase average haulage lengths. Inter-industry trade is more likely to increase average transport distance than intra-industry trade because the source of trade gains - factor differences and comparative advantage - is geographically determined.

The impact of economic growth and increases in per capita income is complex. Of several, partially offsetting effects, that with the greatest environmental significance is likely to be the continuing displacement of bulk commodities by lower lot sizes with higher value-to-weight ratios. Although qualifying his analysis in several ways,

Gabel concludes: "In summary, virtually all of the changes anticipated to accrue from trade liberalisation will probably increase transport output" and "may lead to a shift in the mode of transport to road and air".

Results from studies aimed at projecting the impact of recent EU liberalization and deregulation show similar results. Based on an econometric model, Gabel and Roller forecast impacts on international transport movements of the complete elimination of internal (non-tariff) trade barriers (but not elimination of the EU common external tariff). Elimination of non-tariff barriers was found likely to increase aggregate trade volumes in all industries. Estimates of increase ranged from 16 per cent for pharmaceuticals to 133 per cent for electrical machinery.

In every industry, the percentage increase in intra-EU trade volume was estimated to be larger than the aggregate, suggesting some displacement of imports from non-EU countries. In tonne-kilometre or truck kilometre terms, the effect of eliminating non tariff barriers is to increase international road haulage by 38 per cent. The results confirm the expectations of an EU Task Force, which had predicted that shifts toward liberalization and deregulation might increase trans-frontier truck traffic by 3050 per cent.

Scope for reducing freight volumes

There are many different feasible mechanisms by which to reduce the environmental impact of freight transport. The focus here is on the potential to reduce emissions by reducing the transport intensity of products (mostly through changes in the spatial division of labour) and by increasing the efficiency of use of existing modes - both within the context of existing infrastructural constraints.

The scope for reducing the transport intensity of final products lies in several possible adjustments. One is to reduce the number of transport-intensive components that products embody. Another is to reduce the average length of individual transport movements. This can be done by obtaining raw materials and components locally, serving local markets, reversing current trends in logistics, and revising networking arrangements in respect to contractors and subcontractors in the value-adding chain. Finally, there is also scope to reduce the number of times that the same materials are transported during the process of adding value.

Reductions in the number of transport-intensive components and ingredients can be achieved by substitution. This is particularly im portent in the food industry because of the high quantities of food products now involved in long-distance transport and the high level of substitutability among foods and ingredients. This would imply greater reliance on local/regional produce and on produce in season.

Some physical goods movement can be substituted altogether by using the possibilities provided by flexible technologies and informatics. The possibility exists for information about the design of components embodied within complex products that are manufactured at a distance from the market to be provided with the product or transmitted electronically as need arises. In the event, say, of the product breaking down, a local parts manufacturer is thus able to obtain component design details and make a replacement part rather than having to order and ship this in from a distance.

Similarly, telecommunications can substitute for information-rich but formerly transport-intensive products and services. Just as fax and electronic mail can substitute for conventional mail, similar substitutions can be made in respect to whole industrial sectors. In the newspaper publications industry, for example, a combination of telecommunications and flexible printing plant could do away completely with the need to transport newsprint physically over long distances. It also provides a potentially improved customer service in the form of a greater choice of simultaneously published editions.

The long-distance shipping of goods between world regions could increasingly be replaced by capital flows by encouraging direct foreign investment as an alternative to trade. The attractiveness of direct foreign investment increases with the level of competition in non-standardized products and with the rapidity of market change. Moves toward the strengthening of regional trading blocs could help in this direction. Changing the spatial structure of inter-firm supply networks (the number and relative location of contractors and subcontractors) is important because these needlessly increase the transport intensity of final products. Some argues that such traffic-generating arrangements are currently promoted by EU programmes aimed at integrating European economies, technology transfer, and increasing international marketing opportunities.

Some argues that there is scope for lean production to con tribute to reductions in inter-firm freight transport if reductions in the number of direct suppliers are accompanied by reductions also in average transport distances between them. This depends upon regional concentration of production and supply relations. In a theoretical example based upon German conditions, he contrasts the transport implications of two different inter-firm supply structures. Both are geared toward producing an identical final product. The first represents a traditional relationship between final assembler and several suppliers in which all suppliers deliver directly to the assembler. The second represents a relationship based upon cooperation among suppliers organized into regional value-adding networks. The effect is that more value is added within the region before any components are transported long-haul. Only a small number of high value-density components are finally transported to the assembler.

Average loading ratios for trucks in Europe are typically 75-85 per cent. Empty truck movements account for approximately 1.5 per cent of all domestic freight traffic within countries of the KU. Prior to deregulation and the creation of the Single Market in 1992, one-third of trucks making international journeys on EU roads had empty back-hauls. Of trucks crossing the Dutch-German border, 30 per cent were empty. Although all these data are for the immediate pre-1992 situation, moves to phase out permits and restrictions on cabotage post-1992 were not anticipated to improve loading ratios.

Surveys of hauliers undertaken before 1992 show the main causes of low loading factors to be related not to restrictions but rather to problems in arranging suitable backloads for example, a lack of information on backload opportunities and problems of backload incompatibility. Broadly similar loading ratios are likely to apply currently. The problem of low loading factors is linked to operators' incentives. Some operators prefer to operate large vehicles because this maximizes flexibility and reduces average costs. As size restrictions have been relaxed, the average truck size of some operators' fleets has increased. Once equipped with large vehicles, hauliers use these even with small loads.

The difference between actual and theoretically feasible loading factors implies scope for efficiency gains equivalent to 25 per cent of total kilometrage. While this may not be realizable owing to practical problems of specialization and backloading, these constraints are themselves related to the overall paradigm of which scale economies, long-haul transport, and specialization of transport are part.

Packaging is also part of this paradigm and part of the problem. Goods for final sale are transported together with often bulky packaging. This reduces weight-to-volume ratios and increases truck-kilometres. The scope for efficiency gains is therefore a function not only of truck loading ratios but also of weight-volume ratios.

In principle, the geography of economic activities and the spatial division of labour represent the outcome of choices about the use of transport system improvements and low transport costs. However, choice is contextually constrained. Competitive forces and prevailing relative prices have made a business necessity out of moving materials and goods (often repeatedly) between different points in value adding chains.

To the extent that profit maximizing arrangements differ from those that would be environmentally optimal, this difference arises from the ways in which markets have been constructed (legally, institutionally, and fiscally) and how this affects relative prices. A conclusion now widely drawn is that the social and environmental costs of transport services and energy should be included within their prices.While recognizing the problems involved, an important element of strategy in eco-restructuring must be to take up the opportunities created even by apparently negative developments and trends.

Growing traffic volumes represent a negative development. But the projected growth in traffic under conditions of already congested infrastructure is now focusing policy makers' attention on the need for demand-side management. Similarly, progress toward and actual experience with free trade have highlighted the trade distorting implications both of the under pricing of environmental resources and of differences in national policies toward environmental protection.

As a result, the issues are growing in political importance. They are shifting from being purely domestic policy items to a central position on agendas concerned with the topography of the "playing field" for international competition. This gives them a much higher political priority.

Environmental protection—whether by harmonization of standards or by the use of compensatory mechanisms that would factor differences in national standards into the terms of trade - is now an agenda item for the newly formed World Trade Organization, the successor to the GATT. Differences in national policies affecting transport and energy prices within EU member states are causing these to come under critical scrutiny in ways and to a degree almost unthinkable within a purely national framework.

At the same time, these differences are highlighting that the sources of distortions are often linked to policy interventions through subsidies and tax differentials and that fiscal regimes often bear no clear link to third-party costs. As a result, work is under way to elaborate basic principles for transport and energy pricing from the standpoint of economic theory and optimal resource allocation.

Policy Instruments for Eco-restructuring

The Convention Concerning the Use of White Lead in Paint marks the very beginning of the list of some 140 international environmental agreements. These agreements have established rules for the use of the Antarctic, the exploitation of ocean resources, the protection of migratory and endangered wildlife, the abatement of pollution at sea and in the atmosphere, the management of watersheds, the control of pests and hazardous chemicals, the testing of nuclear weapons, the notification of nuclear accidents, and many other environmental problems that have trans-border complications.

The number of signatory countries averages around 12 but varies from a minimum of 3 to a maximum of 161. The pace of treaty-making has been accelerating. Taking as a divide the 1972 UN Conference on the Human Environment (UNCHE) at Stockholm, which propounded the notion of Only One Earth, the pace has increased from 1.2 treaties per year in the pre-UNCHE decades to some 4.2 per year during the subsequent two decades.

Distinguishing the treaties concerned with the management of commons outside national control from those dealing with within-border or territorial resources, the proportion of the former grew from some 50 per cent before 1973 to nearly 70 per cent during the period since 1973.

Moreover, countries have seemed to demonstrate a willingness to subordinate national controls to the requirements of international agreements. The proportion of treaties that regulate only extra-territorial activities has fallen from 44 per cent before 1973 to 15 per cent since 1973, with those calling for internal controls to internationally agreed standards and criteria rising to 85 per cent.

In spite of the "tragedy of the commons" thesis of rational choice theorists, this may signify that humankind's willingness to assume collective responsibility for the management of common-pool resources has increased, if not radically, and that the exigency of deepening interdependence has begun to erode the concept of the national sovereign state. This does not presage, however, anything like an increased visibility of a Global Government.

Empowerment of a supranational authority for treaty enforcement has occurred only twice so far. And, in most of the cases in which supranational authorities are involved to assist national governments in treaty implementation, their role has been limited to collecting information and conducting research. This is in spite of the fact that the majority of conventions concerned with air pollution, water pollution, marine dumping, and natural resource conservation do not stop at mere coordination of national policies but involve collaboration games in which countries have conflicting interests and solutions entail real distributional costs.

After long debates among ecological scientists, economists, and the policy community, a broad consensus seems to be emerging that the best strategy is to start with "small agreements" and build on their ratchet effects, rather than to struggle for a big, sweeping (and eternally elusive) agreement. One of the important lessons learned from the decade-long "marathon" of the Law of the Sea negotiations is that "to create a universally inclusive process with respect to both issues and participants, together with the requirements for consensus on an overall package deal" can be "a very serious time-consuming mistake". The reason is that the ultimate results of such a heroic endeavour can easily be held hostage to the most reluctant parties on the most difficult issues. The new pattern of interactive planning emerging in that process is roughly as follows.

First, a framework convention is instituted. It defines a commonly shared perception of the problems at issue and sets forth a set of principles and norms to be observed in tackling those problems. This is a precondition for subsequent, more specific rule-making protocols. The process provides enough time for laggard states to become motivated to reassess their respective national interests relative to others. It also allows time for the leading coalitions of interest groups and non-governmental organizations (NGOs) to generate public pressure against resistant institutions and governments. It thus paves the way for protocols and concurrent national and international regulatory activities. This technique was first developed by UNEP's Regional Seas Programme for the Mediterranean in 1975, followed by the subsequent nine regional programmes. A similar approach was adopted for the LongRange Transboundary Air Pollution (LRTAP) Convention in Europe as well as the Vienna Convention to protect the stratospheric ozone layer.

In the process of preparing for the Framework Convention on Climate Change, debates continued for some time among the press and the scientific community as well as within the International Panel on Climate Change (IPCC), formed in 1988. These debates, which still continue, have gradually shifted from their initial focus. At first the issue was whether the available data sets and the existing climate models were really robust enough to base policy on. Now the question at issue is nearer to a matter of strategy: how fast must the level of carbon dioxide emissions be reduced to combat effectively the ongoing degradation of the global atmosphere at the lowest economic cost? The issue has spawned a growing number of global policy scenarios and simulation models. Conceivable options vary greatly.

At one extreme is the approach that just puts a new policy structure into place and leaves aside the question of the uncertainty of costs and benefits. At the other extreme is a comprehensive, stringent, and universalized approach whose benefits might be more certain except that its realization would be politically impossible. The currently considered target of stabilizing the annual emission of greenhouse gases at the 1990 level by the year 2000 would help slow the pace of global warming by just 20 years or so even if the developing countries and the former socialist economies joined the move.

The grace period provided by this target would be no more than five years if the latter groups of countries did not join the protocol! This is due to the long residence time of trace gases in the atmosphere. To stabilize the density of these gases in the atmosphere and thus really stop global warming would require a drastic cut in current emissions, say by as much as 50 per cent within 100 years. So we need to hurry up with both technological and social breakthroughs. That might sound a very relaxed long-term agenda when ecologists keep warning that even a minor change in temperature is likely to have potentially significant impacts on a regional and local basis. But political scientists' reflective cynicism retorts that humankind has not yet learned enough to make any big systemic change in international political systems before a catastrophic signal becomes really palpable.

7

Future Energy Systems

Since the mid-nineteenth century, world energy use has been growing, on average, by 2.1 per cent per year. This growth in energy use has fuelled an annual expansion of the world economy of 3.2 per cent. Most importantly, energy and economic growth have combined to raise world population from 1.2 to 5.3 billion, corresponding to an average growth rate of 1.1 per cent per year. This account of past rates of growth is incomplete as long as it neglects the environmental degradation associated with industrial development, economic growth, and energy use, ranging from local air and water pollution, soil contamination, and reduced biodiversity, to stratospheric ozone depletion and the damage potentially caused by global climate change.

Whereas initially the burdens placed by humans on the environment and their resulting consequences were primarily local, it is now apparent that the adverse impacts of human activity are rapidly approaching global dimensions. Foremost among these impacts is the potential for global climate change caused by a growing concentration of greenhouse gases (GHG) in the atmosphere. Climate change is likely to emerge as one of the greatest threats to the development of mankind during the twenty-first century.

Scientific evidence linking unrestricted fossil fuel use to potential climatic change is increasingly gaining credibility. The Second Assessment Report of the Intergovernmental Panel on Climate Change (IPCC) states that "the balance of evidence suggests a discernible human influence on global climate". However, fundamental disagreement in the scientific community exists as to the eventual impacts of global climatic change, especially at the regional level.

In large part the threat of climatic change is the result of greenhouse gas emissions from the energy system. The energy system is not the sole source of greenhouse gases, but it is the most important one, currently accounting for roughly half of all such emissions. More importantly, the global energy system is the fastest-growing emitter. Stabilization of atmospheric GHG concentrations is a policy objective in several industrialized countries. Present energy research and environmental policy aim at the identification of energy technology options and strategies that mitigate greenhouse gas emissions.

Technology responses analysed by numerous researchers range from efficiency improvements, fuel and technology switching, to GHG emission abatement or removal, and environmentally benign GHG disposal or sequestration. Presently, the discussion centres around issues such as the costs and benefits of different measures, least-cost and hedging strategies, etc. Yet these all focus on incremental and add-on technology fixes within the current energy sector, rather than on a systematic restructuring of the energy system.

What is missing in the current energy-environment debate is a zero-order understanding of the structure of a fully sustainable energy system. Long-term energy and environmental policy requires a reference or target energy system a target beyond the issues of local air pollution and greenhouse gas emission levels. Once established, the long-term reference energy system then plays the role of a beacon for energy policy, for public investment in infrastructure changes beyond the capability of free market forces, for publicly funded research and development activities, as well as for private sector investments.

In a world of continuous technical change, the "reference" energy system is a moving target. Over a period of 50 years and more, technology forecasting based on current knowledge will certainly fail to anticipate future inventions and rates of innovation. The target energy system, therefore, should incorporate least-regret cost features, i.e. it is structured so that future innovation enhances the system's performance rather than making previous infrastructure investments obsolete. Despite the large uncertainties involved, it can be shown that the overall system architecture and some fundamental technological characteristics are quite robust even in a rapidly changing world of technology.

The environmental gains from restructuring the energy system will be compounded if it takes place as an integral part of a fundamental eco-restructuring of the entire economic production and consumption process. Energy is not an end in itself; the prime purpose of energy is to provide energy services such as heating, cooking, mobility, communication, consumption goods, and numerous industrial processes.

Eco-restructuring of the energy system, then, goes hand in hand with changes in settlement patterns and transportation infrastructures, workplace arrangements that include telecommuting, de-materializing of the production process, and recycling. The fundamental features of a sustainable energy system can be defined in terms of the following four compatibility constraints:

1. environmental compatibility,
2. economic compatibility,
3. social compatibility, and
4. geopolitical compatibility.

Regarding environmental compatibility, the fluxes to and from the target energy system should be coherent with nature's energy and material fluxes and should not perturb nature's equilibria. Only then will it be possible to provide for economic growth without environmental costs undermining the gains. On the other hand, economic reasoning demands that the costs of protecting the environment should not exceed the benefits.

An effective and, in the long run, sustainable target energy system should also consider the implications of the historically observed linkage between per capita energy service requirements and demographics. In a world whose population has doubled in a single generation and which continues to grow at alarming rates, even drastic changes that one might be able to engineer in terms of specific energy efficiency improvements or environmental impacts over the next decades could well be swamped by the underlying demographic explosion.

Future energy systems and associated technologies need to be socio-politically acceptable in terms of convenience, level of risk, and economic affordability. Supply security and other potential geopolitical concerns including proliferation issues need also to be effectively resolved. Once a target energy system is defined, the question of managing the transition must be addressed in terms of both energy system evolution and policy. Given the inherently long lifetime of existing energy infrastructures and lead-times from blueprint to operation of a dozen and more years for new production capacity, the energy system does not lend itself to quick adaptation or modification. The transition phase towards a sustainable energy system is likely to last well into the twenty-first century.

As regards policy measures, initiating the shift away from the potentially unacceptable burdens that the present system places on the environment will probably require more than the present measures ranging from energy price manipulations (green taxes), standards, regulated emission levels, and tradable permits to prescribed technology fixes. Present policy focuses primarily on short-term reductions in local air pollution, not on providing the market with guidelines and incentives for a transition toward an environmentally sustainable energy system.

From the perspective of eco-restructuring, one of the most important policy steps would be to get the prices right by internalizing external costs. Still, the enormous changes in infrastructure associated with the transition towards a sustainable energy system are most likely beyond the domain of market forces. Therefore, effective energy policy must be based on a clear understanding of both the eventual shape and structure of the deep future energy system and the implications for the transition phase. This includes our understanding of the energy sources and principal technologies that will be key during this transition phase.

Energy analysts often use the term "energy system" when they are actually referring to the "energy sector." The energy sector is only the upstream part of the energy system. Electric utilities generate and sell kWhs, while the oil sector explores for and produces oil, refines the oil into marketable products, and sells these in the market-place. The success of any particular agent within the energy sector is usually measured in terms of kWh or litres of gasoline sold. However, the reason people purchase kWhs of electricity or litres of gasoline is only indirectly related to these products. What people really want are energy services, i.e. information via electronic mail, the exchange of information through a telephone conversation, or the service of getting back safely from work to a comfortably temperature-conditioned home.

It is important to note that the demand for energy services changes (in quantity and quality) as a function of demographics, income, technology, and location. But their fundamental nature does not change. The supply of energy services depends on two or more interdependent inputs: one or more energy service technologies plus one or more energy currencies. It is the combination of the technology "automobile" and the currency "gasoline" that provides the energy service "transportation" - not the energy product gasoline alone.

The downstream market conditions - in essence oil products' ability to provide the energy services demanded by residential, commercial, and industrial consumers - drive the upstream activities of the oil industry. Oil product demand, end-use competition, and interfuel substitution depend, in all but the shortest term, as much on the techno-economic performance of the energy service technologies providing the services as they do on the actual oil product market prices.

As technologies change, so do the competitive edges of the associated fuels. More precisely, energy services are the product of energy service technologies plus infrastructures (capital), labour (know-how), materials, and energy currencies. Clearly, all these input factors carry a price tag and are substitutes for each other. From the perspective of an energy service consumer, the important issue is the quality and cost of energy services. It matters very little what the energy currency is, and, even less, what the source of that currency was. It is fair to say that most energy services are blind to the upstream activities of the energy system. But, for the development of civilization, it is the end-service technologies, such as automobiles, aircraft, furnaces, electric motors, and computers, that are most important - or at least the most visible. It is these technologies and their mix that determine the quality and quantities of energy services people can buy.

The energy system is service driven, i.e. from the bottom up. Energy, however, flows top-down. Only recently have some energy sector industries begun to adopt a full source-to-service perspective, prompted in most cases by regulatory intervention. "Integrated resource planning" (IRP) and "demand-side management" (DSM) have been promoted to assist the industry in getting out of the energy sector "ghetto." In essence, IRP and DSM explicitly call for the inclusion of the end-use devices into the utilities' investment planning activity. Extending this to an example outside the utility domain, oil company subsidiaries might sell transportation services by leasing out highly efficient vehicles and charging for their use on a mileage basis only.

Energy System Inefficiencies

Most energy services have surprisingly low minimum energy input requirements. The services considered are space heating, transportation, and lighting. There are many difficulties and definitional ambiguities involved in estimating the exergy efficiencies for comprehensive energy source-to-service chains or entire energy systems, and only few exergy efficiency estimates have been attempted to date. All estimates conclude that source-to-service exergy efficiencies are as low as a few percent.

Estimates of global and regional primary-to-service exergy efficiencies vary from 10 per cent to as low as a few percent. The large inefficiency of the system indicates that most services could be provided with considerably lower energy inputs than those represented by current practice. With the exception of the electricity source-to-service chain, the present energy systems exhibit lowest efficiencies at the interface between the traditional energy sector and the domain of energy services. In the case of electricity, the generating process provides the largest potential for efficiency improvement along the electricity source-to-service supply pathway. One should note, however, that electricity also has significant room for improvement at the useful-to-service interface.

Energy and environmental policy should encourage public and private sector investment towards the narrowing of this gap wherever this is techno-economically feasible, because more efficient provision of energy services not only reduces the amount of primary energy required but, in general, also reduces material requirements and emission releases to the environment.

Although efficiency is an important performance parameter influencing investment or purchase decisions, it is not the only one. Other, and often more important, issues include investments, operating costs, lifetime, peak power, ease of installation and operation, plus many other technical, economic, and convenience factors. For entire energy systems, further consideration must be given to regional resource endowments, conversion technologies, geography, information, time, prices, investment finance, operating costs, age of infrastructures, and know-how.

Not only is the energy system driven by service requirements, but the end-use technologies (e.g. the furnace linking final energy and useful energy) and infrastructures (e.g. building codes and insulation standards, which determine the share of useful space heating energy that becomes available for providing these energy services) constitute the system component with the largest potential for narrowing of the efficiency gap. As already mentioned, service technologies are intimately tied to settlement patterns, as well as to housing, transportation, and industrial production infrastructures. These infrastructures are as much responsible for the current inefficiency of the energy system as are the numerous energy conversion technologies associated with these infrastructures.

Structure of a Quasi Zero Pollution Energy System

The term "industrial ecology" reflects the concept of a network of interacting industrial processes that utilize each other's material and energy wastes and byproducts. Revised rules for the selection of technologies, products, and processes provide economic incentives that lead to superior efficiency and productivity in the supply of the goods and services demanded by our societies. Rather than functioning as incremental improvements and add-one, energy efficiency improvements and innovative energy technologies now complement the eco-restructuring process. The net result would be a significant decline in the energy intensity of economic production and consumption, the decarbonization of the energy system, and a drastic reduction in all energy-related GHG emissions. Eco-restructuring of the energy system means adopting industrial ecology features not only within the energy system (e.g. district energy) but also between the energy system and the commercial and industrial sectors.

An energy end-use system based primarily on non-fossil carbon currencies will differ greatly from the present system. Energy conversion efficiency improvements are a necessary but not sufficient prerequisite of the sustainable energy system. Equally important is the restructuring of those infrastructures intimately related to energy services. For example, building and settlement structures affect the quantities and types of service requirements as much as the technology performance of a furnace or vehicle. Although the restructuring of settlement and transportation infrastructures or industrial production processes falls outside the immediate domain of the energy system, these will certainly shape the evolving energy system.

Eco-restructuring of anthropogenic production and consumption in general and the development of sustainable energy systems, therefore, are difficult to pursue independently from each other. Because of this interdependence, the momentum for the eco-restructuring of the energy system must start from the level of energy service technologies and related infrastructures.

In the introduction, sustainable energy systems were defined as systems in which the fluxes to and from the system are coherent with nature's fluxes and do not perturb nature's equilibria. "Coherent" implies that the energy system must mimic nature's energy flows. Coherent in this context means that the energy system utilizes technologies that exploit what nature would "waste" in any case at rates consistent with the natural flows. Nature utilizes a symbiotic relationship between solar energy, hydrogen, oxygen, and carbon. The principal fuel of nature is hydrogen.

Hydrogen fuels the sun. The "technology" photosynthesis utilizes the sun's radiated energy to split water into hydrogen and oxygen and, together with the carbon dioxide extracted from the atmosphere, to produce carbohydrates. Then, hydrogen weakly bonded to carbon fuels biological organisms including man. The human body is made up of some 100 trillion cells, each of which contains tens of thousands of nanobial organisms that use hydrogen to produce nucleic acids and protein. Finally, hydrogen, oxygen, and carbon are emitted or rejected as a variety of differently composed molecules, with carbon, in particular, recycled as carbon dioxide and methane.

A sustainable energy system mimicking nature's approach to energy, therefore, should also be centred on this relationship between solar energy, hydrogen, oxygen, and carbon. Carbon in the deep future energy system would be recycled over time-spans consistent with the natural carbon cycle. In sustainably cultivated plantations, biomass would become the only carbon source in the system and would also serve the carbon sink. Biomass properly managed, e.g. the rate of timber harvesting and reforestation are in balance, is carbon neutral and would not contribute to an increase in atmospheric CO_2 concentrations. This would be coherent with nature's material fluxes.

Alternatively, solar energy technologies engineered by homo technicus to intercept sunlight could provide electric or thermal energy services. The energy of electromagnetic radiation from the sun reaching the earth's surface is in equilibrium with the energy radiated thermally back into space (in the form of infrared radiation). Because most energy services dissipate heat in the form of infrared radiation, this would be coherent with nature's energy fluxes. The main characteristic of the deep future energy system outlined below is to be inherently non-polluting based on highly efficient energy service technologies and sustainable energy sources. This in effect limits the choice of currencies, giving hydrogen an edge over carbon containing currencies.

The conversion of hydrogen into energy services or electricity produces virtually no pollution; the byproduct of electrochemical hydrogen conversion is water. In contrast, hydrogen combustion with air as the oxidant will also produce nitrogen oxide and nitric oxides. Although these pollutants can be effectively controlled by catalytic conversion technology, this represents an end-of-pipe clean-up approach. Likewise, carbon-containing currencies use ambient air as the oxidant and thus generate nitrogen compounds (in addition to carbon dioxide and carbon monoxide plus other emissions).

Moreover, the most efficient use of currencies containing non-fossil carbon involves a reforming step to hydrogen at the point of use. In essence, hydrogen is a universal currency. It can be produced from all energy sources, which, although not all would be non polluting, is of importance for the transition phase, and can meet virtually all energy services. Because a significant share of services require electricity, which, in many instances, can be delivered more efficiently without a hydrogen involvement, hydrogen in the deep future energy system would be complemented by a well-established currency-electricity.

Hydrogen and electricity complement each other as central components in the future energy system in the following ways:

1. Hydrogen can be stored in any quantity; electricity cannot (at least from current technology perspectives; this may change drastically with the eventual advent of high-temperature superconductivity).
2. Hydrogen can be a chemical or material feedstock; electricity cannot.
3. Electricity can process, transmit, and store information; hydrogen cannot.
4. Hydrogen and electricity can be readily converted to one another. These four compatibilities combine to provide excellent synergies between the two currencies. From these synergies it becomes obvious that hydrogen will be a strong candidate currency - in fact probably the candidate - that will substitute for oil-based liquid fuels in the longer term, while electricity will largely continue to do what it does today.

The outlook regarding the exact twenty-first-century energy sources from which the currencies hydrogen and electricity will be derived is less clear. Although the potential deep future options are known - nuclear power (fission and/or fusion), direct solar radiation (photovoltaics, central thermal solar conversion), and indirect solar energy (hydropower, wind, biomass, etc.), at present no single option is superior on all four compatibility constraints mentioned in the introduction.

The potential for nuclear energy to make a substantial contribution hinges upon the satisfaction of public concerns about operational safety, waste disposal, and proliferation.

Without this satisfaction, nuclear power could wither away and play only a transitory role. Moreover, current nuclear fission practice is not necessarily sustainable unless breeding technology is employed. Fusion may become an option by the mid-twenty-first century, but to date has not been shown to be technically feasible - the conditions for a self-sustaining net power production controlled by man have not yet been achieved.

Solar and related renewable technologies are rapidly approaching economic viability in many niche applications, and their future potential is, in principle, enormous. However, uncertainty exists with respect to economic performance, in part related to their low specific-energy densities and intermittent availability, although the utilization of renewable energy sources offers substantial emission benefits compared with the use of fossil sources. One point is likely: eventually, the selection from this source option menu will become a socio-political choice at the regional rather than at the global level.

The lack of certainty or determinism regarding sources, however, is not a vice. Because the shape of future civilization depends on the currencies providing energy services - and not on energy sources per se - today's burning issues surrounding energy sources are put into a different time and priority scale. This may appear counter-intuitive given the current socio-political controversy surrounding the present and future use of nuclear power. But the absence of complementary hydrogen end-use technologies would be a much greater barrier to the sustainable energy system than keeping open the question (and the options) as to its eventual sources.

Certainly, if solar and/or nuclear energy are to replace fossil fuels, hydrogen must become their strategic partner.

Unless solar and nuclear energy can be effectively stored and transported, they will not be able to displace fossil sources and currencies, especially in transportation. The palette is divided into two groups of energy services, one served by chemical fuels and the other served by electricity. Located at its periphery, the palette also contains two groups of energy source options: fossil sources and sustainable energy sources (labelled "new/ old hopes"). Fossil sources have unconstrained access to all services. This is not the case for the new/old hopes sources. Direct solar and most of the indirect solar options operate intermittently and are primarily locked into electricity generation.

In addition, their availability profile is often discordant with the daily electricity load. Some may argue that "new/ old hopes" sources can provide space heating services, or that biomass can be used as a feedstock for liquid fuel production. This is correct. But the relative importance of space heating is declining, and using biomass as the principal source for fuelling the global transportation service requirements of 10 billion people may be difficult to reconcile with sustainability, and may well be constrained by land availability. However, the utilization of solar and nuclear energies for hydrogen production via electrolysis, thermochemical water splitting, or biomass gasification and photolysis enables these non-fossil sources to supply all energy services, including transportation services.

Efficiency of Energy Service Technologies

Improvements in the efficiency of energy service technologies are likely to be needed to counterbalance a potential drawback of the sustainable energy system. Harvesting renewable or nuclear energy sources for hydrogen production inherently shifts inefficiencies to the upstream operation of the energy system. Nuclear technologies utilize either steam or gas cycles for electricity generation and their efficiencies are subject to the limitations of heat engines. Renewable energy sources are dispersed and of low specific-energy density, in terms of joules per square metre, with large conversion capacities necessary to compensate for these low concentration or density levels. With the exception of biomass, the efficiency of renewable technologies is mostly an issue of installed capacity and investment costs and less a question of the actual source-to-currency conversion ratio.

Still, efficiencies matter, especially when suitable siting locations, say for solar systems, become a constraint. Producing carbon-free currencies is less efficient and currently generally more costly than producing carbon-containing ones. However, the efficiency and cost disadvantages would improve substantially if energy service technologies designed to exploit the unique characteristics of hydrogen are used instead of adapting conversion equipment originally designed for hydrocarbon fuels.

Electrochemical and catalytic energy conversion have the potential to become the technologies of choice for the production of many energy services, especially in transportation and distributed combined heat and power applications. The most promising electrochemical technology is the fuel cell. Fuel cells convert hydrogen directly into electricity without first burning it, which enables them to realize much higher conversion efficiencies than heat engines. Compared with internal combustion engines, fuel cells are expected to be twice as efficient, thus compensating for the lower hydrogen delivery efficiencies.

Among the most important changes in energy technologies will be the decline of combustion technologies that close their fuel cycle of fossil carbon oxidation through the atmosphere. The remaining combustion processes will operate on either hydrogen, sustainable biomass, or biomass-derived hydrogenrich fuels. Of course, by the mid-twenty-first century numerous additional environmental technologies will have enriched the menu of technology options.

Carbon scrubbing and fossil-sourced hydrogen-rich fuel production may well eke out the fossil era. In any case, technological invention and innovation, in part stimulated by revised energy market prices that reflect their full social costs, will ensure a high degree of technology diversity. From the perspective of sustainable energy systems and eco-restructuring, the coming of the hydrogen age seems inevitable. However, as the twentieth century draws to a close, the energy system is in the middle of the fossil era and its end is not apparently in sight.

Transition of Energy System

The historical development of global primary energy production and use has essentially been a sequence of technology replacements. sources and infrastructures (embodied technologies) are intimately interrelated and the degree of use of any energy source is also a mirror of both upstream and downstream technology. Energy infrastructures have inherently long lifetimes of several decades and more. To obtain a better understanding of the rate at which the energy system can evolve, it is necessary to take a long term quantitative perspective spanning a century or more both backward and forward in time. On a market share basis, wood, once the dominant primary fuel, was replaced by coal. Then coal was replaced by oil.

Today, natural gas is seriously cutting into oil's market leadership, and nuclear power is rising rapidly. These transitions have occurred despite the fact that resources of wood, coal, and oil were and are still plentiful. Today, well over a century after wood lost its pre-eminence, the world's annual biomass production exceeds the needs to fuel the world many-fold. Likewise, coal was displaced by oil not because the world was running out of coal - the conventional view is that coal is by far the world's most abundant fossil resource.

Wood was abandoned because the first industrial revolution demanded a fuel with higher energy density and better transport and storage possibilities. Simultaneously, on the supply side, coal-mining and coal-use technology, notably the steam engine, developed to a point at which coal became a readily available energy source. Similarly, oil displaced coal once a set of new and superior technologies both upstream and downstream were made available. Refined oil products proved superior to coal for powering trains, cars, and aircraft, generating electricity, heating homes and large buildings, etc. Except for aircraft, all these end-use applications can be, and initially were, served by coal. Refined oil products, however, are much better suited for these purposes (energy services), so that societies progressively abandoned coal for oil. The historical inter-source substitutions were caused by innovation and technical change and not by global resource scarcity. Fossil energy resource availability is unlikely to be the driver for future shifts either; rather, the fact that fossil resources are plentiful and inexpensive is likely to be a delaying factor in the transition towards sustainable sources.

The cumulative carbon content of identified and inferred conventional oil, natural gas, and coal occurrences has been estimated to exceed 20,000 gigatonnes (Gt) of carbon. The application of a dynamic resource concept that accounts for long run technical change in the exploration for, and extraction of, fossil sources shows a global fossil availability of some 3,000 Gt of carbon, which can be produced for less than US$30 per barrel of oil equivalent. To put this resource volume into perspective: the cumulative use of carbon by mankind to date amounts to some 230 Gt. If 200300 Gt of carbon emissions give reason for severe concern about climate stability, it is obvious that most of the indicated 3,000 Gt of carbon will have to remain untapped in the ground.

Natural gas resources are plentiful and accessible by all the major economic centres worldwide. Natural gas is an established energy source with basically no public acceptance problem. Because natural gas is by far the cleanest fossil energy source, it is increasingly being touted as the fuel of least environmental resistance. As regards the build-up of greenhouse gases in the atmosphere, natural gas represents the ideal hedging strategy. It automatically reduces CO_2 emissions (versus other fossil fuels) and thus buys time for sustainable energy sources and technologies to mature.

The CO_2 benefits of natural gas, however, may not accrue if its enhanced use is accompanied by an increase in methane (CH_4) emissions. Methane, the chief component of natural gas, is itself a greenhouse gas, with a greenhouse forcing potential per molecule up to two orders of magnitude larger than CO_2 depending on the time-horizon and the decay response of the underlying carbon model. IPCC reports a 56 times higher warming potential for methane over a 20-year time-horizon and 6.5 times over a period of 500 years. Leakages from extraction, transmission, and distribution systems, as well as from end-use devices, therefore, need to be curbed substantially from present practice in order not to undermine the CO_2 gains.

The dynamics of the energy source substitution model suggest that the fossil era will extend far into the twenty-first century - that a deep future hydrogen age will be preceded by a "methane age". In fact, natural gas is the ideal bridge towards hydrogen for two reasons. First, a global market share of 50 per cent or more requires natural gas to expand into other than the traditional residential, commercial, and industrial markets. Electricity generation is certainly the market offering the largest opportunity for expansion in the short run. On a global scale, however, the electricity generation market is unlikely to be large enough to lift the gas market share to the level suggested by the substitution model. If gas is to achieve a 50+ per cent market share, natural gas would have to become a major source of transportation fuels.

Today, natural gas already contributes to transportation fuel supply in three ways: as a feedstock in oil refining to improve the premium yield of the barrel; as a feedstock for upgrading heavy hydrocarbon sources such as oil sand bitumen; and directly as a vehicle fuel in the form of compressed natural gas (CNG). In absolute terms, however, the present market share in transportation is negligible.

The large-scale use of natural gas as a direct transportation fuel will foster fundamental and far-reaching infrastructure changes that eventually would assist the hydrogen age. The path-breaking function of natural gas is the second reason the methane age is essential to a future hydrogen age. Both natural gas and hydrogen are gaseous currencies at ambient conditions. A natural gas market share of 50 per cent or more would advance gas-handling infrastructures and technologies. Innovative liquefaction technologies and cryogenic storage of liquefied natural gas (LNG) would become commonplace. Moreover, because the methane age may have a life cycle of 40-60 years, societies would have sufficient time to familiarize themselves with gaseous and cryogenic fuels. All these events would ease the large-scale introduction of hydrogen, especially with fuel cells being a key energy service technology. Finally, during the century-long transition phase towards a non-fossil energy system, natural gas is likely to become the predominant source for hydrogen production.

A 40-60-year methane window would also provide sufficient time for non-fossil technologies currently lacking economic feasibility to move down the technology learning curve and become commercially viable. For nuclear power, this time-horizon should suffice for the nuclear industry to develop and demonstrate new, possibly smaller scale reactor designs incorporating "inherently safe" and "walk away" features as well as efficient fuel cycles and waste disposal solutions. Also, fusion may become a viable option by the mid-twenty-first century.

Other technology developments that enable the continued use of fossil sources even in a future of severely constrained greenhouse gas emissions may have advanced and their environmental implications become better understood. For example, although the technology to capture CO_2 after combustion is available, it is unclear whether the present storage and/or disposal options are environmentally acceptable or the capacities are large enough for long-term CO_2 disposal. Although the storage potential in oceans is estimated to be in excess of 1,200 Gt of carbon, not much is known about potential adverse environmental effects 8 or the actual ocean's CO_2 retention time. Offsetting CO_2 emissions through reforestation and forest management (carbon sequestration) is likely to be one of the least cost mitigation options. The carbon captured from the atmosphere and fixed during the growth of forest, however, would have to be stored for a long time, and land availability may eventually limit the extent of carbon sequestration.

De-materialization and Decarbonization

De-materialization is a major cornerstone of the global economic eco-restructuring process. Within the energy system, decarbonization can be viewed as analogous to de-materialization. De-materialization implies a shift in emphasis from quantity to quality, from inefficiency to efficiency. Decarbonization of the energy system implies a shift in initiatives from energy supply to quality energy services. Despite the exponential growth of energy-related carbon dioxide emissions since the early days of the industrial revolution, the energy system, in terms of carbon per unit of primary energy use, has been decarbonized at an average rate of 0.2 per cent per year.

The carbon-to-hydrogen (C/H) ratio declined steadily between 1920 and 1975, a trend that slowed down after the mid-1970s as a result of energy policy in many OECD countries. The oil price shocks of the 1970s and early 1980s were perceived as signs of oil and natural gas resource depletion. As a consequence, energy policy banned oil and natural gas from electricity generation and endorsed the use of coal as a secure and inexpensive under-boiler fuel in industry and electricity generation. Decarbonization of the energy system is likely to continue as natural gas, chiefly methane (CH_4), nuclear, and renewable energy sources take on a growing share in global energy supplies. In a methane age, with global primary energy supply dominated by natural gas, the C/H ratio would approach 0.25. Yet, given an expected world population of 10 billion people by 2050 and a corresponding increase in energy service demand, a C/H ratio of 0.25 may well be insufficient for the long-term target of stabilizing atmospheric greenhouse gas concentrations. Any reduction in carbon intensity well beyond a value of 0.25 requires non-fossil energy sources - nuclear power (fission and/or fusion), direct solar radiation (photovoltaics, central thermal solar conversion), and indirect solar energy (hydropower, wind, biomass, etc.).

Sustainable Energy Systems

The globalization of environmental deterioration is the direct consequence of population growth and industrialization. In 1990, some 23 per cent of the world population living in industrialized countries were responsible for some 80 per cent of GHG emissions. Future demographic developments will likely push global population close to 10 billion people by the year 2050. Clearly, with 96 per cent of the incremental population growth taking place in the developing countries, the historical link between population, industrialization, and environmental degradation must be decoupled. Yet, present per capita income and per capita energy use in the developing world are about one-tenth of the respective values for the OECD.

In the light of the disparities, we must ask how the deep future energy system fits the realities of the developing countries. No doubt, at face value the sheer capital intensiveness of the sustainable energy system, in addition to the capital resources needed for the industrialization process, will far exceed their economic capability. In the past, environmental degradation has been a steady companion of industrialization and urbanization.

At a certain level of prosperity and income, however, societies appear to express a preference for environmental amenities. This preference manifests itself as an internalization of external costs. Clean air acts, mandatory zero emission vehicles, or legislated flue gas desulphurization of coal-fired power stations are representative historical examples of the emergence of environmental awareness in the developed world. To a certain extent the industrialized societies have begun to pay a small part of the interest on the mortgaged environment used to establish their wealth. Most of the interest, not to mention the principal, is still owed.

The industrialized world may well have harvested the benefits of the environment to the point of rapidly decreasing returns. It would add insult to injury for the rich North to withdraw to a position where the developing countries are expected to forgo the benefits of industrialization so that the North can live an enjoyable life in a clean world that the South cannot afford. For sure the South will not consider the preservation of the North's wealth at the expense of their own development as equitable burden sharing. Still, there is growing concern about a potential conflict between economic advance in the developing countries and the protection of the environment. The industrialized and developing countries are faced with the following dilemma.

Successful business-as-usual industrialization will take its toll on the environment. Compounded by the anticipated population growth, even small per capita income improvements may soon put the South on a par with the North, in terms of GHG emissions. However, lack of economic growth and development translate into increased poverty and population growth, which in turn lead to accelerated environmental deterioration through deforestation, soil erosion, and groundwater degradation. Moreover, agriculture-based economies may be more vulnerable to climatic hazards than industrialized economies where agriculture accounts for less than 3 per cent of gross domestic product (GDP) and the bulk of production is little affected by climate conditions.

Is a clean environment a matter of affordability? The answer is yes. Thus, economic development of the South is a necessary prerequisite for global environmental stability. Sustainable energy system development in the developing countries, therefore, is likely to depend on international action such as science and technology transfer. The costs of this transfer should, to the extent it is benefiting the protection of the atmosphere, be borne by the North. It can be said that the North's environment mortgage has matured and the principal including the accrued interest is now due for redemption.

Ideally, this repayment would be financed from the revenue generated by the monetary incentives, green taxes, or other mechanisms deemed suitable for correcting the present market imperfection of free use of the environment. Consequently, the concept of an internalization of external costs that is neutral in terms of tax revenue would have to be abandoned in favour of a capital transfer to the developing countries. Economic potency demands that the North initiate the transition to the deep future energy system. From the perspective of system evolution, the initial step is under way already - the increasing role of natural gas in meeting global energy service requirements. The redemption of the North's environment mortgage will assist the South in the development of sustainable energy systems. In addition, the combating of global environment degradation may lead to the recognition that a dollar spent in the South may generate higher marginal environmental returns than one spent in the North.

Challenge of Stabilizing the Atmosphere

Since the pre-industrial era, the concentration of CO_2 in the atmosphere has increased from 280 parts per million (ppm) to 350 ppm, mainly as a result of the burning of fossil fuels. The consequences of the ongoing build-up are troubling though uncertain. Stabilizing the atmosphere at less than a doubling of the atmospheric concentration of CO_2 would require radical change in global energy technology. According to the Intergovernmental Panel on Climate Change (IPCC), stabilizing the atmospheric concentration of CO_2 at 450 ppm would require that cumulative emissions over the period 1990-2100 be no more than 630-650 GtC, corresponding to an average emission rate of 5.7-5.9 GtC/year. For comparison the mean estimate of actual emissions in 1990 is 7.4 GtC (of which 6.0 GtC was due to fossil fuel burning).

Recent advances relating to the prospects for renewable electric power-generating technologies - especially wind, photovoltaic, solar thermal electric, and biomass power technologies - have led various groups to be optimistic about the prospects for curbing emissions from the electric power sector over a period of many decades. Although this new outlook for renewable electric technologies is auspicious, successful development of a wide range of renewable electric technologies by itself would not make it possible to stabilize the atmosphere at near current levels, because most CO_2 emissions are from non-electric sources. The major greenhouse challenge will be to avoid enormous increases in CO_2 emissions arising from the production of synthetic fuels from coal. In the IS92a scenario, synthetic fluids account for 75 per cent of all liquid and gaseous fuels used in 2100, and the amount of coal used for synthetic liquid and gaseous fuels production then is 4.2 times the total amount of coal use in 1990.

Synthetic fuels can be produced from non-fossil fuel sources. The prospect that low-cost photovoltaic (PV) power systems could become available with amorphous silicon and/or other thin-film PV technologies led in the late 1980s to a detailed technical/economic analysis painting a picture of a world energy economy in which PV technology would be widely used not only to provide electricity that is used directly but also to provide hydrogen derived electrolytically from this electricity, for transport and various stationary markets.

The growing of biomass for use with modern energy conversion technologies, either in large plantations or on many small energy farms, has been identified as an attractive climate friendly energy strategy that simultaneously could provide an energy base for rural industrialization and employment generation in the developing world and make it possible to phase out agricultural subsidies in the industrialized world. Although it is inherently easier to grow biomass for energy in environmentally acceptable ways than is the case for food production, various groups are sceptical that biomass can be produced for energy at large scales in environmentally acceptable ways.

Flue gas decarbonization vs. fuel gas decarbonization

A technically feasible but costly option for achieving deep reductions in greenhouse gas emissions is to extract the CO_2 from flue gases of large fossil fuel combustors (e.g. at fossil fuel power plants) and to isolate the CO_2 so recovered from the atmosphere. This "flue gas decarbonization" strategy is costly largely because of the expenses associated with separation of the CO_2 from flue gases (in which the concentration of CO_2 is only 8-15 per cent); once the CO_2 is separated out, the incremental cost of isolating the recovered CO_2 from the atmosphere can often be relatively modest.

A much more promising approach involves fuel decarbonization: the production of hydrogen or a hydrogen-rich fuel from a carbon rich fuel, in the process of which a stream of essentially pure CO_2 is separated as a byproduct at low incremental cost - a process that might more appropriately be labelled "fuel gas decarbonization". Although the cost penalty for fuel decarbonization and sequestration of the separated CO_2 with this approach is far less than that for various flue gas decarbonization schemes, the electricity produced this way would nevertheless be about 30 per cent more costly than with a conventional coal integrated gasifier/combined cycle power plant, simply because there are no direct economic benefits (only environmental benefits) arising from fuel gas decarbonization.

Because the production of hydrogen is inherently costly, it is desirable to use it in conversion equipment where it is worth more than conventional fluid fuels-especially because there is little prospect that the prices of conventional hydrocarbon fuels will rise high enough in the foreseeable future to the point where hydrogen will be able to compete on a \$-per-GJ-equivalent basis. The true value of hydrogen should be determined not by a comparison of fuel costs but by a comparison of the costs of providing an energy service such as the cost per vehicle km of travel. The use of hydrogen in low-temperature fuel cells for transport and distributed combined heat and power applications could provide the needed high value. Fuel cells offer high thermodynamic efficiency and zero or near zero local pollutant emissions without the need for pollution control equipment. Moreover, for combined heat and power applications, the absence of scale economies for production units, the lack of need for operating personnel, low maintenance requirements, and low noise levels make it possible to site low-temperature fuel cells near users where the produced energy is more valuable than at centralized facilities.

Until recently it has not been practical to take advantage of these attributes. The only commercial fuel cell is the phosphoric acid fuel cell. Its power density is too low for it to be considered for automotive applications, and its prospective costs in mass production are not especially low. However, recent advances relating to the proton exchange-membrane (PEM) fuel cell indicate a hopeful future for this technology for both distributed combined heat and power and transport applications.

When mass produced for transport applications, its costs could be low, approaching the costs of internal combustion engines. Low-temperature PEM fuel cells can very efficiently utilize hydrogen or methanol that is reformed with steam to produce a gaseous H_2/CO_2 mixture onsite or, in transport applications, onboard the vehicle. Such fuels have good prospects for becoming major energy carriers in the "post-combustion" era, when electrochemically based fuel cells will have become well established in the energy economy. The least costly ways of producing these energy carriers are from chemical fuel feed stock's - initially natural gas and later coal and biomass.

Whereas the alchemists failed in their attempts to transmute base metals into gold, the technology for making hydrogen from carbon is well established. Specifically, a carbon-rich fuel feedstock can be processed to produce hydrogen or methanol (a hydrogen carrier) by first converting the feedstock into "syugas" (a mixture of CO and H_2) via steam re-forming (in the case of natural gas) or via thermochemical gasification (in the case of coal or biomass) and then shifting the energy contained in the CO to H_2 by reacting the CO with steam - a process requiring very little net energy input. If there were no greenhouse problem, this stream of pure CO_2 would be vented to the atmosphere. In a greenhouse-constrained world, consideration might be given to isolating this CO_2 from the atmosphere because of the large potential and relatively low costs involved. If this stream of separated CO_2 could be stored in isolation from the atmosphere, CO_2 emissions would be sharply reduced.

CO_2 emissions - Without and with CO_2 Sequestration

Without sequestration of the separated CO_2 there would be no significant reduction in lifecycle CO_2 emissions per GJ of fuel provided, in shifting from reformulated gasoline to methanol or hydrogen derived from natural gas; moreover, lifecycle emissions would roughly double in shifting from reformulated gasoline to methanol or hydrogen derived from coal. The only options based on the thermochemical conversion of fuels that offer significant greenhouse benefits without sequestration of the separated CO_2 are methanol and hydrogen derived from biomass that is grown on a sustainable basis; in these instances lifecycle emissions are just 5 and 10 per cent of those for reformulated gasoline. With sequestering, the balances are sharply changed. Lifecycle emissions for methanol produced from coal would be no more than for gasoline or for methanol produced from natural gas, while life cycle emissions for hydrogen produced from either natural gas or coal with sequestering would be only about half of the emissions from gasoline.

In the case of biomass grown on a sustainable basis, net lifecycle emissions with sequestering would be strongly negative (because the carbon in the plant matter was originally extracted from the atmosphere in photosynthesis) and, absolutely, more than twice as large for hydrogen production10 as for methanol production. This characteristic of systems that involve the production of hydrogen-rich fuels from biomass with sequestering of the separated CO_2 makes it possible to achieve deep net reductions in global greenhouse gas emissions even if some countries are unable to achieve deep reductions or choose to ignore the greenhouse problem. If the end-use technology is taken into account, the emissions reduction potential with sequestration can be even more dramatic.

Consider lifecycle emissions, measured in gr C per km of vehicular travel, for fuels used in fuel cell vehicles (FCVs) compared with emissions for gasoline internal combustion engine vehicles (ICEVs). Operated on gasoline, methanol, and compressed hydrogen, FCVs are expected to be, respectively, 1.8, 2.4, and 2.8 times as energy efficient as comparable gasoline ICEVs.

As a result, lifecycle emissions per km of travel for FCVs operated on methanol derived from coal with CO_2 sequestering are only two-fifths as large as for gasoline ICEVs. For FCVs operated on hydrogen derived from natural gas or coal with CO_2 sequestering, emissions per km are less than one-fifth of those for gasoline ICEVs and one-third of those for gasoline FCVs.

Options for sequestering CO_2

The most-discussed option for CO_2 disposal has been piping CO_2 to depths greater than 3 km in deep ocean basins. So doing would eliminate the rapid transient build-up of CO_2 in the atmosphere and delay equilibration with the atmosphere by several hundred years; resulting interactions with calcite-rich sediments would probably reduce the long-term (> 2000-year) atmospheric concentration by a significant amount (~50 per cent).

But many questions remain about the dynamics of the processes involved, and many environmental issues have been raised - including concerns about the effects on ocean life of pH change from CO_2 injection, and the impacts on benthic organisms and ecosystems as hydrate particles are deposited on the ocean floor. Much more research is needed on such issues before deep ocean disposal can be pursued with confidence that the environmental risks are acceptable.

Among other options, disposal in depleted natural gas and oil fields stands out as being especially secure, as long as the original reservoir pressures are not exceeded, and potentially low in cost. The global sequestering capacity associated with past production, proved reserves, plus estimated undiscovered resources is estimated to be 410 GtC for natural gas fields and 105 GtC for oil fields. For comparison, global CO_2 emissions from fossil fuel burning totalled 6.0 GtC in 1990.

The capacity of natural gas fields to sequester carbon at the original reservoir pressure is generally greater than the carbon content of the original natural gas and depends on the depth of the reservoir, the geothermal gradient, and the pressure gradient. Hendriks has shown that, for typical gradients, the ratio of carbon in CO_2 to that in the original natural gas is 3.0, 1.8, and 1.4 for depths of 1, 2, and 3 km, respectively, and that worldwide, on average, about twice as much carbon can be stored (as CO_2) in depleted reservoirs as was in the original natural gas. If a hydrogen production facility could be sited near a depleted natural gas field the costs of long-distance pipeline transport of CO_2 could be avoided. Moreover, the cost of injection into the reservoir could be offset to some extent by recovery of additional natural gas.

When primary production of natural gas at a reservoir ceases, it is not because the contained natural gas has been exhausted but rather because the reservoir pressure falls below a certain level (typically of the order of 30 bar) at which it is no longer economic to continue pumping out natural gas. But with CO_2 injection, the reservoir is depressurized, so that enhanced natural gas recovery is possible. Because of the order of 80 per cent of the natural gas in place is recovered in primary production, the amount of additional natural gas that can be produced is not large - but the enhanced production could pay for part of the incremental costs of CO_2 storage.

There would be considerable capacity in depleted natural gas fields for sequestering CO_2 recovered from decarbonizing fuels other than natural gas. For example, when hydrogen is produced from natural gas, the CO_2 recovery rate -10.7 kg C/GJ of produced hydrogen or 9.0 kg C/GJ of the natural gas from which it is derived (assuming all energy inputs are provided by natural gas) - is equivalent to just two-thirds of the carbon in the original natural gas (13.5 kg C/GJ).

Since, on average, the CO_2 sequestering capacity is equivalent to about twice the carbon contained in the original natural gas, the production of hydrogen from natural gas would thus leave about two thirds of the sequestering capacity available for CO_2 derived from other sources. In addition, the sequestering capacity associated with past natural gas production and future production that will not be associated with the manufacture of hydrogen and the sequestering of the separated CO_2 would be available.

The limitation on strategies for CO_2 sequestration in depleted natural gas and oil fields is their limited geographical availability. This should not be a significant constraint on hydrogen manufactured from fuel conversion facilities sited near the natural gas fields, because the produced hydrogen could be distributed long distances via pipeline at acceptable costs, serving markets just as natural gas pipelines do today. However, it would be desirable to have sequestering options that are more widely available as well.

The most widely distributed reservoirs for potential sequestering of CO_2 are saline aquifers located deep below the earth's surface underlying most of the area of sedimentary basins throughout the world. The areal extent of these basins is equivalent to nearly half of the land area of the inhabited continents.

Aquifers are porous underground beds, consisting mainly of sand, that are permeable to the flow of fluids. The pore spaces are usually filled with water and, occasionally, with petroleum or natural gas as well. In order to be able to store the CO_2 at high supercritical fluid densities, only aquifers deeper than 750 metres are considered as potential storage reservoirs for CO_2. Aquifers containing fresh water are normally found at much shallower depths. If CO_2 were stored at a depth of 750 metres or deeper, it would generally take 2,000 years or more to reach a freshwater reservoir, and even then it will probably reach the freshwater reservoir in low concentrations; the main effect of the CO_2 that would enter the freshwater reservoir would be to increase the hardness of the water, because carbonates will dissolve.

Hendriks has estimated the CO_2 storage capacity of such aquifers under the assumption that the injected CO_2 displaces water. He has made alternative estimates that depend on the extent to which structural traps are needed for secure storage. Without a structural trap, the injected CO_2 might eventually migrate from the injection site to other subterranean sites where storage is not desirable or even to where it can escape to the atmosphere. If structural traps are not needed, the estimated worldwide sequestering capacity of aquifers is about 15,000 GtC; if structural traps are necessary, the sequestering capacity is 60 GtC.

A recent multinational, multi-institutional study carried out for the European Commission concluded that structural traps might not be necessary to achieve a reasonably high degree of confidence in the security of aquifer storage, if the CO_2 is injected far enough from the aquifer boundary that it is predicted not to reach the boundary.

It estimated that the underground CO_2 storage potential for the European Union plus Norway is more than 200 GtC - equivalent to 250 years of total CO_2 emissions for all of OECD Europe; most of this storage capacity is in aquifers under the North Sea. The study pointed out, however, that, to ensure adequate storage security in large aquifers, large amounts of data would be needed regarding reservoir integrity.

Cost analysis for CO_2 sequestration

The costs of alternative options for hydrogen production and use/ CO_2 disposal are estimated here for hydrogen produced from natural gas, coal, and biomass, with a focus on automotive applications of the produced hydrogen. Storage of CO_2 in both depleted natural gas fields and saline aquifers is considered. Various hydrogen production/ CO_2 disposal scenarios are investigated. Costs are estimated for hydrogen production, for delivering hydrogen to users, and for using hydrogen. The estimated costs for CO_2 sequestration include the costs for drying and compressing the CO_2 to the pressures required for CO_2 transport and injection,13 the costs of pipelines for transporting the CO_2 to the sequestering sites, and the costs for wells and surface facilities at the storage sites.

For hydrogen production from natural gas with sequestration, it is assumed that the hydrogen plant is sited at a depleted natural gas field, in which the recovered CO_2 is sequestered, thereby avoiding long-distance CO_2 transport costs.

Credit is taken for the modest increase in natural gas production that results from depressurization of the natural gas reservoir. It is assumed that: (i) as in the analysis of Blok et al., the increased natural gas production would contribute between 3.5 and 8.5 per cent of the natural gas feedstock requirements for the hydrogen production plant; (ii) increased production takes place after 20 years of primary production; (iii) after 15 years of CO_2 injection there is no more increased production; and (iv) the benefits of increased production accrue to producers of hydrogen from natural gas for the situation where conversion plants are located near the disposal site.

Because natural gas field disposal sites are geographically limited, it is assumed for the base case scenarios that in order to reach typical final consumers the produced hydrogen is transported 1,000 km further than is required for hydrogen that might be produced from coal or biomass at sites other than at depleted natural gas fields. To take advantage of the scale economies of pipeline transport of hydrogen, it is assumed for the base case scenarios that the outputs of five large production plants (each having a production capacity of 19.1 PJ of hydrogen per year are combined for hydrogen transport in a single 1,000 km pipeline.

Costs for hydrogen from natural gas with sequestration are compared with costs for two alternative configurations for making hydrogen from natural gas without sequestration: one in which hydrogen is produced near the natural gas field and piped to distant markets; and another in which natural gas is piped to a hydrogen production facility near these distant markets. Siting the facility for producing hydrogen from natural gas near hydrogen markets for one of the cases without sequestration is included because pipeline transport is less costly for natural gas than for hydrogen.

8

Sectoral Approach to Economic Balance

Over the past few decades the globalization of the world's societies has become a physical reality and one that has relatively quickly become apparent to the general public. The two principal reasons for globalization are attributable to technological advances. Through modern telecommunications, people in all but the most remote locations are exposed instantaneously to the world's crisis situations and familiarized with the day-to-day realities in far-away places; and modern transportation has made it possible to travel, and to trade and shift investments, among distant locations more quickly and more extensively than ever before. The other major stimulus to global thinking was the ability to view the whole planet from space and to measure and anticipate the possible effects of human activities not only on the water, the soil, and the minerals buried in it but especially on the quintessential global commons, the atmosphere. The desire to "save the planet" reflects a concern that is not just environmental but specifically global.

Eco-restructuring is an attempt to promote social well-being by designing and implementing technologies in a way that disrupts the bio-geochemical systems of the planet as little as possible. Eco-restructuring is undoubtedly influencing the design considerations and the content of engineering for the twenty-first century, but it is not yet evident what forms this influence will take and how extensive the changes will be.

Economics provides a powerful conceptual framework for describing the world system in terms of the interdependence of human activities and decisions. An economic modelling framework can be used to analyse and evaluate alternative, more or less detailed stories - or scenarios - about the future, based, in part, on alternative initiatives that originate in eco-restructuring. A framework capable of playing this role needs to go beyond the concepts of equilibrium and marginal changes that still dominate economists' thinking and practices today. The framework needs to be guided by a broad conception of economic theory that describes the material structure, as well as the social structure, of the global economy. Scenarios need to be capable of reflecting substantive policy options related to major potential structural changes, and the challenges related to them. The overall structure has to be sufficiently integrated to capture the inter dependencies that characterize this complex and dynamically changing system.

Economic Growth

The basic political and economic objective of the modern liberal state is to achieve increased prosperity through economic growth, which in turn is pursued through improvements in efficiency, new technology, and free trade. This outlook has prevailed in the two centuries since the industrial revolution, a period that has experienced accelerated growth of both population and material well-being. With the fall of communism, economic liberalization is virtually unopposed as a global political and economic philosophy. However, as population growth levels off, at least in the affluent societies, it is timely to consider the prospect for a levelling off of economic growth as well and new global agreements and institutions that govern the operation of more or less self-regulating markets.

Economists distinguish three categories of factor inputs needed for the production of goods and services: capital, labour, and land, where "land" is interpreted as shorthand for all categories of inputs from the natural world. For an economy operating with a given set of technologies, growth in the delivery of goods and services to final users requires more factor inputs. Clearly, population growth can generate economic growth with the simple replication of existing methods and a larger labour force, as well as more land and other inputs. Of course, on a per capita basis, consumption might not increase.

Malthus's concern about running out of land and food was at least temporarily put to rest by the enormous increases in yields resulting from new technology. "Artificial manure" proved remarkably successful in assuring "big and ever increasing harvests lasting eternally". Such confidence in unlimited increases in prosperity already sound dated, however. There is surely the possibility of continued advances and even dramatic breakthroughs in our ingenuity for wresting a living from nature. But there is also precedent for the collapse of entire ecosystems. In the analysis of actual activities, economists in the twentieth century have focused their investigation of growth almost exclusively on changing inputs of capital and labour both in theoretical discussion and in the "production functions" chosen for most empirical analysis.

This emphasis is largely explained by the fact that the extraction of primary materials in agriculture and mining utilizes a very small portion of the labour force in the rich, industrialized economies that have been taken as the model for development, and air and water were considered free of charge.

However, demographic and environmental pressures are already shifting the attention of economists to the third factor of production, natural resources. Its operational definition will require attention to the distinctions among the individual energy raw materials that are neither renewable nor recyclable; the numerous mineral resources that are potentially recyclable; and water and soils of different qualities.

The different categories of pollution and environmental degradation that are delivered back to the natural world also need to be accounted for as factors of production; they can be viewed as "negative inputs." Although capital and labour obviously cannot be ignored, the primary materials that increasingly occupy economists are also the inputs at the centre of attention in eco-restructuring.

A major reason for the developing countries taking on a new importance in the world economy is that they will continue to be the locus for virtually all population growth over the twenty-first century and therefore offer the easiest targets for the expansion of both production and consumption. The affluent societies can increase per capita consumption further through employing higher-quality factor inputs; the most practical avenue to exploit this option is through the upgrading of the skills and satisfaction of the labour force.

New technologies can promote growth by enhancing the "productivity" of factor inputs; but they invariably involve not only a decrease in factor quantities per unit of output but also a change in the quality or at least the mix of inputs. Some consequences include the generation of novel wastes - such as chlorine containing compounds.

However, the opportunities for actually implementing new technologies are limited when they are applied to the upgrading of capacity that is already in place (in the industrialized countries) rather than the construction of entirely new facilities to expand capacity (in the developing countries). individuals or firms in the rich countries may be able to generate more profit, if they are free to do so, by supplying the requirements of other countries with faster-growing populations rather than by investing in incremental improvements in production for domestic markets.

The size of the population may level off in the developing countries too in the course of the twenty-first century. With less political pressure continually to "create jobs" for increasing numbers of labour force entrants, concerns about depleting resources or degrading the physical environment could lead to a shift in emphasis from growth to improvements in the quality of life. For the medium term, however, the asymmetry in population dynamics between the rich and poor countries will strongly influence the nature of their interactions.

Environmental Pressures for Global Economic Change

Darwin's identification of competition as the mechanism for natural selection was influenced by the ideas of Malthus. The mutual reinforcement of the dominant role assigned to competition as the mechanism for change in both the biological and economic world views assured its fundamental role in Western thinking over the past century. It is significant that at the present time this view is being substantially moderated in our understanding of both the natural and the social spheres, as these reinforcing changes in perspective will be more influential than either one could be alone. Increasing numbers of contemporary biologists are subscribing to Margulis's view that accommodation through symbiosis is a major mechanism for evolutionary change: life "did not take over the world by combat but by networking". The parallels are striking with the emergence of the global economy.

The global economy is emerging at a time of great transformation as the ideological confrontation of East and West is replaced by economic conflict and negotiation (largely over trade and aid) between North and South. The countries in transition to a market economy are aiming to join the ranks of the developed economies over the next several decades as Europe - Central and Eastern, as well as Western - proceeds toward increasing unification along various dimensions. Regional economic blocs, based initially on trade and investment agreements, are also developing in America, in Asia, and among the Pacific Rim countries. The international competition associated with laissez-faire capitalism is if anything more fierce than ever. At the same time, it is undeniably operating within a context of long-term regional integration and emerging global institutional arrangements and constraints.

Environmental concerns about the "global commons" will strongly reinforce other pressures toward global dialogue and negotiation. Only a small number of environmental disputes has so far been brought to court within the international trade community, but it is already clear that these conflicts raise questions far more complex than what conventional trade law can readily resolve.

In anticipation of the avalanche of cases to come, the Secretariat of the General Agreement on Tariffs and Trade (GATT) was led to call for discussions about multilateral consensus on environmental objectives in the hopes of bypassing bilateral, case-by-case haggling in instances where new environmental concerns conflict with the older objective of removing barriers to trade to promote growth independently of any other considerations. The tuna and dolphin dispute between the United States and Mexico or the Danish bottle law and the reaction to it in Europe are two early examples. In surprisingly blunt language, the GATT Secretariat stated that it is "no longer possible for a country to create an appropriate environmental policy entirely on its own".

Environmental concerns (coupled with the attempt to protect domestic producers) are leading countries to erect barriers to trade based on the production process and not just on the characteristics of the traded product. These pressures to provide a product produced using a particular technology are a potent force for the further globalization of technology. There is already a tendency to adopt modern technologies in new manufacturing sectors in developing countries, especially in foreign-owned factories. But the pressures for international use of common techniques are likely to spread beyond manufacturing into areas that have until now been largely shielded from globalization by cultural differences.

For example, trade-related requirements about the use of recycled materials affect people's lifestyles because recycling involves common procedures to be followed by individuals in their capacities as citizens and consumers;

likewise, legislation governing water pollution is bound to be similar in different societies because it will need to promote compliance with common process specifications. Other pressures toward uniform social practices can also be observed. One example is a universal concept of human rights; another is the state's assumption of responsibility for social welfare, which today absorbs roughly similar proportions of national income in the rich economies and in the formerly socialist economies but is virtually non-existent in most developing countries.

Challenge for Eco-restructuring

Much of the primary material that passes through the economic system, from automobiles to packaging or sewage pipes, ends up sooner or later as solid waste. There are several emerging rules of thumb for solid waste management: use less material in the first place (i.e. source reduction), re-use products or at least recycle materials to the extent that is practical, and dispose of remaining wastes in a manner that is environmentally benign. It is often necessary to reconceived product design and manufacturing to facilitate recycling, for example by preferring a single material to composites. It is clear that practices in several countries, which have already begun to move in these directions, will spread in the twenty-first century. But these prescriptions are far more complicated than they appear because there are many different ways of proceeding, all of which have different consequences that affect not only a single sector but many parts of an economy.

We can expect a relatively rapid globalization of those solutions that appear to be successful. Then, for better or worse, there will tend to be a "lock-in" on a global scale to these solutions, which will make it hard to replace them by superior ones for many decades to come. One of the obstacles to the effective recycling of any material is the difficulty of assuring a uniform waste stream of predictable volume. The investment in recycling facilities cannot be justified from a business or from a social point of view unless a steady, reliable source of inputs can be assured. This problem is faced for many materials but none more so than plastics, and they provide an instructive case-study of the challenges for eco-restructuring.

All parties today agree about the need to reduce polymer solid waste in landfills by some combination of source reduction, degradability of the material, and recycling. The problems arise in achieving an appropriate and stable mix because the steps taken to satisfy one objective tend to thwart the other objectives. One mechanism for source reduction is the substitution of other materials for plastics.

However, the most celebrated comparisons, such as McDonald's former polystyrene foam "clamshell" package vs. the replacement of bleached paper/polyethylene wrappers, or disposable vs. cloth diapers, are inconclusive as to their environmental effects - in part because they have not yet been analysed within a sufficiently complete and integrated economy-wide framework. Source reduction can be achieved by lowering consumption; but, after the initial economies, this option is likely to require significant changes in lifestyle that consumers may be reluctant to make. Refilling plastic containers is another option that requires behavioural changes. Achieving degradability is similarly complicated. Petrochemical based polymers are not intrinsically degradable, and truly degradable ones are still in early stages of commercialization.

Of course, very little of the potential for degradation is actually realized in waste disposal sites designed and managed as landfills rather than composting facilities. Furthermore, the shift in feedstock from hydrocarbons to biomass would have massive implications for the global economy. A significant problem in the recycling of plastics is the expense of collection and the cost and difficulty of separation even among apparently homogeneous objects and polymers, not to mention objects of mixed composition and composite materials. The relative importance of different polymers, and the material composition of many objects, would need to change substantially if large-scale recycling of polymers were to be implemented. Further technical development would be necessary for the separation of mixed plastics.

Of course, in the unlikely event of a massive substitution away from plastics in many uses, coupled with a reliance on biodegradable plastics, there would be inadequate raw material to justify investing in recycling. One current prospect is for the development of completely biodegradable polymers from biomass. Polymers derived from starches of annual crops such as corn and potatoes are already in use in several applications such as golf tees and pharmaceutical capsules. A significant programme is also under way to commercialize polymers based on the jute crop of Bangladesh and India; it is hoped that this market will be able to replace the traditional uses of jute, which are lost as polypropylene displaces jute sacks for packaging grain, sugar, fertilizer, and cement. Plastics are still displacing other primary materials and paper even in the rich economies, and their use is growing rapidly in developing countries. To the extent that polymers are fabricated from biomass, the demand for the hydrocarbon feedstock is reduced. It could also reduce the solid waste that needs to be disposed of and precipitate the shift from landfills to composting facilities. But it puts pressure back on the land used to grow renewable crops.

The alternative roles that plastics might play in the global economy over the next 50 years may be a particularly fruitful case to study from both a technological and a social and economic point of view. What actually happens, by conscious decision or otherwise, may be only one small contributing factor to the global "big picture," but the range of alternatives that were sketched in the previous few paragraphs demonstrates that although engineering innovation is necessary it is hardly sufficient.

Agriculture and Food Production

In nearly all scenarios of global development food supply is the major critical factor. At the same time mainstream agriculture is now increasingly considered to be not sustainable. There is overwhelming evidence that "efficient" (industrial) agriculture is not only mining the natural resource base but also influencing other parts of the environment in ways that are detrimental to the well-being of humankind. In addition, the availability of external inputs such as phosphates, fossil hydrocarbons (the current source of synthetic nitrates), and potash is limited. The characteristic signs of unsustainability include soil erosion, deterioration of soil structure, exhaustion of soil nutrients, salinization of irrigated areas, overuse of water resources, desertification, deforestation, reduction of biodiversity, pest and disease build-up, and pollution from agricultural chemicals in groundwater. Toxic chemicals are finding their way into our food supply. Synthetic nitrogen fertilizer also contributes (via denitrification bacteria) to nitrous oxide emissions and climate warming. On the other hand, it is argued that this intensive pattern of production is necessary to feed the growing world population and, especially, the rapidly growing megacities.

Limiting Factors

One limiting factor is traditional basic cultivation patterns and mind sets. In different social and ecological conditions very different cultivation methods and philosophies have evolved. The most marked difference is that between intensive gardening-like agriculture in densely populated areas of Asia and "industrial" agriculture in those areas of the world that were brought under cultivation by European emigrants or colonizers within the past 500 years.

In the old cultures, land was scarce and population was dense. Thus, a high yield per surface unit was the overriding need. In the Americas, on the other hand, land was abundant, the population was low, and labour was in short supply. Thus mechanization and large scale agriculture were appropriate and successful.

At present the latter model dominates world agriculture. Its domination is fortified by mainstream economic theory and international trade interests and rules, as well as by cheap transport and telecommunications. But will it be the proper long-term strategy for feeding the dramatically growing world population in a sustainable way? Would not the "outdated" agricultural models from China, (peasant) Europe, India, and Japan be a more appropriate starting point? Could these older models be modernized and adapted to the needs of the future?

Another limiting factor is underestimation of the real importance of agriculture in the industrialized economies. Owing to its minor contribution to the GNP of industrialized economies (typically 2-5 per cent), agriculture is largely neglected in mainstream economic analysis. But agriculture plays a key role in every scenario as the essential life-support system. This is due to five major features:

1. Because agriculture is the industry nearest to nature, ecological deficits become apparent much earlier here than in any other branch of the economy.
2. Agriculture satisfies the most basic needs of humankind: it feeds us.
3. The consequences of disregarding sustainable patterns have been more serious in agriculture than in any other sector of the economy; "modern" industrialized agriculture has turned out to be unsustainable within two generations.
4. The long-term prospects for the world food situation are so critical that, if civilized humankind is to survive, corrective action is urgent.
5. Agriculture is the indispensable source of organic material streams in a sustainable future world economy.

A further limiting factor is that modern economics and management theory have encouraged a short-term and reductionist view of agriculture. Successful industrial strategies, characterized by "lean production," rapidly changing technologies, short depreciation periods, and minimization of external influences in process design, are now being transferred to agriculture. The evaluation of agricultural production strategies (systems) by impersonal "market forces" leads to a short-term calculus. But the physical and biological nature of the system itself implies that the appropriate time-frame for measuring sustainable and economically viable agricultural supply systems is much longer: at least 20 years (for example, to observe three periods of a seven-fold crop rotation requires 21 years) and perhaps as much as 100 years.

Agriculture is an inherently interacting system that should make use of all natural synergism's. To evaluate agricultural strategy on a short-term basis is to create inappropriate expectations. Thus agriculture is globally being driven towards the industrial model. But this systems coercion is in blunt contradiction to eco-system needs, which require biodiversity, site orientation, and a massive reduction of material flows.

There is a high degree of consensus that sustainable land use in developing countries should rely on small-scale mixed agriculture in order to husband environments with a low ecological buffering capacity as well as to feed and employ the population. But the opposite is demanded for industrialized countries. The negative reaction of leaders in developing countries is not surprising. They consider this advice to be self-interested and neo-colonialist; they regard it as an attempt to preserve the oligarchic economic structure of the world economy. Hence they unwisely imitate the inappropriate patterns of the industrial world, even when they are not directly imposed by "Western-style" agro-business.

A logical consequence is that soil erosion and the leaching of agrochemical into groundwater are out of control in non-OECD countries. In fact, more than three-quarters of world soil destruction takes place in the third world. The massive problem of soil erosion demands a drastic change in production systems towards more stewardship and husbandry of soils and landscapes. The present pattern of production is leading to a decrease in the productive agricultural area by up to 16 million ha per year. Therefore, without change, a higher production volume for an increasing population would (will) have to be achieved on a decreasing area.

Another limiting factor is water. The exploitation of water resources, which brought nearly a 2 per cent increase in productivity in the first three post World War II decades, cannot be augmented, at least not without major investments and dislocations. Pollution of water resources by wasteful agricultural practices (especially excessive use of synthetic nitrogen fertilizers and pesticides) will have to be reduced in many cases in order to save drinking water reserves. Inputs of agrochemical must also to be limited in order to guarantee the integrity of food chains.

To compound the difficulties, most mainstream cultivation systems have been brought to a rather high level of productivity. This means that the law of diminishing returns has to be taken into account in planning the future. In the context of the standard model, this implies that higher industrial inputs will be necessary to increase productivity further, thus shortening the time-horizon within which non-renewable external resources (oil, natural gas, phosphates, potash) will still be available.

These are the major raw materials for agrochemical (fertilizers, pesticides, and herbicides). These fossil resources are finite and will last at most for some 100 years, if consumption is not slowed down. But the opposite (i.e. acceleration) is the probable outcome of present policies.

Yet another limiting factor is that the food potential of the oceans (and aquaculture) will not be a sufficient alternative at least as far as fish is concerned. There is strong evidence that the world's traditional fishery resources are also already overexploited. Is a collapse of the agricultural system inevitable? The logic of the curve of population growth suggests that either humans are already overtaxing the carrying capacity of the environment, or they soon will. This implies a real danger that we will eventually consume our own "seed corn," i.e. our life-support system.

Without a basic change in population growth rates, consumption patterns ("lifestyle"), and supply technology, present developments resemble a forest fire in a strong wind. The system's breakdown can be expected. As far as agriculture is concerned, the limiting factors enumerated above can be summarized in a nutshell: intensified conventional mainstream high-in-put/high-output agriculture is not sustainable in the long run. This is because short-term advantages are offset by long-term disadvantages in the form of increasing destruction and loss of soil and water resources. In addition, the pattern of ever increasing inputs of fossil energy and raw materials cannot continue indefinitely, for reasons of eventual scarcity as well as environmental reasons.

The food needs of an exponentially increasing world population could not be met, in the long run, even if we assume the most optimistic possible increases in area productivity. Besides slowing down population growth, increasing the efficiency of nutrition will be an indispensable supplementary measure (especially the reduction in luxury meat consumption). If the present trends of soil degradation and population growth are projected without change, there would be very few regions in the world in 2025 able to satisfy the nutritional needs of their own population, even relying on a diet of grain, tubers, and legumes (i.e. cutting meat consumption to a minimum). Therefore the often-heard argument that there is only one way to avoid serious social upheavals in the future, namely to feed the growing world population by employing intensified industrial patterns of production, cannot be a realistic solution.

This judgement is supported by the annual "State of the World Reports" by the Worldwatch Institute, which point to an approaching crisis. In recent times several events and studies have underlined the view that agriculture will be the crucial sector in world economic development.

In 1991 the Conference on Agriculture and the Environment, organized by the Food and Agriculture Organization of the United Nations (FAO) and the Government of the Netherlands, analysed the world situation and worked out an Agenda for Action to meet food needs without mining the natural resource base and thus consuming the life-support systems of future generations and probably even of our own. The loss of 5-7 million hectares of arable land per year through soil degradation was reported, with an annual global loss of topsoil running at 24 billion tons.

There was a general consensus that the situation demands urgent action. It was generally agreed that it is not only the symptoms of unsustainability in agriculture (land degradation, desertification and deforestation, water pollution, loss of soil productivity and natural processes, diminishing wildlife habitats and genetic diversity, air and climate effects, etc.) that have to be changed. The change must extend to the underlying dynamics of our societies.

Some other studies support this position. The reduction in vital agricultural reserve capacity implied by "business-as-usual" scenarios is likely to lead to increased starvation in developing countries and to mass migration. It may also to social, economic, political, and - last but not least - military conflicts. In worst-case scenarios, such catastrophes could destroy the social achievements that most countries value so highly and assume to be guaranteed. Some economists dismiss these warning studies with epithets such as "neo-Malthusian," the implication being that Malthus was long ago disproved or discredited.

As to the food surplus scenarios, it has to be pointed out that all these scenarios are based on the assumption that industrialized countries will continue to run their economies unsustainably. Societies that cover basic demands for organic raw materials and energy by plundering non-renewable fossil resources within a few generations have no need to reserve land for an enduring harvest of solar energy. By limiting agricultural production to the food sector and by boosting food production via cheap fossil-based inputs (chemicals and energy), they can and do produce artificial, but temporary, surpluses. These are not sustainable, however.

Because the introduction of general conditions of sustainability cannot be circumvented in the long run, agricultural politics is confronted with a (politically) painful dilemma. The choice is between short-term maximization even to the point of generating unwanted surpluses - and long-term sufficiency. This dilemma cannot be resolved by relying on market forces alone, because the latter are unavoidably short term and private in nature and do not reflect the larger public interest. Anticipatory strategies leading the market to a long-term optimum are therefore necessary. The reasons are evident: population growth cannot be stopped quickly; water resources have already become scarce, especially in developing countries; the use of chemical fertilizers and pesticides in agriculture has to be controlled and curtailed in order to protect the groundwater, especially in developed countries. The accepted principles of precaution and plausibility in risk management underline this position.

In this context a few remarks on international trade policy as it concerns agriculture are appropriate. The results of the Uruguay Round of the General Agreement in Tariffs and Trade (GATT) reflect the short-term market calculus. Calls by environmentalists for measures allowing protection of future-oriented long-term sustainable agricultural systems within a system of fair trade are denounced by trade negotiators as "green protectionism."

Trade negotiators argue that agriculture must accept the same rules as the industrial sector. Yet industrial undertakings normally do not need a site-oriented design. Their adaptation time to changing circumstances is shorter, and the same holds for the depreciation period. Further, the co-production of public goods (such as harmonious landscapes, biodiversity, and potable water) is, for practical purposes, non-existent in industry. The timeframe of the trade calculus is even shorter than the industrial one.

In addition, long-term food security concerns seem inconsistent with providing favourable trade treatment to regions that gain a short-term comparative advantage by operating unsubstainably. Examples include risking soil erosion through irrigation with "fossil" groundwater and clearing rain forests and steep hillsides to provide cattle pasture for less than a decade before the thin layer of topsoil is lost. Myopic decisions in international economic development planning are the rule, rather than the exception.

Proven and sustainable cultivation systems are routinely sacrificed for unsustainable short term advantages, not only in the Amazon or Central America and in disadvantaged areas such as the European Alpes-Maritimes and Ligurian Alps, terrace agriculture in Yemen, or mountain agriculture in India and Pakistan, but also in the advantaged areas of the northern hemisphere. The so-called "green box" measures are an attempt to mitigate some symptoms. This has broadly the character of a "social end-of-the-pipe treatment strategy," because the listed measures are strictly palliative. They leave the underlying dynamics unchanged. Therefore the environmental impacts of agriculture are not changed at the roots.

Does this mean that agriculturalists, as a minority that cannot significantly influence the economic mainstream, must be advocates of intensification of the presently dominating patterns of agricultural production in order to keep humanity alive and fed in the short run, in spite of the warnings of ecologists, environmentalists, and rural developers? The key to a strategy of hope is the answer to the following crucial question: Are there other systems of sustainable agriculture at our disposal that can achieve the high area productivity of mainstream (high-input/high-output) agriculture but that have the potential to feed the growing mega-cities of the future?

Towards Sustainable Agriculture

An essential characteristic of sustainable future economic systems must be to minimize the energy and material inputs per service (production) unit, in all sectors. In the realm of food production, organic agriculture is the most appropriate concept. By careful husbanding of soils and landscapes, by relying on site-oriented biodiversity in order to be able to use a maximum of natural synergisms, and by intensive nutrient recycling it minimizes external inputs. Thus, it achieves a maximum net harvest of solar energy in forms usable to humans. In this way it preserves and even improves the soil and achieves the highest possible yields in a way that can be practiced for a virtually unlimited time-horizon.

There is evidence that a gardening-like cultivation system with a high input of labour (~0.3 persons per ha), a high turnover of nutrients, and a balanced pattern of mixed cropping is capable of out producing low-labour (mechanized) agricultural production systems by at least three-fold. In times of worldwide structural unemployment it would be a wise strategy to rely on this concept in order to meet future food shortages.

But the intelligent intermediate step would be to preserve the skills needed to manage highly productive mixed agricultural systems that later can be more easily intensified towards a gardening like pattern of cultivation. In this light, small-scale mixed agriculture can be seen as the starting block for stepping up agricultural productivity in the future in a sustainable way.

Potential of Organic Agriculture

Some preliminary remarks have to be made with respect to the validity of existing comparisons between conventional and organic agriculture. First there is a general tendency to underestimate the productivity of organic agriculture for four reasons:

1. Organic agriculture stems from a revolutionary "bottom-up" movement. It still has relatively little scientific support, because R&D funding by government and industry is directed to support mainstream activities.

2. In order to achieve full productivity by building up the humus content of soils and optimizing the farmer's skills (including the choice of appropriate crop rotations and intermediate crops), a "learning" period of about 10 years is typically necessary.

3. Organic farmers have always asked for support because of the initial yield-lag during the transformation phase.

4. In many cases shortage of affordable labour is a limiting factor, because the question of labour intensity cannot be addressed within the present system of agricultural support and mainstream economic philosophy. This bottleneck could be overcome by a future ecological tax reform that taxed the consumption of nonrenewable materials and primary energy carriers on the one side and reduced the direct and indirect taxation of labour on the other.

Thus assessment of the productivity potential of organic agriculture has also to take into account these short-term temporary disadvantages. Comparisons between conventional and organic agriculture, assuming similar endowments of labour and machinery, suggest a much higher energy efficiency for organic agriculture. The improvement ranges from 48 per cent to 64 per cent. But there is a corresponding short-term drop in yield of up to 30 per cent.

One study observed a 10 per cent reduction in natural produce yields when comparing 14 pairs of conventional and organic farms in the eastern central states of the United States. A 1980 study by the US Department of Agriculture in the US Midwest found not only a much higher energy efficiency for organic agriculture but also similar or better average yields per surface area unit. In the case of wheat there was no significant difference between the two. In the case of soybeans, organic methods produced 14 per cent higher average yields.

In Europe a number of similar studies have been made. They have estimated a 20-30 per cent reduction in yields, based on the average performance of organic farms. Based on the facts it is possible to make the following rough judgements. The earth is now providing about 4.6 billion ha of land usable for agricultural purposes.

About one-third is arable land and two-thirds permanent grassland. Divided by a world population of 5.77 billion in 1996, the current world per capita endowment amounts to 0.25 ha of arable land and 0.50 ha of grassland. Thus there is still sufficient (but not ample) room for adjustment towards a global eco-restructuring of the agricultural supply systems without the threat of increased starvation. On the contrary, given appropriate incentives, humanity could save its resource base for future generations and still achieve food security.

In assessing future potentials, the performance of the best farmers should serve as a measuring rod, because they are the spearhead of future development. Personal observation of Austrian organic farms, especially the well-documented model farm of Hermann Pennwieser, shows that within a period of 10 years the humus content of soils increased by one-third (1.5-2 per cent per annum), and that soil life, soil structure, and water storage capacity also increased significantly.

One surprising effect is also that the incidence of plant diseases actually decreased, which indicates a strengthening of the plant's immune systems. The average yields of these organic farms are at the same high level as in comparable Austrian conventional farms. Besides estimating the potential of sustainable organic agriculture, it is also important to assess the resource conservation potential of organic agriculture if it were adopted globally.

The contribution of organic farming vis-à-vis soil erosion is vitally important. There is clear evidence that soil erosion can be drastically reduced. Erosion is reduced by three major characteristics of organic agriculture:

— crop rotation, the concept of evergreen agriculture, mixed cropping, and underseeding reduce the susceptibility of soil to erosion;

— augmentation of the humus results in a better soil structure, a higher stability of aggregates, greater penetration by roots, and better water storage capacity;

— careful (soft) soil cultivation also cuts the risk of erosion.

Higher plant nutrient efficiency

It is usually argued that there are no alternatives to the present high inputs of nitrogen, phosphorus, and potassium (NPK). If all farmers of the world were to follow the high-input model, the minable deposits of phosphorus would be exhausted in about 80 years. The same holds for potassium and for fossil organic resources, which are the base of nitrogen fertilizers. In addition, the high energy input for the supply of mineral fertilizers has to be taken into account. Nutrient-efficient cultivation techniques are, therefore, a conditio sine qua non for long-term sustainable food supply.

Organic agriculture tries to achieve maximum nutrient recycling by integrating plant and animal production and by using all by-products and wastes. Following this concept, nearly balanced nutrient cycles can be achieved. As far as phosphorus and potassium are concerned, use of the nutrient reserves in the soils and of their geo genous potential, combined with the recycling of organic residuals, can be considered to be a proper intermediate strategy. In the very long term, agriculture must achieve a near closure of nutrient material cycles. Nitrogen efficiency deserves a separate comment.

Conventional agriculture now imports nutrients in nearly unlimited quantities, which have resulted in a nitrogen surplus (N-surplus) in areas where this has been going on for many years. In contrast, organic agriculture limits itself to nutrient recycling and to legumes as sources of nitrogen. In addition, organic farms normally observe the restriction of not more than two large animal units per hectare. Because organic farms are forced to economize on nitrogen inputs, the N-surplus on organic farms is much lower.

Agriculture has always tried to optimize the living conditions of plants and animals and to protect them. Organic agriculture has the same aim. Enlightened organic agriculture therefore does not refuse external aids completely (as some fundamentalists do), but it cuts them to a minimum and tries to rely mainly on the employment of natural synergisms and intensive care. Under these auspices, further increases in the effectiveness and productivity of organic agriculture can be expected. This judgement is underpinned by the fact that political support and public funding of research work in this field are also increasing.

Based on the above evidence, it can be said that pragmatic organic agriculture is a realistic pathway to feed the growing world population and to secure the natural resource base needed for a long term sustainable future. But it has to be complemented by other measures, especially efficiency of food distribution. Most important of all, there must be effective measures to stabilize world population in order to secure a high quality of life for all citizens of the globe in the long term.

All basic strategies need a rather long time-horizon in order to implement the necessary changes. As pointed out by Leo Jansen, a realistic approach has to start simultaneously on three basic fronts:

— good housekeeping in the short term, i.e. increasing efficiency within the present patterns of supply and consumption;

— designing new more efficient and environmentally benign processes that are compatible with the envisaged future supply systems in the medium term;

— designing new supply systems for the long term, in harmony with the ethical demand for global ecological, social, and economic sustainability and respecting the governing principles of the biosphere. In order to do this efficiently, an orientation grid (a "mental map") can be helpful to guide research, politics, and entrepreneurial activity.

The sustainability discussion in agriculture has so far developed in a rather casual and informal manner. There is some risk of failing to see the wood for being too fascinated by the trees. Therefore some general "guidelines" should be established. A narrowing "grid" for evaluation is therefore proposed. Accepting intergenerational and global solidarity as overriding principles implies that human supply systems should be designed in such a way as to be practicable for all people at all times. In order to come up with practical management rules, more specific guidelines should be derived from this very general imperative. A constraint is that the biosystem has to maintain itself in balance, such that material flows are integrated by recycling mechanisms and driven mainly by solar energy. A set of general rules for sustainable action can be derived from this starting point.

A second essential guideline can be deduced from further discernible characteristics of the ecosystem to which humans are adapted. It may be called "respect for the governing principles of the biosphere". These governing principles are characteristics of the ecosystem earth that cannot be altered by humans. They constitute boundary conditions for human action, as noted below.

The above broad principles imply that ecological principles have to be respected even more firmly than the social rules that have been developed within the past 200 years, if we are to give future generations a fair chance. The market mechanism should be acknowledged as the best proven vehicle for economic development. It can encourage human creativity and foster a multitude of options and flexible interactions. But its benefits can be steered towards the commonweal only if it is directed to operate within the domain allowed by ecological (and social) constraints. Therefore the World Trade Organization (WTO), regional trade agreements, supranational institutions, and national constitutions should take into account the principles of sustainable action.

In view of the conflict between present-day economic pressures and expected future conditions it would be unwise to attempt instant change. The best strategy is to put the unavoidable rules definitely into force, to "send a message," but to "turn them on" gradually, so as to discourage new investment in unsustainable technologies. It is important to provide for a long transition (depreciation) period, in order to avoid unnecessary destruction of capital that has been invested according to the old rules of the game. The basic rules can be easily cast in a normative form usable for national and international negotiation and legislation.

Restructuring of Tropical Land-use Systems

Rural land use in the tropics is dominated by agriculture (used here in its broad sense to include forestry, animal production, and other related topics). Rural land use, and particularly agriculture, represents perhaps the most intense and intimate link between society and nature. The dynamics of ecosystems, and the fact that they respond in an active, rather than a passive, way to human actions, are particularly visible in the tropics. Agricultural activities have been, of necessity, more aware of the ecological or natural resources dynamics, opportunities, and limitations than have industrial activities. However, this does not mean that integration was (or is) a basic characteristic of the activity. On the contrary, the prevailing conceptualization is vertical, by product or crop, with specified priorities and policies, as if the production situations were ecologically, economically, and socially homogeneous.

Eco-restructuring in general, and more so in the case of tropical agriculture, will have to involve much more than marginal improvements and mitigating measures recognized by many orthodox economists and politicians. Eco-restructuring is, or should be, about the deep changes required to advance towards sustainable development.

In moving towards sustainable agriculture, three partially overlapping degrees of progress can be distinguished: efficiency changes, substitution changes, and fundamental redesign changes. Efficiency changes progress towards sustainability by reducing inputs for the same output, increasing output for the same input, and/ or reducing wastes (spot rather than whole-field applications of pesticides, avoidance of over fertilization, efficiency of water use, etc.).

The advantages that efficiency increases provide towards sustainability (and often also towards economic gains) are generally accepted. However, maximizing efficiency can be a deadend path if the system being made more efficient is intrinsically unsustainable. Besides, efficiency gains can be offset by increases in the total volume of the activity if it grows faster than efficiency.

Substitution changes can increase sustainability by replacing limited or environmentally damaging inputs with healthier, or less limited, alternatives. Substitution changes may involve replacing herbicides with mechanical weed control, or using legumes to replace fertilization with inorganic nitrogen. Redesign changes are more fundamental and involve whole production systems.

In agriculture, the emphasis would be on cropping systems and farming systems as a whole. In some cases, even whole landscape systems should be redesigned. Redesign changes are likely also to incorporate efficiency and substitution changes. For example, changing from a mono-cultural grain production system to a multi year crop rotation system can involve numerous substitution and efficiency effects.

The general approaches of efficiency, substitution, and redesign changes apply to agriculture as well as to industry and services. However, there is a major difference between agricultural and industrial eco-restructuring. Although modern agriculture is in many senses becoming similar to an industrial activity, it is still fundamentally based upon the management of agricultural ecosystems, including living and non-living components.

The functioning of those ecosystems under management depends upon (and affects) larger ecological cycles and processes, and also depends upon their own internal bio-geochemical dynamics and capacity of response. This is particularly true in the case of the tropical agro-ecosystems, and in reference to complex agro-forestry production systems that mimic many of the features of natural ecosystems. The capacity of living systems for spontaneous behaviour and unexpected changes makes eco-restructuring in agriculture potentially more complex than in industry.

Rural Development Models

Different approaches to rural development, including land use, have been applied in tropical regions. Although the specific examples used here will mostly draw from the Latin American experience, some of the lessons have wider applicability. Historically, the concept of agricultural development included the sum of the efforts directed towards the growth and diversification of production and towards increases in productivity.

The conceptual base of agricultural development was essentially technical, mostly associated with yield increases through the Green Revolution, the expansion of the physical capital, and the creation of an institutional context coherent with the requirements of a continuously increasing agricultural output.

The concept of rural development arose as a response to the realization that agricultural development, as applied, did not lead to an overall improvement in the living standards of rural people and did not "trickle down" to the poor.Rural development was associated with a set of actions (including improvement in production systems, the availability of credit facilities for commercialization of harvesting, and the expansion of the physical infrastructure) specifically directed towards poor rural producers.

Different approaches to rural development were tried in Latin America. From the mid-1950s to the early 1960s, the United Nations promoted the community development approach, directed mainly at the integration of rural communities (particularly the indigenous people) in the national socioeconomic context, the utilization of their potential for development through education, social organization, and social action, and participation. The strong dependence upon external financing and foreign experts, the failure to pursue rapid increases in production (to avoid conflicts with national agricultural policies), and the political struggles associated with the empowerment of communities in some countries seem to be among the major factors that contributed to the abandonment of this model.

In the 1960s agrarian reform was considered by many experts (and governments) to be the major instrument to lead to new rural structures that would be stable, efficient, and participative and result in a quantum leap in production and equity. The results have been mixed. The reform was concretely applied to no more than 20 per cent of appropriable land; today, Latin America is still the region of the world with the highest concentration of land ownership. The impacts on production were also non-conclusive: in some countries the impacts were positive, in others negative. Sustainability of the natural resource base and relations between the social changes triggered and the available technological package and credit, technical assistance, and training were neglected.

The prevailing approach during the 1970s was that of agricultural modernization, which led to economic concentration and the expulsion of labour, which is still happening in many countries of the region. Large and medium agricultural production was integrated into the national economy, as well as becoming more dependent on the market. Strong processes of proletarization, social differentiation, and recomposition affected, and still affect, the peasant economies.

The concept of integrated rural development (IRD) emerged in the early 1970s, and is still in use. It implies the definition of multiple goals: increases in production and productivity, social improvement, and physical capital formation. It also involved attempts to integrate action on different factors, institutional coordination, and strong participation by the beneficiaries. The approach was conceived as an integral state intervention, specifically targeting poor rural producers.

Many of the projects operated at the micro level, in isolation. By the end of the 1970s, the need to link IRD projects with an explicit national policy coherent with national and sectoral development strategies gained political support. During the 1980s (officially known as "the lost decade" for development in Latin America), the economic crisis and recession led to the application of structural adjustment policies, including severe reductions in public expenditure. This also strongly affected IRD projects, in particular because they require substantial and sustained investments with long maturation periods.

The impacts of the adjustment process upon the theoretical basis of IRD, as well as dissatisfaction with the results achieved in terms of the total rural economy and society, led to new analytical proposals in the late 1980s.

These emphasized the need to focus on less complex projects, directed at a narrower target population, and to look for technical solutions that are economically viable for poor farmers and allow increases in production and income within the context of current macroeconomic and agricultural policies.

During the 1980s, a more integrated approach, "social forestry," started to be implemented as a response to the problems generated in ecologically fragile areas with high demographic pressures and a high incidence of poverty. A number of successful experiments exist. These projects emphasize the active participation of small and medium farmers in the design, implementation, and control of the project; the goals of the project are defined by the community; the projects integrate many relevant components (such as crops and farm animals associated with trees and other woody plants, small industries, marketing, training, agro-forestry, social organization of the population); the concept of the sustainability of the productive system is incorporated in the design of the projects as a prerequisite for rural development; and the projects explicitly attempt to reach synergy between the resources of the community (land, labour, appropriate traditional technologies, and organization). In general, they are not intensive in financial resources per person or per hectare.

In general in Latin America the generic policies for rural development had few explicit linkages with macroeconomic policies (particularly with those defining urban rural exchange relations) and with public investment. They also suffered from a lack of complementarily with the policy instruments applied to foster agricultural modernization. They concentrated too much on the productive aspects, without addressing the issue of the sustainability of production, and sometimes resulted in increased environmental degradation. They did not address the linkages between international agricultural trade and the degradation of natural resources within prevailing economic patterns. And, finally, they were often biased towards expensive and unconnected projects, which ended when the external financial resources were exhausted.

Need of Integrated Solutions in Tropical Land Use

Tropical agriculture is not limited to the humid tropics; it also includes dry zones. However, it is in the humid tropics that the major challenges for eco-restructuring lie. Humid tropic conditions are found over nearly 50 per cent of the tropical land mass and 20 per cent of the earth's total land surface an area of about 3 billion hectares. Tropical Central and South America contain about 45 per cent of the world's humid tropics, Africa about 30 per cent, and Asia about 25 per cent. As many as 62 countries are located partly or entirely within the humid tropics.

Land transformation in temperate zones from its natural state to its present intensive agriculture and land use occurred over thousands of years. Changes in the tropics are occurring at a much faster rate; in some cases, areas are completely transformed and often degraded beyond economically feasible restoration within one generation. Sustainable land use in the humid tropics will require an approach that recognizes the characteristic cultural and biological diversity of these lands, respects their complex ecological processes, involves local people at all stages of the development process, and promotes cooperation among biologists, agricultural scientists, and social scientists. The easing of rigid disciplinary boundaries is of special importance in the humid tropics.

Most public sector agricultural research and development programmes in the humid tropics have in the past used a commodity oriented approach, aiming to maximize the production of cereals and a limited number of root and pulse crops. This approach has led to striking increases in food production in areas with good soil and water resources. However, by focusing attention on particular crops and agro-ecosystem components, it has tended to neglect the range of physical and biotic interactions that influence crop production, the ecological impacts of intensive production practices, and broader social and economic aspects. This commodity-oriented approach has also ignored lessons from the performance of traditional agricultural systems.

Many traditional resource management techniques and systems, often dismissed as primitive, are highly sophisticated and well suited to the opportunities and limitations facing farmers in the tropics. Their durability, adaptability, diversity, and resilience often provide critical insights into the sustainable management of all tropical agro-ecosystems. Although many of these systems have been deeply modified or abandoned owing to economic, cultural, and social pressures, some could, with modification, contribute significantly to the sustainability and productivity of agriculture in many tropical countries.

Agricultural systems and techniques that have evolved from ancient times to meet the special environmental conditions of the humid tropics include the paddy rice of South-East Asia, terrace, mound, and drained field systems, raised bed systems (such as the chinampas of Mexico and Central America), and a variety of agroforestry, shifting cultivation, home garden, and natural forest systems. Although diverse in their adaptations, these systems share common elements, such as high retention of essential nutrients, maintenance of vegetative cover, high diversity of crops and crop varieties, complex spatial and temporal cropping patterns, and the integration of domestic and wild animals into the system.

Many of the required activities are highly knowledge intensive, even if based on empirical knowledge. This diversified holistic, empirical knowledge, or socio-diversity as it is sometimes referred to, is being lost in the tropics as fast as, and often faster than, biodiversity. This is a precious resource receiving insufficient attention.

It is generally agreed that sustainable agriculture typically will require more information, more and better trained labour, and more diverse management skills per unit of production than conventional farming. This is because diversification into each additional crop and additional animal species requires additional and different skills.

A diversified farm requires better production management and a different kind of labour resource than a similar-sized farm growing only one or two crops. This is one of the major limiting factors. In the case of integrated pest management (IPM), based on sound scientific principles, it is argued that, when problems arise in its practice, they are usually associated with the large amount of knowledge and expertise needed to develop, implement, and improve an IPM programme and with a tendency to rely too heavily on strategies developed from inadequate knowledge and without sufficient consideration of all the consequences of their use.

It is also recognized that sustainable agriculture must be based in large part on site-specific information and knowledge. It seems ironic that modern agriculture in many cases has lost (and, in the tropics, is still losing) site-specific skills for managing complex agro-ecosystems in its quest for standardization and commoditization, and that the same skill factor (albeit with the incorporation of modern scientific knowledge) is limiting the transition to sustainable agriculture.

Sustainable Land Use

One significant background fact is that the world is currently moving through a period of extraordinary turbulence reflecting the genesis and intensification of deep changes associated with the current techno-economic revolution, led by micro-electronics and accompanied by a constellation of developments based upon new, science intensive technologies.

This situation implies that sustainable land use must aim not only at preserving and maintaining the ecological base for development and habitability, but also at increasing the social and ecological capacity to cope with change and the ability to retain and enlarge the available options in the face of a natural and social world in permanent transformation.

Sustainable land use in a rapidly changing world requires the capacity to confront many different types of change at the same time, without compromising the social, economic, and ecological sources of renewal, as well as to reduce vulnerability and retain or enlarge the range of available options. Thus, the concept of sustainable land use cannot mean merely perpetuation. The central question is what is to be sustained and what is to be changed.

Approaching sustainable land use, and sustainable development, requires:

(1) getting rid of accumulated rigidities and impediments;

(2) identifying and protecting the accumulated foundations of knowledge and experience that are important as a basis upon which to build;

(3) sustaining the social and natural foundations for adaptation and renewal, and identifying and enhancing the lost renewal capacity needed;

(4) stimulating innovation, experimentation, and social creativity.

For sustainable land use, the issues of technological pluralism (complementary use of traditional, "modern," and high technology) and technological blending (constructive integration of high technology into existing technologies, such as using biotechnology to improve the yield and pest resistance of traditional crops - thus increasing efficiency and substituting for pesticides - or applying advanced ecological theory to redesign production systems based on shifting cultivation to improve sustainability) assume paramount importance, requiring new forms of organization and an integral strategy for technological development and diffusion.

The upgrading of traditional technology and empirical knowledge will become especially important for the medium- and small-scale sectors of rural areas. Many traditional technologies are already better adapted to local conditions and ecological cycles than the expanding "modern" technology.

Technological blending could improve yields and avoid some of the limitations of traditional techniques. Such technological integration could reduce conflicts, promote self sustainable technological innovation, be easily absorbed and adapted to local situations, and favour social, cultural, economic, and environmental sustainability. Special emphasis should be allocated to developing systems of production for the already altered ecosystems, including "neo-ecosystems" generated by human activities. Strategies should be developed for choosing areas for protection involving large-scale ecological functions and processes.

A general criterion is the maintenance of productive pluralism, with the coexistence of different major types of agriculture integrated through sub-national, national, and regional policies. Structural reforms and technological innovations directed to the transformation of the present subsistence agricultural sector into an efficient and sustainable peasant agriculture will be required. New forms of high-technology diversified agriculture should be developed, directed to the selective exploitation of local genetic resources for food, medicine, industry, etc. It will imply the development of technologies for a new efficient recollection agriculture in diversified ecosystems, as well as new ranching and wildlife management systems, viewing ecological diversity, heterogeneity, variability, and singularities as resources rather than as hindrances or constraints. Forestry should emphasize the revalorization of the forests as multi-purpose producers (wood, energy, wildlife, special products, ecological functions).

This will require deep changes in storage and commercialization systems. Today, market and consumer demand are geared to guaranteeing uniformity in products. This has favoured the dominance of mono-cropping, which is highly vulnerable to pests and genetic erosion. The challenge is now to ensure uniformity in quality and delivery at the consumer level while managing and even nurturing variability at the production system level. This implies a completely different approach to the whole system of production/distribution of agricultural produce.

The case of peasant agriculture is a good illustration of the potential role of technical change for sustainable development if integrated with socioeconomic policies. Peasant agriculture is important in terms of the number of people involved, the intense environmental pressures it generates in many countries of the region, and the concentration of rural poverty.

The problem cannot be solved through technological fixes. An integral strategy for the transformation of the current subsistence agriculture into a sustainable and profitable peasant agriculture would need to include efforts in:

(a) facilitating access to the means of production,

(b) eco-restructuring of the national economies and of the marketing and distribution systems,

(c) community empowerment, as well as

(d) research and development.

The strategy proposed here might be labelled Utopian by some readers. However, one should consider that technical innovation and diffusion have already occurred in the past few decades on a greater scale than implied in this section. Many remote areas are already being connected through radio, TV, and telephone networks, and communication costs are fast declining. The next decade or two will almost certainly involve tremendous additional technological change. The need to address the fact that fundamental, rather than incremental, changes in policy and values are required to move towards sustainable development is increasingly obvious.

The means of production include not only the land, agricultural inputs, capital, and technology but also (and this is likely to become increasingly important) information and knowledge. In the initial stages, the availability and redistribution of land for use through community management will be a key element, together with strategies for the restoration and rehabilitation of ecologically degraded lands. An agriculture under ecological management could in many cases lower requirements for material and energy inputs. Access to appropriate technology, and the stimulation of the social creativity to improve on it, should be supported.

Finally, access to information in rural communities may be greatly improved through telematic networks connecting communal nodes. This includes quick access to information about the prices of products and inputs, the monitoring of weather conditions, of the condition of crops, and of erosion, meteorological forecasts, and the anticipation of natural disasters, besides programmes of education and capacity-building (local and at a distance). The same telematic networks could also be used to collect information about the state of the agro-ecosystems and of the population to facilitate regional and national planning.

Eco-restructuring of the national economies and marketing systems implies a redesign in order to benefit from technological and productive pluralism. This represents an important theoretical and organizational challenge. Many traits of the current economic systems rest on the homogenization of both production (e.g. monocultures) and consumption, which has often generated serious environmental problems and increased vulnerability to pests.

Productive and distributive systems must be restructured in such a way that they will operate efficiently in situations where rural products are highly diversified (particularly in the tropics) and where the production of a given agricultural commodity is based on myriad dispersed exploitations, distributed in time and space.

The new technologies, used within new forms of interlinked but decentralized social organizations, make possible sophisticated productive and distributive management making full use of variability and heterogeneity as assets rather than constraints. It will also be necessary to develop mechanisms for the articulation of large-scale, homogeneous agricultural production (which will continue to exist, directed particularly to urban consumption and agro-industry and to export) with diversified small-scale production (thus minimizing or reversing the expulsion of rural labour to marginal land).

A proportion of the diversified rural production would be used for self consumption by the peasant populations, contributing to a balanced diet. The marketable surplus would be composed in large part of food or industrial crops of high unit value made possible by local germplasm and ecological conditions; many of these products would not have competition at the international level.

Active exploration and measures to open up new national and international markets will be necessary. Peasant agriculture will increasingly focus on the ecological comparative advantages rather than on the comparative advantage of cheap labour (the latter, besides often being associated with low standards of living, is rapidly losing importance at the world level).

Creative programmes to improve the living conditions of the peasant populations will be essential. The role of the new communication system is essential here, in synergy with the fostering of social participation and communal self-reliance. Access to health, housing, and education services should be improved, as well as access to the means for family planning.

Technological advances, in a participative and decentralized context, can open up huge opportunities for the discovery of new, flexible, and adaptive solutions to the traditional liabilities of rural populations, while respecting their cultural identity. Support for the peasant populations will in many cases require the implementation of financial systems capable of managing thousands of small loans and investments, rather than only a few massive investments, as is typical of the majority of the national and international agencies for rural development and financing.

A strong push to scientific and technological research will be required, directed to improving yields and the profitability of agricultural systems based (as appropriate) on traditional, modern, or even completely new systems and making use of local cultural and ecological comparative advantages. The systematic and comparative study of the potential of the regional germplasm is a priority area of research. Another priority is the implementation of an annotated catalogue or database of the traditional and modern technologies used in the region and, whenever possible, those that were used in the past. Such a catalogue should include the social and ecological conditions to which these technologies are adapted, their degree of environmental sustainability and social suitability, the type of products and their possible yields, and the major economic, social, cultural, political, or ecological constraints on their wide utilization.

Comparison with other regions of comparable ecology could be of great utility. On the basis of the comparative analysis of the relative advantages of the different technologies, it should be possible to select a menu of technologies as a basis for the development of suitable solutions for each ecological zone and socio-cultural realm, improving them on the basis of technological, ecological, and social research. These would help the development of diversified production, adapted to the different local conditions but integrated through regional, national, and international systems of capacity-building, information, transport, storage, and distribution.

The improvement of crop varieties through biotechnology and the relaxation of environmental constraints through the use of agro-technology, biotechnology, and informatics could include, for instance: the selection or creation of nitrogen-fixing or phosphorus concentrating bacterial strains, which are easy to reproduce and have little environmental impact; the application of biological pest control; genetic manipulation to increase crop resistance to pests or drought; and social and anthropological research directed at improving the cultural and social suitability of production systems and the quality of the information and capacity-building systems.

New technologies such as informatics and telematics could play a crucial role. For instance, serious attention should be given to the possibility of facilitating access to microcomputers and expert systems by local communities, to aid fertilizer and irrigation dosage, pest control, the management and administration of complex agro-ecosystems, medical diagnosis, education, etc.

The current level of technological development would make it possible to keep costs within a reasonable level, provided a decentralized and collective design is adopted, with computers run by community-based rural units and linked through telecommunication networks. The research requirements for the success of this strategy are significant.

It suffices to consider the challenge represented by the need to develop efficient software for rural populations who are often illiterate or, as is the case with some peasant communities in Latin America, have a culture based on magical thinking, distant from Western logic. This would require new modes of research and interaction, interdisciplinary teams that include participation by local farmers (participatory research), the development of sophisticated forms of iconic communication, and the simultaneous utilization of alternative cultural paradigms.

Regarding hardware, it will be necessary to develop inexpensive but very robust equipment, of low obsolescence and easy to update. Ecological research in combination with anthropological research, making use both of the empirical knowledge accumulated by the peasant cultures of the region and of modern science, would allow sophisticated new forms of ecosystem management.

The sequence and localization of human activities and of the germplasm would allow effective management of the local bio-geochemical cycles - for instance, crops grown in a temporal sequence designed to regenerate their own nutrients, in a spatial mosaic designed so as to benefit from diversity and heterogeneity in order to minimize the growth of pest populations, and in a vertical architecture allowing fuller use of resources. The net result of such a strategy directly focused on peasant agriculture would be an improvement in the rural quality of life, an associated decrease in the migratory flows to the urban centres, an important decrease in ecological degradation, and the utilization of an economic potential that is currently barely tapped.

Bibliography

Berthold-Bond, Daniel. "The Ethics of "Place": Reflections on Bioregionalism." *Environmental Ethics* 22. Spring 2000.

Brandenburg, A.M., and M.S. Carroll. "Your place, or mine: the effect of place creation on environmental values and landscape meanings." *Society and Natural Resources* 8:5. 1995.

Cantrill, J.G. "The environmental self and a sense of place: communication foundations for regional ecosystem management." *Journal of Applied Communication Research* 26. 1998.

Chawla, L. "Reaching Home: Reflections on Environmental Autobiography." *Environmental and Architectural Phenomenology*, 6:2.1995.

Cheney, J. "Postmodern Environmental Ethics: Ethics as Bioregional Narrative." *Environmental Ethics*, 11. 1989.

Curry, Leslie. "Information in geographical systems." *Geographical and Environmental Modelling* 2:1. 1998.

Curry, Michael. *Digital Places: Living with Geographic Information Technologies*. New York: Routledge, 1998.

Dovey, Kimberly. "The Quest for Authenticity and the Replication of Environmental Meaning." Seamon, David & Robert Mugerauer, *Dwelling, Place, and Environment: Toward a Phenomenology of Person and World*. Dordrecht: Martinus Nijhoff, 1985.

Feld, Steven and Keith H. Basso. *Senses of Place*. Santa Fe, NM: School of American Research Press, 1996.

Halls, Peter. *Spatial Information and the Environment.* Routledge, 2001.

Hannon, B. "Sense of Place: Geographic Discounting by People, Animals and Plants." *Ecological Economics* 10:2.1994.

Million, Louise. "A World of Many Places." *Environmental and Architectural Phenomenology* 7:3. Fall 1996.

Norton, B.G., and B. Hannon. "Environmental values: a place-based theory." *Environmental Ethics* 19:3. 1997.

Norton, Bryan and Bruce Hannon. "Democracy and Sense of Place Values in Environmental Policy" in Light, Andrew & Jonathan Smith, eds. *Philosophies of Place: Philosophy and Geography III.* Lanham: Rowman and Littlefield, 1999.

Paterson, Douglas. "Place and Placelessness: Fabulous Frustrations." Environmental and Architectural Phenomenology 7:3. Fall 1996.

Relph, Edward. "Reflections on Place and Placelessness." *Environmental and Architectural Phenomenology* 7:3. Fall 1996.

Seamon, D. "Humanistic and Phenomenological Advances in Environmental Design." *Humanistic Psychology* 17. 1989.

Seamon, D. "Phenomenology and Environment-behavior Research." in G. T. Moore and E. Zube, eds., *Advances in Environment, Behavior and Design,* vol. 1. New York: Plenum, 1987.

Seamon, David & Robert Mugerauer, *Dwelling, Place, and Environment: Toward a Phenomenology of Person and World.* Dordrecht: Martinus Nijhoff, 1985; Florida: Krieger Publishing, 2000.

Seamon, David, ed. *Dwelling, Seeing, and Designing: Towards a Phenomenological Ecology.* Albany: SUNY Press, 1993.

Williams, D.R., and S.I. Stewart. "Sense of place: an elusive concept that is finding a home in ecosystem management." *Journal of Forestry* 96:5. 1998.

Index